ESTABLISHING ZION:

PREPARING THE EARTH FOR THE RETURN OF JESUS CHRIST

RANDAL S. CHASE

EDITED BY
MICHAEL D. CHASE

Establishing Zion:
Preparing the Earth fo the Return of Jesus Christ

Send inquiries to:
Plain and Precious Publishing
3378 E. Sweetwater Springs Drive
Washington, UT 84780

Send e-mail: info@ldsgospelsource.com

For more copies visit www.ldsgospelsource.com

For a listing of all Plain and Precious Publishing products,
visit www.ldsgospelsource.com
or call 435–275–8005.

Printed in the United States of America

ISBN: 978-1-937901-18-9

Cover: *The New Jerusalem Descending from the Heavens*
Artist Unknown

ESTABLISHING ZION:

PREPARING THE EARTH FOR THE RETURN OF JESUS CHRIST

TABLE OF CONTENTS

The New Jerusalem Descending from the Heavens

INTRODUCTION

Establishing Zion

The Prophet Joseph Smith declared:

IN HIS GLORY, © DEL PARSON, USED BY PERMISSION

> The building up of Zion is a cause that has interested the people of God in every age; it is a theme upon which prophets, priests, and kings have dwelt with peculiar delight; they have looked forward with joyful anticipation to the day in which we live; and . . . have sung and written and prophesied of this our day; but they died without the sight; we are the favored people that God has made choice of to bring about the latter-day glory. . . . Generations yet unborn will dwell with peculiar delight upon the scenes that we have passed through, the privations that we have endured . . . in laying the foundation of a work that brought about the glory and blessing which they will realize.[1]
>
> We ought to have the building up of Zion as our greatest object. When wars come, we shall have to flee to Zion. The cry is to make haste. The last revelation says, Ye shall not have time to have gone over the earth, until these things come. It will come as did the cholera, war, fires, and earthquakes; one pestilence after another, until the Ancient of Days comes, then judgment will be given to the Saints.[2]

As Latter-day Saints, we covenant in sacred places to sacrifice and consecrate all that is asked of us in order to bring about the establishment of Zion.

What does this mean? We understand what it means to sacrifice and consecrate, but what can we do to establish Zion in our own day?

THE DEFINITION OF "ZION"

(Moses 7:2, 19, 21, 62–63, 69; D&C 97:21)

Zion is defined in various ways—as a city, as a nation, as a continent, and as people who are "pure in heart." The following are described in the scriptures:

—	The city built by Enoch	(Moses 7:19)
—	Jerusalem and its mount	(1 Kings 8:1)
—	North and South America	Joseph Smith[3]
—	The Church of Jesus Christ	(D&C 113:7–8)
—	The New Jerusalem in Jackson County, Missouri	(D&C 57:1–5; 101:67–73
—	The pure in heart	(D&C 97:21)

Elder Bruce R. McConkie stated:

> Zion is people; Zion is the Saints of God; Zion is those who have been baptized; Zion is those who have received the Holy Ghost; Zion is those who keep the commandments; Zion is the righteous; or in other words, as our revelation recites: 'This is Zion—THE PURE IN HEART' (D&C 97:21)."[4]

Zion Is the Pure in Heart

Elder McConkie wrote:

> *Zion* is the name given by the Lord to His Saints; it is the name by which the Lord's people are always identified. Of the Saints in Enoch's day the record says: *"And the Lord called his people ZION, because they were of one heart and one mind, and dwelt in righteousness; and there was no poor among them"* (Moses 7:18). *"This is Zion—THE PURE IN HEART,"* He said in this day (D&C 97:21). Thus The Church of Jesus Christ of Latter-day Saints is Zion. . . .
>
> Many revelations speak of Zion in this sense. Before the organization of the Church, the command was given to a number of brethren, "Seek to bring forth and establish the cause of Zion" (D&C 6:6; 11:6; 12:6; 14:6). On the day of its organization, the

Lord commended the Prophet [Joseph Smith] for his diligence, prayers, and labors in bringing forth Zion (D&C 21:7–8). After its organization various brethren were commanded to labor in Zion with all their power and strength (D&C 24:7; 30:11; 93:53).[5]

Elder Dale E. Miller remarked:

> In one context, Zion is geographic, having a center, while enlarging its boundaries to eventually fill the earth.... Another context shows Zion as an organization wherein we work to strengthen its stakes through our callings.... The scriptures suggest that Zion has a third context, an intensely personal one. It is the perfecting process within us. Those willing to serve are invited to labor in the vineyard of the Lord, steadily transforming themselves to become the pure in heart.[6]

And President Brigham Young observed:

> When we are swallowed up in the will of Him who has called us; when we enjoy the peace and the smiles of our Father in Heaven, the things of His Spirit, and all the blessings we are capacitated to receive and improve upon, then are we in Zion, that is Zion.[7]

Notes

1. *Teachings of Presidents of the Church: Joseph Smith* (2007), 513,514–15.
2. Joseph Smith, in *History of the Church,*3:390–91.
3. See Joseph Smith, in *History of the Church,* 6:318–19.
4. Bruce R. McConkie, "Come: Let Israel Build Zion," *Ensign,* May 1977, 117.
5. Bruce R. McConkie, *Mormon Doctrine,* 2nd ed. (1966), 854.
6. Dale E. Miller, "The Kingdom's Perfecting Pathway," *Ensign,* May 1998, 29, 30.
7. Brigham Young, "A Discourse," *Deseret News,* Apr. 13, 1854, 41.

SECTION ONE

Zion In Previous Dispensations

EFFORTS TO ESTABLISH ZION

In every dispensation of the world the Lord has sought to establish a Zion people that will worship Him in truth and qualify themselves to have Him dwell among them. The reason for this is plain: only such a people can qualify to dwell in His presence in eternity.

Professor Keith H. Meservy wrote:

> Calling Israel to be holy was God's invitation to them to be like Him. "Ye shall be holy: for I the Lord your God am holy" (Leviticus 19:2). Their fathers—Abraham, Isaac, and Jacob—had all been sanctified (made holy) and entered into God's presence. When Moses "sought diligently to sanctify [the Israelites] that

they might behold the face of God" (D&C 84:23), they learned that it was within their capacity to do the same.

Since God is holy and His children are not, His work with them is preparatory in nature, to help them become holy. Whenever He succeeds in doing this, a society of the pure in heart is produced. While God's challenge to His people is not always expressed in these words, this is His oft-expressed goal—to build up a holy people—God's kind of people. Such a community of people is called *Zion.* To help meet this end, God's people often are commanded to build temporary sanctuaries (tabernacles and temples set apart as holy places), so that He, the Holy God, might reside in their midst. This is to be the first step in establishing Zion.[1]

And the Prophet Joseph Smith said:

> The building up of Zion is a cause that has interested the people of God in every age; it is a theme upon which prophets, priests, and kings have dwelt with peculiar delight; they have looked forward with joyful anticipation to the day in which we live; and . . . have sung and written and prophesied of this our day; but they died without the sight; we are the favored people that God has made choice of to bring about the latter-day glory.[2]

Because we are expected to build up Zion in these last days, we would do well to study efforts in previous dispensations—some successful and some not successful—in order that we might not fail to accomplish the task that lies before us.

Notes

1. Keith H. Meservy, "The Good News of Moses," in Kent P. Jackson and Robert L. Millet, eds., *Studies in Scripture, Volume Three: Genesis to 2 Samuel* (1985), 212.
2. *Teachings of Presidents of the Church: Joseph Smith* (2007), 186.

CHAPTER 1

The Zion of Enoch

(GENESIS 5; MOSES 6–7; LUKE 3; HEBREWS 11; JUDE; DOCTRINE AND COVENANTS 107)

The Book of Enoch

"ENOCH & HIS CITY TAKEN UP," DEL PARSON, © IRI, USED BY PERMISSION

- **Genesis 5:21–24** In the Bible we get only four verses about Enoch and his people. They tell us that Enoch was 65 when Methuselah was born (v. 21). They tell us that he continued to "walk with God" after Methuselah was born for 300 years while having other sons and daughters" (v. 22). They say that his total life span was 365 years (v. 23). And they tell us that he was translated (v. 24). See the table above for an explanation of why the 365 years mentioned in verse 23 is an error. He actually lived 430 years before he was translated.
- **Moses 6–7** The story of Enoch is greatly expanded in the Book of Moses. Moses was very interested in Enoch and he skipped rapidly to his day in the Book of Moses. Even these two verses are a summary of a larger record called the Book of Enoch, which we do not have in its fullness today.

- The Book of Enoch was once prominent in scripture. Enoch is mentioned frequently in the New Testament, sometimes quoting from the Book of Enoch. The Christian sectarians rejected the Book of Enoch in the centuries following Christ because they did not like the doctrines it contained, considering them to be heretical. Most copies of it were destroyed.

G.HOET

  — **Luke 3:37** Luke mentions Enoch in his recitation of the line of patriarchs after Adam.

  — **Hebrews 11:5** Paul tells us that through faith "Enoch was translated that he should not see death."

  — **Jude 14–15** Jude says that "Enoch . . . the seventh from Adam, prophesied . . . Behold, the Lord cometh with ten thousands of his saints, to execute judgment upon all, and to convince all that are ungodly among them of all their ungodly deeds."

  — **D&C 107:56–57** The Book of Enoch is also mentioned in the Doctrine and Covenants. During his final meeting with and blessing of his posterity, before his death, "Adam stood up in the midst of the congregation; and, notwithstanding he was bowed down with age, being full of the Holy Ghost, predicted whatsoever should befall his posterity unto the latest generation. These things were all written in the book of Enoch, and are to be testified of in due time."

Dr. Hugh W. Nibley wrote:

> Early Christian writers knew all about the book of Enoch: indeed, "nearly all the writers of the New Testament were familiar with it, and . . . it had all the weight of a canonical book."[1] Its influence is apparent in no less than 128 places in the New Testament. . . . [But

> to the apostate Christian church, the book of Enoch] "contained much of a questionable character," writes R. H. Charles with a sigh, "and from the fourth century of our era onward it fell into discredit; and under the ban of such authorities as Hilary, Jerome, and Augustine, it gradually passed out of circulation, and became lost to the knowledge of Western Christendom."[2] . . . They were all learned schoolmen steeped in the rhetorical and sophistic education of the time, admitting quite freely that the Christians of an earlier time held ideas and beliefs quite different from theirs. They also knew that Enoch was treasured as a canonical book by the early Christians, but they would have none of it. . . . "From the 4th century on, the Latin Church ceased to concern itself"[3] with Enoch.[4]

Today, versions of the ancient book of Enoch are coming back to light, and not surprisingly, they reveal exactly the same themes and doctrines as those found in the Pearl of Great Price.

The Patriarchs From Adam to Noah

Patriarch	Year Born	Age When Adam Died	Years Lived	Year Died
ADAM	0	930	930 yrs	930
ABEL SETH	130	800	912 yrs	1042
ENOS	235	695	905 yrs	1140
CAINAN	325	605	910 yrs	1235
MAHALALEEL	395	535	895 yrs	1290
JARED	460	470	962 yrs	1422
ENOCH	622	308	430 yrs *	1052 translated
METHUSELAH	687	243	969 yrs	1656 year of flood
LAMECH	874	56	777 yrs	1651
NOAH	1056			

- **Interesting things which the above facts tell us:**

  1. All of the patriarchs from Adam to Lamech (father of Noah) knew Adam personally.

  *2. Enoch was 430 years old when the City of Zion was translated, according to D&C 107:49, which means that in his case the biblical account (which says that he was 365) is wrong. It was the City of Zion that was 365 years old when translated, according to Moses 7:68.

  3. All of the patriarchs from Seth to Lamech (father of Noah) were on the earth when the city of Enoch was translated. They were left on the earth to continue to preach repentance, in Methuselah's case until the very time of the flood.

  4. Noah was born just 4 years after Enoch and his city were taken, just 14 years after Seth's death, and just 126 years after Adam's death. At Noah's birth, all of the patriarchs except Adam and Seth were on the earth.

  5. Methuselah died (or was possibly translated) in the year in which the flood came. There is some indication (Moses 7:27) that after Zion was taken, any righteous person who listened to the words of the patriarchs and repented was also translated or "caught up by the powers of heaven unto Zion." At Methuselah's death, Noah and his family were indeed the only righteous people left on earth.

The Calling of the Prophet Enoch

"Four generations and some five hundred years later, according to Adam's book of remembrance, Enoch, of Seth's line, was called to become a great prophet-missionary-reformer. His ministry was needed, for the followers of the line and cult of Cain had become numerous, and violence was rampant already in the fifth generation after Cain (Moses 5:28– 31, 47–57). Unto those who had become sensual and devilish Enoch preached repentance."[5]

- **Moses 6:21–26 Enoch was taught by his father, Jared,** "in all the ways of God" (v. 21). In fact, all the patriarchs in the direct line of descent from Adam to Enoch preached righteousness (v. 23).

- **D&C 107:48 Enoch was ordained by Adam at the age of 25.** He was 65 when Adam blessed him with his final blessing. Our present Pearl of Great Price text of the Book of Enoch starts when he was 65.

- **Moses 6:27–30 The Lord calls Enoch to prophesy unto the people.** Enoch heard a voice from heaven which said, "Enoch, my son, prophesy unto this people, and say unto them—Repent, for thus saith the Lord: I am angry with this people, and my fierce anger is kindled against them; for their hearts have waxed hard, and their ears are dull of hearing, and their eyes cannot see afar off" (v. 27). This is a very similar statement to the one the Lord made to Joseph Smith in our own day. Enoch, like Joseph Smith, was a dispensational prophet, called to reestablish a righteous kingdom among an apostate people. The Lord's complaints against the people of Enoch's day sound familiar to us.

  — "They have gone astray, and have denied me, and have sought their own counsels in the dark; and in their own abominations have they devised murder, and have not kept the commandments, which I gave unto their father, Adam" (v. 28).

  — "They have foresworn themselves, and, by their oaths, they have brought upon themselves death; and a hell I have prepared for them, if they repent not" (v. 29).

  The Lord decreed to Enoch that the people must repent or would be utterly destroyed. And He had declared this message from the "beginning of the world, from my own mouth, from the foundation thereof, and by the mouths of my servants, thy fathers, have I decreed it, even as it shall be sent forth in the world, unto the ends thereof" (v. 30).

- **Moses 6:31 Enoch's fearful response to his call.** Enoch was greatly humbled by his call, bowing to the earth and saying, "Why is it that I have found favor in thy sight, and am but a lad, and all the people hate me; for I am slow of speech; wherefore am I thy servant?" (v. 31). These would be familiar fears to Moses because he had some of the same weaknesses. In particular, both were "slow of speech" (Exodus 4:10; Moses 6:31), which means that they were stutterers.

- **Moses 6:32–34 The Lord's promises to Enoch.** The Lord's response to Enoch was essentially the same as the one to Moses, "Go forth and do as I have commanded thee, and no man shall pierce thee. Open thy mouth, and it shall be filled, and I will give thee utterance, for all flesh is in my hands, and I will do as seemeth me good" (v. 32). The message was clear and precise: "Choose ye this day, to serve the Lord God who made you" (v. 33). He promised Enoch that "my Spirit is upon you, wherefore all thy words will I justify; and the mountains shall flee before you, and the rivers shall turn from their course; and thou shalt abide in me, and I in you; therefore walk with me" (v. 34).

The Visions of Enoch

- **Moses 6:35 Enoch sees all of God's spirit children.** The Lord invited Enoch to "Anoint thine eyes with clay, and wash them, and thou shalt see." When he did so, "he beheld the spirits that God had created." This is very similar to the vision that Moses saw when he received his call—another reason why Moses related so well to the story of Enoch and wanted it included in the Book of Moses.
- **Moses 6:36 Enoch becomes a "seer."** Enoch was also able to see "things which were not visible to the natural eye; and from thenceforth came the saying abroad in the land: A seer hath the Lord raised up unto his people."
- **Moses 6:42–45 Enoch's vision of God, who is our Father and the Creator.** Enoch testified that "as I journeyed from the land of Cainan, by the sea east, I beheld a vision; and lo, the heavens I saw, and the Lord spake with me, and gave me commandment" (v. 42). "The Lord which spake with me, the same is the God of heaven, and he is my God, and your God, and ye are my brethren" (v. 43). Furthermore, he taught that God created the heavens and the earth, which is His footstool, and that "an host of men hath he brought in upon the face thereof" (v. 44). And he testified concerning all their predecessors who had died, going all the way back to Adam (v. 45).

The Teachings of the Prophet Enoch

- **Moses 6:37–39 Enoch begins to preach.** He boldly went forward among the people, "standing upon the hills and the high places," and crying "with a loud voice . . . against their works; and all men were offended because of him" (v. 37). They called him a "seer" but did not take him seriously, referring to him as the "wild man [that] hath come among us" (v. 38). Yet they feared him and would not touch him because it was clear that "he walked with God" (v. 39).

We do not have time or space to cover in detail all the teachings and doings of Enoch that are recorded in the Book of Moses. Suffice it to say that few people have held the powers bestowed upon Enoch.

— Was given power to control the elements (Moses 7:13–17).

— Was able to see things from the beginning to the end of time (Moses 7:21).

— He also became a very powerful preacher.

The teachings of Enoch cover seven major categories and include some information found nowhere else in scripture:

(1) The Fall of man and its results.
(2) The nature of salvation and the means of achieving it.
(3) Sin, as seen in the evils of his times, in contrast to the righteousness of the godly who were his followers.
(4) The cause, purpose, and effects of the anticipated flood of Noah.
(5) The scope of Satan's triumph and the resultant sorrows of God.
(6) The first advent of the Messiah.
(7) The second advent of the Messiah and his peaceful, millennial reign.

- **Moses 6:46 A Book of Remembrance**. The book of remembrance mentioned in the days of Seth, the son of Adam, still existed. It had been written "according to the pattern given by the finger of God" and "in our own language" (meaning the Adamic language). These writings were the "scriptures" of Enoch's day.

- **Moses 6:48 The Fall of Adam and Eve.** Enoch's summary of the fall of Adam and Eve is short and succinct. "Because that Adam fell, we are; and by his fall came death; and we are made partakers of misery and woe."

- **Moses 6:49 The influence of Satan**. His description of the role of Satan is equally to the point: "Behold Satan hath come among the children of men, and tempteth them to worship him; and men have become carnal, sensual, and devilish, and are shut out from the presence of God."

- **Moses 6:52 First principles and ordinances**. Adam was fully aware of the first principles of the gospel. Enoch quotes God as saying to Adam, "If thou wilt turn unto me, and hearken unto my voice, and believe, and repent of all thy transgressions, and be baptized, even in water, in the name of mine Only Begotten Son, . . . ye shall receive the gift of the Holy Ghost, asking all things in his name, and whatsoever ye shall ask, it shall be given you." Adam also knew that Jesus Christ [is] the only name which shall be given under heaven, whereby salvation shall come unto the children of men."
- **Moses 6:57 The names of God and Christ are Ahman, and Son of Ahman.** While speaking of what is required in order to inherit the kingdom of God, where "no unclean thing can dwell . . . in his presence," we are given the names of the Father and the Son. In the language of Adam, "Man of Holiness is [the Father's] name, and the name of his Only Begotten is the Son of Man, meaning the Son of Man of Holiness. This gives insight into why Enoch's city was called the "City of Holiness" (Moses 7:19)—it was the city of the Lord.

  Elder Orson Pratt said

  > There is one revelation that this people are not generally acquainted with. I think it has never been published, but probably it will be in the Church History. It is given in questions and answers. The first question is, "What is the name of God in the pure language?" The answer says, "Ahman." "What is the name of the Son of God?' Answer, "Son Ahman[6]—the greatest of all the parts of God excepting Ahman."[7]

  President Joseph Fielding Smith said:

  > Jesus Christ is also called Son Ahman [see D&C 95:17]. Therefore His name is connected with the name of the place where Adam dwelt [Adam-ondi-Ahman]. For that reason Elder Orson Pratt gives it the interpretation of "The Valley of God."[8]

- **Moses 6:58 Teach your children.** Enoch commanded his people to "teach these things freely unto your children." With the degree of wickedness that existed, it is obvious that children were not being properly taught and did not have an understanding of who they were, where they came from, or what their destiny might be. They were growing up in a carnal, sensual, and devilish society—one very much like the one we live in today.

- **Moses 6:63 Symbolism is everywhere.** I have studied and taught learning theory for many years. One of the principles established by considerable research is that human beings learn through symbolism. Even our very words are symbols—things which stand for something else and allow us to remember and process meanings. Thus, it should not be surprising that He who created us knows all about the power of symbolism. Notice how the Lord uses symbolism in all of His ordinances and in all of His parables. Thus, by being constantly reminded of eternal principles by everyday things and activities, we can more easily remember these eternal life-saving principles.

  Enoch tells us in this verse that everything on the earth has a "likeness, and all things are created and made to bear record of me." In other words, the very earth and all things in it symbolize our Heavenly Father's plan for us—"things which are temporal, and things which are spiritual; things which are in the heavens above, and things which are on the earth, and things which are in the earth, and things which are under the earth, both above and beneath: all things bear record of me." As just one example we can consider the seasons of the year and how they symbolize the seasons of life, and the fact that after the death of winter comes the resurrection of life in the spring. There are messages all around us if we have the spiritual eyes to see them.

- **Moses 6:59–62 Enoch describes what Adam learned** about the Atonement (vv. 59–60), the Gift of the Holy Ghost (v. 61), and the plan of salvation (v. 62).

- **Moses 6:64–65 Adam was baptized.** We learn that after Adam had been taught these things by the Lord, he was "caught away by the Spirit of the Lord, and was carried down into the water, and was laid under the water, and was brought forth out of the water. And thus he was baptized" (vv. 64–65).

- **Moses 6:66 Adam was "born again" spiritually.** After his baptism in water, "the Spirit of God descended upon [Adam], and thus he was born of the Spirit, and became quickened in the inner man. And he heard a voice out of heaven, saying: Thou art baptized with fire, and with the Holy Ghost. This is the record of the Father, and the Son, from henceforth and forever."

More Visions of Enoch

- **Moses 6:38–39 Enoch received mighty visions** and the people recognized that he was a seer who "walked with God" (v. 39). But they considered him a "wild man" that prophesied "strange things" (v. 38).
- **Moses 7:2–4 Enoch sees the world's history.** While Enoch was out preaching, he called upon God in prayer while in a place called Mahujah, whereupon he was instructed to go "upon the mount Simeon" (v. 2). He was "clothed with glory" (transfigured) and "beheld the heavens open" (v. 3). In this vision, he "saw the Lord" who "stood before my face, and . . . talked with me, even as a man talketh one with another, face to face" (v. 4). The Lord then showed him "the world for the space of many generations" (v. 4).

  This vision was similar to the one Moses had when he beheld "all the children of men" (Moses 1:8). It is yet another reason why Moses could relate so well to the prophet Enoch. Both Enoch and Moses were shown "all the children of men which are, and which were created" (Moses 1:8) and "there was not a soul which [they] beheld not" (Moses 1:27), despite the fact that "their numbers were great, even numberless as the sand upon the sea shore" (Moses 1:28).

  Dr. Rodney Turner explained:

  > [Moses] did [not] simply view them en masse as one might look at a vast concourse of people without discerning any one individual. By the incomprehensible power of the Holy Ghost he perceived each man, woman, and child comprising the human race *at one and the same time!* In doing so, he experienced something of the omnipresent nature of the Spirit of the Lord.[9] The same would have been true for Enoch's vision.

The Greatness of Enoch

- **Moses 7:10–12 Enoch is commanded to preach repentance.** The Lord was preparing to destroy the wicked from off the face of the earth. He therefore sent Enoch out to warn them, "Repent, lest I come out and smite them with a curse, and they die" (v. 10). Those who listened to him he was commanded to "baptize in the name of the Father, and of the Son, . . . and of the Holy Ghost" (v. 11). This Enoch did among all of the people except "the people of Canaan" (v. 12).

- **Moses 7:13 Enoch's great faith moves mountains and rivers.** As we might imagine, the forces of evil were so great and so angry that they "came to battle" against "the people of God" who had chosen to follow the prophet Enoch" (v. 13). But when Enoch "spake the word of the Lord, . . . the earth trembled, and the mountains fled, even according to his command; and the rivers of water were turned out of their course; and the roar of the lions was heard out of the wilderness" (v. 13). He had been promised by the Lord that "the mountains shall flee before you, and the rivers shall turn from their course; and thou shalt abide in me, and I in you; therefore walk with me" (Moses 6:34). And now we see the fulfillment of those promises.

- **Moses 7:14 Enoch's great faith against the armies of the wicked.** The display of Enoch's mighty power put fear in the hearts of all of his enemies. They did not dare come up against "the people of God" for fear of annihilation. Some took refuge on land that had recently come up "out of the depth of the sea," perhaps as a result of the great tectonic movements Enoch had set off when he moved mountains and rivers.

- **Moses 7:15 "Giants" came up on the land** to afflict the sons of God. They "stood afar off" out of fear of Enoch's mighty power. These cursed people were still around in Noah's day (8:18). These "giants" were not huge and scary monsters. They were people in opposition to Noah and the gospel he was teaching, and they were a cursed people.

The English word	The Hebrew word	The Hebrew meaning
"giants"	"nephalim"	"those who cause to fall" or "tyrants"

The City of Enoch Was Translated

- **Moses 7:16–17 War ensued among the wicked, but Enoch's Zion dwelt in peace.** As seems to always be the case, "wars and bloodshed" became the norm among the wicked. But among the people of God, "the Lord came and dwelt with his people, and they dwelt in righteousness" (v. 16). In other words, their righteousness reached a point where they became a Zion people. The "glory of the Lord . . . was upon his people. And the Lord blessed the land, and they were blessed upon the mountains, and upon the high places, and did flourish" (v. 17).

- **Moses 7:18–21 Enoch established the city of Zion, which was translated.** The Lord gave Enoch's righteous people a new name: "Zion, because they were of one heart and one mind, and dwelt in righteousness; and there was no poor among them" (v. 18). They built a city which was called "the City of Holiness, even ZION" (v. 19). Thus, both the *people* and the *place* where they dwelt were designated as Zion. The Lord blessed them with safety and peace, "but the residue of the people [He] cursed" (v. 20). And eventually, "in process of time" the city and people of Zion were "taken up into heaven" (translated) (v. 21).

  Elder Bruce R. McConkie said:

  > After the Lord called his people Zion, the scripture says that Enoch "built a city that was called the City of Holiness, even ZION"; that Zion "was taken up into heaven" where "God received it up into his own bosom"; and that "from thence went forth the saying, Zion is fled." (Moses 7:19, 21, 69). . . .
  >
  > This same Zion which was taken up into heaven shall return during the Millennium, when the Lord brings again Zion; and its inhabitants shall join with the New Jerusalem which shall then be established. (Moses 7:62–63).[10]

- **Hebrews 11:5 Enoch was translated by faith.** The only information we have in the Bible concerning Enoch, aside from this statement of Paul's, is that given in Genesis 5:24: "And Enoch walked with God: and he was not; for God took him." This one passage, together with Paul's inspired comment, has given rise to endless speculation regarding Enoch's destiny. What is the meaning of "and he was not; for

God took him"? Took him whereto heaven? to paradise? Once again Joseph Smith, the great prophet of the last dispensation, has helped provide the answer: Enoch and his entire city was so righteous that they were taken from the earth to a place where they could "dwell in safety forever." (Moses 7:18–21; see especially verse 20.)

The Prophet Joseph Smith said:

> Now this Enoch God reserved unto Himself, that he should not die at that time, and appointed unto him a ministry unto terrestrial bodies, of whom there has been but little revealed. . . . Many have supposed that the doctrine of translation was a doctrine whereby men were taken immediately into the presence of God, and into an eternal fullness, but this is a mistaken idea. Their place of habitation is that of the terrestrial order, and a place prepared for such characters He held in reserve to be ministering angels unto many planets, and who as yet have not entered into so great a fullness as those who are resurrected from the dead.[11]

- **Hebrews 11:10, 16 Zion was "a city . . . whose builder and maker is God."** The city referred to in this passage is the "city of Zion" or the city which Enoch and his people built. Translated from the earth because of the righteousness of its inhabitants, the city of Enoch became an example of that to which all men who studied and practiced righteousness might seek. Abraham certainly did, as Paul informs us here.
- **Moses 7:67–69 "Zion is fled."** We are told that "the Lord showed Enoch all things, even unto the end of the world" (v. 67). We are told again that "Enoch and all his people walked with God, and he dwelt in the midst of Zion" while the city was on the earth (v. 69). And then, and after 365 years of its existence, the city of "Zion was not, for God received it up into his own bosom; and from thence went forth the saying, Zion is fled" (vv. 68–69).
- **Moses 7:62–63 The City of Enoch will return again at the Second Coming.** The scriptures contain a promise that the city of Enoch shall someday return to earth. This promise is reserved for fulfillment during the coming millennium of peace. The Lord told Enoch that in the latter days of earth, He would prepare "an Holy City . . . and it shall be called Zion, a New Jerusalem. . . . Then shalt thou and all thy

city meet them there, and we will receive them into our bosom, and they shall see us." The city of Enoch shall return to earth.

- **JST Gen. 9:21–25 The rainbow was set in heaven as a sign of God's covenant to Enoch concerning Zion.** The rainbow is usually associated with God's covenant to Noah after the flood. But actually, the covenant was made first with Enoch, "who, seeing that the world would be flooded, sought God's reassurance. He said to Noah that in the last days "when men should keep all my commandments, Zion should again come on the Earth, the city of Enoch which I have caught up unto myself. And this is mine everlasting covenant that I establish with you," The City of Enoch will come down and join the city of New Jerusalem.

  Thus, "in addition to being a sign that God will no longer destroy the world by flood, the rainbow is a sign of the return of the city of Enoch. This is unique restored doctrine not appreciated (or known) by most Latter-day Saints. When we see a rainbow in the sky, we should see it as a sign that Zion will return."[12]

- **Moses 7:62–64 Enoch's Zion will join with the New Jerusalem.** Kent Jackson said:

  > Enoch's city cannot return until its counterpart, the latter-day Zion on earth, is established and ready to receive it. . . . "Then shalt thou and all thy city meet them there, and we will receive them into our bosom, and they shall see us; and we will fall upon their necks, and they shall fall upon our necks, and we will kiss each other; and there shall be mine abode, and it shall be Zion, which shall come forth out of all the creations which I have made; and for the space of a thousand years the earth shall rest" [Moses 7:63–64].[13]

What Does It Mean to be Translated?

We might wonder when we hear about Enoch and his people what happened to them. And what is the condition of all translated beings?

- **3 Nephi 28 We Know the Following About Translated Persons** from the description of the Three Nephites in the Book of Mormon.

  — They never taste of death or endure the pains of death (vv. 7–8, 37–38).

— They will be changed from mortality to immortality in the twinkling of an eye (v. 8).

— They experience no pain while in the flesh and no sorrow except for the sins of the world (v. 9).

— They have power over the evil men of the earth (v. 19–22).

— They are like the angels of God, administering to whomsoever they will (v. 30).

— A change is effected on their bodies so that Satan can have no power over them, and they are sanctified in the flesh and are holy (v. 39).

— They remain in a translated state until the Judgment Day (v. 40).

— Translated beings are also transfigured (vv. 13–15)

Elder Bruce R. McConkie wrote:

> Some mortals have been translated. In this state they are not subject to sorrow [except for the sins of the world] or to disease or to death. No longer does blood (the life-giving element of our present mortality) flow in their veins. Procreation ceases. If they then had children, their offspring would be denied a mortal probation, which all worthy spirits must receive in due course. They have power to move and live in both a mortal and an unseen sphere. All translated beings undergo another change in their bodies when they gain full immortality. This change is the equivalent of a resurrection. . . . Millennial man will live in a state akin to translation. His body will be changed so that it is no longer subject to disease or death as we know it, although he will be changed in the twinkling of an eye to full immortality when he is a hundred years of age.[14]
>
> All translated beings [eventually] receive what amounts to an instantaneous death and resurrection. Those who were translated before the Resurrection of our Lord "were with Christ in his resurrection" (D&C 133:55). Those who have been translated since the Resurrection of Christ shall continue to live as mortals

> until the Second Coming when they shall receive their immortal glory.[15]

The Prophet Joseph Smith said:

> Now this Enoch God reserved unto Himself, that he should not die at that time, and appointed unto him a ministry unto terrestrial bodies, of whom there has been but little revealed.... He is a ministering angel, to minister to those who shall be heirs of salvation....
>
> Many have supposed that the doctrine of translation was a doctrine whereby men were taken immediately into the presence of God, and into an eternal fulness, but this is a mistaken idea. Their place of habitation is that of the terrestrial order, and a place prepared for such characters He held in reserve to be ministering angels unto many planets, and who as yet have not entered into so great a fulness as those who are resurrected from the dead.[16]

Translated Persons Will Eventually Die and Be Resurrected

Jesus promised the Three Nephites, "Ye shall never taste of death" (v. 7). This does not mean they will never die. All men and women die. No person, not even a translated being immunity from death.

The Prophet Joseph Smith taught that "translated bodies cannot enter into rest until they have undergone a change equivalent to death."[17]

Drs. Joseph Fielding McConkie and Robert L. Millet wrote:

> It would appear that all persons who were translated before the Resurrection of Christ—Enoch and his city, Melchizedek and his city, Elijah, Moses, Alma the Younger, Nephi, and so forth—were resurrected at the time of Christ's Resurrection.[18] Persons who were translated after the time of Christ's Resurrection will minister in their terrestrial state until the Second Advent. At that time they will be changed in the twinkling of an eye, transformed instantaneously from their mortal (still subject to death) terrestrial condition to a resurrected fully immortal condition.[19]

Conditions after Zion was "Taken"

- **Moses 7:22–26 The power of Satan was upon all the earth.** All of the children of Adam had intermixed by this point in history, except for the descendants of Cain, who had been marked with a black skin and lived separately from all other peoples (v. 22). From his vantage point "high and lifted up, even in the bosom of the Father, and of the Son of Man" Enoch could see that "the power of Satan was upon all the face of the earth" (v. 24). The children of God had reached the point of no return, when their wickedness was fully ripe and ready for destruction. No child born into the world had any chance of hearing the truth and making a choice. Wickedness was everywhere. As part of this vision, "he beheld Satan; and he had a great chain in his hand, and it veiled the whole face of the earth with darkness; and he looked up and laughed, and his angels rejoiced" (v. 26). It makes Satan happy when we are miserable. They think it's funny when we suffer. They rejoice when wickedness prevails.

- **Moses 7:28–30 God weeps.** We can only imagine the sorrow of our Father when he saw his children so thoroughly engulfed in wickedness. Enoch saw and bore record that as "the God of heaven looked upon the residue of the people . . . he wept" (v. 28). This surprised Enoch, who wondered how someone as mighty as God could weep (vv. 29–39).

- **Moses 7:32–34 God explains why he wept.** The Lord explained to Enoch that "these thy brethren; they are the workmanship of mine own hands, and I gave unto them their knowledge, in the day I created them; and in the Garden of Eden, gave I unto man his agency" (v. 32). Furthermore, He had commanded His children "that they should love one another, and that they should choose me, their Father; but behold, they are without affection, and they hate their own blood" (v. 33). Thus, the Father had no choice but to remove them from the earth and start again. Agency was now not possible in a cesspool of wickedness. God said, "mine indignation is kindled against them; and in my hot displeasure will I send in the floods upon them" (v. 34).

- **Moses 7:38–40 The promised redemption of Christ will apply also to the wicked of Enoch's day.** From an earthly perspective, physical death is great tragedy. It feels like it is the end. But from God's perspective it is simply a choice to move a spirit child from one estate into another. The wicked in the days of Enoch and Noah would "perish in the floods" physically, but their spirits would live on in "a prison [which] have I prepared for them"—the spirit prison (v. 38). And while they would have to remain there "in torment" for a long time, eventually the Savior who "suffereth for their sins" will teach them the truth there so that they can have a realistic chance to repent (v. 39).

METHUSELAH AND LAMECH

Thus ended the dispensation of Enoch. He and his people were removed from the earth to protect them from the coming flood. Two righteous prophets remained to preach the gospel and to carry on the patriarchal bloodline down to Noah. These were Methuselah, the son of Enoch, and Methuselah's son Lamech, who was Noah's father.

Methuselah

Methuselah was the son of Enoch, and is mentioned in only six verses in the Old Testament (see Gen. 5:21-22, 25-27; 1 Chr. 1:3). These verses tell us very little about him. From modern revelation, we know that Methuselah was ordained to the priesthood by Adam (D&C 107:50), and he, in turn, ordained his grandson Noah (D&C 107:52). Methuselah was present at the great meeting at Adam-ondi-Ahman three years before Adam's death at which Adam gave his righteous posterity "his last blessing" (D&C 107:53). Methuselah provided the link between Adam and Noah, who would become a "new Adam"—father of the human family— following the Flood.[20]

When Enoch's city was translated, Methuselah "was not taken, that the covenants of the Lord might be fulfilled, which he made to Enoch" (Moses 8:2). Dr. Kent P. Jackson explained this covenant:

> Enoch had learned through revelation that the Flood would destroy the population of the earth. The covenant referred to in this verse [Moses 8:2] was that from his lineage a faithful family would survive to repopulate the planet, and thus all the people thereafter would stem from him [see Moses 7:42, 50–52; Genesis 6:18[21]]. Of necessity a family line from Enoch—presumably worthy to

be translated—would remain behind. Methuselah prophesied correctly that all the human family would descend from him, but "he took glory unto himself" (Moses 8:3).[22]

- **Genesis 5:21,27 Methuselah died in the year of the Flood.** "Methuselah lived till the very year in which the Flood came, of which his name is supposed to have been prophetical ... *methu,* 'he dieth,' and *shalach,* 'he *sendeth out*'; as if God had designed to teach men that as soon as Methuselah died the Flood should be sent forth to drown an ungodly world. . . . Even the *name* of this patriarch contained in it a *gracious warning.*"[23]
- **JST Genesis 14:34 The people of Melchizedek were also translated.** They were contemporaries of Abraham who also "wrought righteousness, and obtained heaven, and sought for the city of Enoch which God had before taken, separating it from the earth, having reserved it unto the latter days, or the end of the world."

  Those of succeeding generations likewise continued to seek for this standard, but as the Lord informs us in latter-day scripture, they "found it not because of wickedness and abominations; And confessed that they were strangers and pilgrims on the earth; But obtained a promise that they should find it and see it in their flesh." (D&C 45:12–14.)

NOAH AND THE COVENANT

Noah and his three sons—Japheth, Shem, and Ham—were called "the sons of God" (Moses 8:13) because they were righteous men. They "walked with God" (Moses 8:27), a phrase also used to describe Enoch and his people in Zion (Moses 7:69).

Noah received the priesthood from his grandfather Methuselah when he was ten years old (D&C 107:52). Later, "the Lord ordained Noah after his own order"—the priesthood after the order of the Son of God (Melchizedek Priesthood) in preparation for his calling to "declare his Gospel unto the children of men, even as it was given unto Enoch" (Moses 8:19).

The Prophet Joseph Smith said: "As Noah was a preacher of righteousness he must have been baptized and ordained to the priesthood by the laying on of the hands. . . ." Indeed, God "continued to [Noah] the keys, the covenants, the power, and the glory with which he blessed Adam at the beginning."[24]

Noah "taught the things of God" (Moses 8:16), including faith, repentance, baptism, and the reception of the Holy Ghost (Moses 8:24). This is verified by the Prophet Joseph Smith when he said: "Now taking it for granted that the scriptures say what they mean and mean what they say, we have sufficient grounds to go on and prove from the Bible that the gospel has always been the same, the ordinances to fulfill its requirements the same, and the officers to officiate the same, and the signs and fruits resulting from the promises the same."[25]

Dr. Kent P. Jackson said:

> The Latter-day Saint view that ancient righteous people had the gospel is not shared by other Christians. But how else could it be? If God spoke with worthy men like Noah, and if accepting the gospel of Christ is the only means of salvation, as the Bible teaches (see John 3:16, 36; 1 John 5:11–12), then why would God deny its blessings to honorable men and women who lived before Jesus? These considerations should cause all Christians to conclude, as Joseph Smith did, that "much instruction has been given to man since the beginning which we have not."[26]
>
> We are certainly blessed by the restored scriptures that teach us of believers in Christ from earlier days[27]

Noah warned the people that rejection of his message would bring destruction: "If men do not repent, [the Lord] will send in the floods upon them" (Moses 8:17). "Noah called upon the children of men that they should repent; but they hearkened not unto his words" (Moses 8:20). "And if ye do not this, the floods will come in upon you." But still, "they hearkened not" (Moses 8:24). This puts the Flood in its proper context. The Lord through his servant Noah (and others before him) gave the people of the world every opportunity to change before bringing in the floods upon them.

The Covenant and the Rainbow

The Joseph Smith Translation makes several references to a covenant God made with Enoch and later renewed with Noah. From the evidence preserved in the text, it appears that this covenant had several parts:

1. **The entire human family will descend from Enoch and Noah.** We have already seen this promise in the account concerning Enoch's son (and Noah's grandfather) Methuselah (see Moses 8:2-3). The Lord told Noah, "With thee will I establish my covenant, even as I have sworn unto thy father, Enoch, that of thy posterity shall come all nations" (JST Genesis 6:18–19).

2. **The inhabitants of the earth will never again be destroyed by flood.** The Joseph Smith Translation teaches that this promise was made earlier to Enoch (Moses 7:50-51; JST Gen. 9:9, 12), but it provides an interesting context—not found in the Bible—for the renewal of the blessing to Noah.

   The Joseph Smith Translation change to Genesis 8:21 shows that the promise came as the result of Noah's request to the Lord in behalf of the living things of the earth. Noah said, "I will call on the name of the Lord, that he will not again curse the ground any more for man's sake, . . . and that he will not again smite any more every thing living, as he hath done."[28]

   The Lord honored Noah's request and promised that he would never again send a flood to destroy all the humans and animals (see JST at Gen. 9:9-15). Noah served as an intercessor in behalf of his descendants and the rest of life on earth, as is shown in several changes in the Joseph Smith Translation (see JST at Gen. 9:9, 12, 15, 17"). Just as Adam at the beginning of human history was God's representative and vice-regent on earth, so Noah, the new Adam, made covenants with God in behalf of his children and all other life.

3. **"This promise came with a sign. The rainbow,** which even now often shows that a rainstorm is ending, would signify that God would never again destroy the world by flood (see Genesis 9:12–15[29])."[30] Dr. Kent P. Jackson said, "Concerning the destruction of the world that will take place in the last days, Joseph Smith taught: 'I have asked of the Lord concerning His coming; and while asking the Lord, He gave me a sign and said, "In the days of Noah I set a bow in the heavens as a sign and token that in any year that the bow should be seen the Lord would not come; but there should be seed time and harvest during that year: but whenever you see the bow withdrawn, it shall be a token that there shall be famine, pestilence, and great distress among the nations'[31]."[32]

The Greatness of Noah

Dr. Kent P. Jackson wrote:

> Noah was a great man, chosen to preach the gospel of repentance, to preserve a faithful family through the Flood, to lead God's people in his generation, and to father all the human race that would come after him. Yet there is more to Noah's significance than can be gleaned from the scriptures.
>
> Joseph Smith taught, "Christ is the Great High Priest; Adam next."[33] And, "The Priesthood was first given to Adam . . . then to Noah, who is Gabriel; he stands next in authority to Adam in the Priesthood; he was called of God to this office, and was the father of all living in his day, and to him was given the dominion."[34]
>
> Hence, the hierarchy of God's priesthood holders in the human family begins with Christ, then Adam, and then Noah—making

Noah third in rank among all the bearers of the holy priesthood. Moreover, Noah was Gabriel.

How fitting that this great man would have the assignment to return to earth as a spirit messenger (see D&C 129:1, 3; 130:5) to prepare selected participants for the coming of the Savior in the flesh (see Luke 1:11–20, 26– 38; and probably Matthew 1:20–24; 2:13, 19–20; and possibly Luke 2:8–14).[35]

Notes:

1. R. H. Charles, *The Book of Enoch* (1913), page ix, note 1.
2. R. H. Charles, *The Book of Enoch,* page ix.
3. G. B., "Livre d'Henoch," in J.-P. Migne, *Dictionnaire des Apocryphes,* 2 vols. (Paris: Migne, 1856), 1:396, in *Troisième et Dernière Encyclopédie Théologique,* Tomes 23 and 24.
4. Hugh W. Nibley, *Enoch the Prophet,* ed. Stephen D. Ricks (1986), 95, 97, 98, 99.
5. Ellis T. Rasmussen, *An Introduction to the Old Testament and Its Teachings,* 2nd ed., 2 vols. (1972–74), 1:24–25.
6. See Doctrine and Covenants 78:20; 95:17.
7. Orson Pratt, "Discourse," *Deseret News,* May 23, 1855, 82.
8. Joseph Fielding Smith, *Church History and Modern Revelation*, 2 vols. (1953), 1:310.
9. Rodney Turner, "The Visions of Moses," in Robert L. Millet and Kent P. Jackson, eds., *Studies in Scripture, Volume Two: The Pearl of Great Price* (1985), 55.
10. Bruce R. McConkie, "Come: Let Israel Build Zion," *Ensign,* May 1977, 117.
11. Joseph Smith, in *History of the Church,* 4:209, 210.
12. Kent P. Jackson, "Methuselah, Noah, and Melchizedek," in *The Restored Gospel and the Book of Genesis*, Chapter 10, 111-126.
13. Kent P. Jackson, *The Restored Gospel and the Book of Genesis,* Chapter 10, 111-126.
14. Bruce R. McConkie, *The Millennial Messiah: The Second Coming of the Son of Man* (1982), 644.
15. Bruce R. McConkie, *Mormon Doctrine,* 803, 807–8.
16. Joseph Smith, in *History of the Church,* 4:209, 210.

17. Joseph Smith, in *History of the Church,* 4:425.

18. See Doctrine and Covenants 133:54–55. See also Bruce R. McConkie, *Mormon Doctrine,* 807–8.

19. Joseph Fielding McConkie, Robert L. Millet, and Brent L. Top, *Doctrinal Commentary on the Book of Mormon,* 4 vols. (1987–92), 4:190.

20. Kent P. Jackson, *The Restored Gospel and the Book of Genesis,* 111–126.

21. Compare Joseph Smith Translation (JST), Genesis 8:23–24.

22. Kent P. Jackson, *The Restored Gospel and the Book of Genesis,* 112.

23. Adam Clarke, *The Holy Bible . . . with a Commentary and Critical Notes,* 6 vols. (n.d.), 1:68.

24. *Times and Seasons,* 1 September 1842, 904; spelling and punctuation standardized.

25. *Times and Seasons,* 1 September 1842, 904; spelling and punctuation standardized.

26. Joseph Smith, in *The Evening and the Morning Star,* Mar. 1834, 143.

27. Kent P. Jackson, *The Restored Gospel and the Book of Genesis,* 113–14.

28. Joseph Smith Translation (JST) Genesis 9:6.

29. See also Joseph Smith Translation (JST), Genesis 9:15–20.

30. Kent P. Jackson, *The Restored Gospel and the Book of Genesis,* 115.

31. *Teachings of Presidents of the Church: Joseph Smith* (2007), 252.

32. Kent P. Jackson, *The Restored Gospel and the Book of Genesis,* 115–16.

33. *Teachings of Presidents of the Church: Joseph Smith,* 105.

34. *Teachings of Presidents of the Church: Joseph Smith,* 104.

35. Kent P. Jackson, *The Restored Gospel and the Book of Genesis,* 118.

CHAPTER 2

The Zion of Melchizedek

(GENESIS 14; PSALM 110; HEBREWS 5–7; ALMA 13; DOCTRINE AND COVENANTS 76; 84; 107)

Dr. Kent P. Jackson wrote:

> The translation of the city of Enoch did not end God's work to build Zion on earth, for, as Joseph Smith taught, "The building up of Zion is a cause that has interested the people of God in every age."[1] Though the Flood would delay the creation of other Zion communities until after the waters subsided, Zion on earth was always the objective.[2]

MELCHIZEDEK

Melchizedek's name appears only one time in Genesis (14:18), leading the world to believe that he played only a very minor role in the history of Abraham. Yet he is mentioned both in Psalms (110:4) and in the New Testament (see Hebrews 5:6, 10; 6:20; 7:1–28), and there is a discussion of him in the Book of Mormon (see Alma 13:14–19). These references show that much was known of him in antiquity that has not survived in our Bible.[3]

Medieval mosaic of Melchizedek at an altar

Dr. Daniel H. Ludlow commented:

> Melchizedek is one of the most misinterpreted persons in the Bible. He lived approximately 2000 B.C., was a contemporary of Abraham, and was one of the most righteous men who ever lived on the earth. Yet little is known about him, and the little that is said about him in the Bible has been misunderstood by most biblical scholars.[4]

THE GREATNESS OF MELCHIZEDEK

The King of Salem

Melchizedek was a king and (high) priest of the Lord's people in pre-Israelite Canaan. He was the prophet-leader in Salem (later called Jerusalem).[5]

Salem was located exactly where Jerusalem stands today

He was a prince because he "reign[ed] under his father" (the former king) (Alma 13:18). He was the prince of peace because of the name of his city—Salem—which means "peace" (see Hebrews 7:2).

This exalted title—"The Prince of Peace"[6]—was later to grace only one other person: our Lord and Savior Jesus Christ, of whom Melchizedek was a prototype.

"In the days of Melchizedek and Abraham, the area of Syria and Canaan constituted not a country but a collection of small city-states ruled by kings. Melchizedek was apparently one such king, ruling a nation that the Book of Mormon describes as 'full of all manner of wickedness' (Alma 13:17)."[7]

"But Melchizedek having exercised mighty faith, and received the office of the high priesthood according to the holy order of God, did preach repentance unto his people. And behold, they did repent; and Melchizedek did establish peace in the land in his days; therefore he was called the prince of peace, for he was the king of Salem; and he did reign under his father" (Alma 13:18).

Where Did Melchizedek Reign?

Drs. D. Kelly Ogden and Andrew C. Skinner observed:

> Abraham's instruction to go to the "land of Moriah" for the offering of his son [Isaac] (Genesis 22:2) is the first biblical reference to a place called Moriah. Numerous and long-standing Jewish and Christian traditions, as well as the historian Josephus, all support the thesis that Moriah is the same place as Jerusalem's Temple Mount. The biblical record itself indicates that "Solomon began to build the house of the Lord at Jerusalem in mount Moriah, where the Lord appeared unto David" (2 Chronicles 3:1).
>
> Partly because of the sanctity of the place, David purchased the rock on Moriah to make an altar to the Lord (see 2 Samuel 24:18– 25), and he instructed Solomon to build the holiest edifice in ancient Israel at that spot (see 1 Kings 5:5). . . . We do know that Abraham had met with Melchizedek sometime before "at the valley of Shaveh, which is the king's dale" identified in Bible times and today as the confluence of the Kidron, Tyropoeon, and Hinnom Valleys southeast of the City of David—that is, Old Testament Jerusalem (see Genesis 14:17). We know, too, that Melchizedek ruled over his people at Salem, later called Jerusalem. . . .

The Rock of Sacrifice on Mt. Moriah was inside Solomon's Temple in the Holy of Holies

> Is it possible that a Temple or sanctuary existed on Moriah during Abraham's lifetime? One early historian wrote that "[Melchizedek] the Righteous King, for such he really was; on which account he was [there] the first priest of God, and first built a temple [there],

and called the city Jerusalem, which was formerly called Salem" [Josephus, *Wars of the Jews,* book 6, chapter 10, paragraph 1].[8]

- **Alma 13:14–18 Alma used Melchizedek's people as an example of a wicked people who repented and were blessed.** The people in Salem were just as wicked as the people in Ammonihah, but because the people in Salem chose to repent, they were forgiven and blessed. Because the people of Ammonihah did not do this, they were eventually utterly destroyed (see Alma 16).

  Melchizedek's people and city became righteous enough to be translated. The great high priest established righteousness among his people, eventually making them a Zion people (see JST, Genesis 14:25–40 [in the Bible appendix]).

A Prince and King of Peace

By preaching repentance to his people, Melchizedek established peace. He was therefore called "the prince of peace" (Alma 13:18), and the "King of Salem, which is, King of peace" (Hebrews 7:2).

- **JST, Genesis 14:36 Melchizedek was also called "the king of heaven by his people, or, in other words, the King of peace."**

  "Joseph Smith taught that the name 'Salem' for Melchizedek's community [had nothing] to do . . . with geography but [rather] with the quality of the people who made up its citizenry: 'In the original it reads "king of Shalom," which signifies king of peace or righteousness.'[9]"[10]

  "Melchizedek apparently began with the kingdom over which he ruled 'under his father' (Alma 13:18). But as his land was transformed into a covenant community of Saints, it is likely that it attracted believers from many separate political entities, just as Enoch's city did and just as the Lord's kingdom does today."[11]

  Elder Bruce R. McConkie shared these insights about Melchizedek:

  > Paul, very obviously knowing much more about Melchizedek than he happened to record in his epistles, gave as an illustration of great faith some unnamed person who "wrought righteousness,

obtained promises, stopped the mouths of lions, quenched the violence of fire" (Hebrews 11:33–34). From the [Prophet Joseph Smith's] inspired additions to the Old Testament we learn that Paul's reference was to Melchizedek [see JST, Genesis 14:26 (in the Bible appendix)].[12]

A Great High Priest

Concerning Melchizedek, Elder McConkie continued:

> Of all God's ancient high priests "none were greater" (Alma 13:19) [than Melchizedek]. His position in the priestly hierarchy of God's earthly kingdom was like unto that of Abraham (Hebrews 7:4–10), his contemporary whom he blessed [Genesis 14:18–20; Hebrews 7:1; JST, Genesis 14:17–40], and upon whom he conferred the priesthood (D&C 84:14). Indeed, so exalted and high was the position of Melchizedek in the eyes of the Lord and of his people that he stood as a prototype of the Son of God Himself.[13]

- **Genesis 14:18–20 Abraham knew that Melchizedek "was the priest of the most high God"** (meaning he held the keys of the high priesthood) (v. 18), and that he (Abraham) was accountable to him. It was for this reason that he paid him his tithes (v. 20). Unfortunately, this is about all we get from the Old Testament regarding Melchizedek.
- **JST, Genesis 14:37–39 Melchizedek was the presiding high priest over Abraham.** Melchizedek blessed Abraham, and Abraham gave him tithes. "He blessed Abram, being the high priest, and the keeper of the storehouse of God; him whom God had appointed to receive tithes for the poor. Wherefore, Abram paid unto him tithes of all that he had, of all the riches which he possessed."

"Aside from Abraham and his family members, Melchizedek is the only other mortal mentioned in this part of the Bible who worshipped the true God. . . . As great as Father Abraham was, to whom the Bible dedicates thirteen chapters, our text leads to the conclusion that Melchizedek was the presiding authority, again suggesting that there is much about this period we do not know."[14]

- **Abraham 1:2–3 Abraham sought for the blessings of the priesthood from the time of his youth.** He recognized that he was a descendant of Enoch and Noah and therefore was entitled to be ordained and to lead God's people as His prophet and their patriarch.

  In response, the Lord led Abraham to the land of Canaan, which the Lord promised to give to him and his posterity. There he sought out Melchizedek in order to receive the priesthood.

  Another revelation tells us that Abraham received the priesthood from Melchizedek, "who received it through the lineage of his fathers, even till Noah" (D&C 84:14).

  Abraham tells us:

  > I sought for the blessings of the fathers, and the right whereunto I should be ordained to administer the same; having been myself a follower of righteousness, desiring also to be one who possessed great knowledge, and to be a greater follower of righteousness, and to possess a greater knowledge, and to be a father of many nations, a prince of peace, and desiring to receive instructions, and to keep the commandments of God, I became a rightful heir, a High Priest, holding the right belonging to the fathers. It was conferred upon me from the fathers (Abraham 1:2–3).

Joseph Smith taught that Abraham "received a blessing under the hands of Melchizedek, even the last law, or a fulness of the law or priesthood, which constituted him a king and priest after the order of Melchizedek, or an endless life."[15]

MELCHIZEDEK BLESSES ABRAM, © WALTER RANE. USED BY PERMISSION.

Abraham received the priesthood from Melchizedek

The Prophet Joseph also said:

> "Abraham [told] Melchizedek, I believe

all that thou hast taught me concerning the priesthood and the coming of the Son of Man; so Melchizedek ordained Abraham and sent him away. Abraham rejoiced, saying, Now I have [the] priesthood."[16]

And Drs. D. Kelly Ogden and Andrew C. Skinner noted:

> Abraham received the priesthood from Melchizedek (see D&C 84:14), though we do not know when or where. . . . We understand . . . that Melchizedek bestowed on [Abraham] the priesthood either in the land of the Chaldeans or in the land of Salem. When Abraham "sought for [his] appointment unto the Priesthood" (Abraham 1:4), he either traveled to Canaan or else Melchizedek traveled to Mesopotamia.[17]

The blessing Abraham received from Melchizedek is an example of "the blessing of being sealed [up unto] exaltation, administered under the hands of one holding the keys of this power. This 'was not the power of a prophet, nor apostle, nor patriarch only, but of [a] king and priest to God—to open the windows of heaven and pour out the peace and law of endless life to man.'[18] Indeed Melchizedek, whose true kingship was of the kingdom of God, 'stood as God to give laws to the people, administering endless lives to the sons and daughters of Adam [by] kingly powers of anointing.'[19]"[20]

"It is in this sense that those who will be the heirs of the celestial kingdom 'are they who are priests and kings, who have received of his fulness, and of his glory; and are priests of the Most High, after the order of Melchizedek, which was after the order of Enoch, which was after the order of the Only Begotten Son' (D&C 76:56–57)."[21]

GIOVANNI BATTISTA, 1740, PUBLIC DOMAIN

Administering the Sacrament

"The Bible tells us that when Abraham returned from a battle to rescue his nephew Lot from capture, he encountered Melchizedek, the king of Salem. At their meeting, Melchizedek 'brought forth bread and wine.' The Bible suggests only incidentally a connection between the bread and wine and the fact that Melchizedek 'was the priest of the most high God' (Genesis 14:18)."[22]

"Melchizedek 'brought forth bread and wine; and he break bread and blest it; and he blest the wine, he being the priest of the most high God' [JST, Genesis 14:17]. The bread and wine were thus obviously not a meal but an ordinance conducted by virtue of the priesthood. This was certainly the sacrament, which commemorates (in this case in advance) the atoning flesh and blood of Christ, and this passage is the earliest reference to the sacrament in the scriptures."[23]

In the Joseph Smith Translation of Genesis 14, several verses are added about Melchizedek that greatly increase the available knowledge of this great high priest [see JST, Genesis 14:25–40 (in the Bible appendix)]. Following are four such verses:

- **JST, Genesis 14:26–29**

> "Now Melchizedek was a man of faith, who wrought righteousness; and when a child he feared God, and stopped the mouths of lions, and quenched the violence of fire.
>
> "And thus, having been approved of God, he was ordained an high priest after the order of the covenant which God made with Enoch,
>
> "It being after the order of the Son of God; which order came, not by man, nor the will of man; neither by father nor mother; neither by beginning of days nor end of years; but of God;
>
> "And it was delivered unto men by the calling of his own voice, according to his own will, unto as many as believed on his name."

A Symbol of Christ

Dr. Kent P. Jackson tells us:

> Melchizedek's name, like that of most others from ancient Semitic-speaking peoples, can be translated as a sentence and gives praises to his God. The first part, *Melchi-* (Hebrew *malkî*), means "My King" and has reference to God. *Zedek* (Hebrew *sedek*) means "righteousness." [Therefore,] the name means "My (Divine) King Is Righteousness." . . . [Both of these names are used to describe Jesus also. Thus,] Melchizedek, being both a "great high priest" (D&C 107:2) and a priest-king, serves as a [symbol] of Christ, as we learn from the Joseph Smith Translation of Hebrews 7:3.[24]

Was Melchizedek Actually Shem?

Noah's sons Shem, Ham, and Japheth

Based primarily on the phrases "Melchizedek was such a great high priest" (D&C 107:2) and "Shem, the great high priest" (D&C 138:41), some have suggested that Shem and Melchizedek are the same person.

There are some issues with this analysis, but in some ancient Jewish traditions, Melchizedek is thought to be Shem, the son of Noah. Melchizedek is a title meaning "king of righteousness," even though it is also used as a proper name. A modern writer examined the question of whether Shem and Melchizedek could be the same person and concluded that, while we cannot say for sure, the possibility is clearly there.

Alma E. Gygi wrote:

> Let us examine first what we know about Shem. Although the Bible names Shem as the eldest son of Noah (Genesis 5:32), modern-day revelation places Japheth as the eldest (Moses 8:12). Both reports, however, are harmonious in naming Shem as the

progenitor of Israel and in the fact that the priesthood descended through Shem to all the great patriarchs after Noah (1 Chronicles 1:24–27). In this patriarchal order of priesthood, Shem stands next to Noah. He held the keys to the priesthood and was the great high priest of his day.[25]

Living contemporary with Shem was a man known as Melchizedek, who was also known as the great high priest.[26] The scriptures give us the details of Shem's birth and ancestry but are silent as to his ministry and later life. Of Melchizedek, however, the opposite is true.

Nothing is recorded about his birth or ancestry, even though the Book of Mormon states that he did have a father (Alma 13:17–18). Concerning his ministry and life we have several interesting and important facts (Genesis 14:18– 20; Hebrews 7:1–4; Alma 13:17–18).

All of this provokes some questions and calls for answers. Were there two high priests presiding at the same time? Why is the record silent concerning Shem's ministry? Why is nothing known concerning Melchizedek's ancestry?

Because of this state of knowledge on our part, many Saints and gospel scholars have wondered if these men were the same person. The truth is, we do not know the answer. But an examination of the scriptures is fascinating, because it seems to indicate that these men may have been one and the same. . . . Here is the case for their oneness:

1. The inheritance given to Shem included the land of Salem. Melchizedek appears in scripture as the king of Salem, who reigns over this area.

2. Shem, according to later revelation, reigned in righteousness and the priesthood came through him. Melchizedek appears on the scene with a title that means "king of righteousness."

3. Shem was the great high priest of his day. Abraham honored the high priest Melchizedek by seeking a blessing at his hands and paying him tithes.

4. Abraham stands next to Shem in the patriarchal order of the priesthood and would surely have received the priesthood from Shem, but D&C 84:5–17 says Abraham received the priesthood from Melchizedek.
5. Jewish tradition identifies Shem as Melchizedek.[27]
6. President Joseph F. Smith's remarkable vision names Shem among the great patriarchs, but no mention is made of Melchizedek.
7. *Times and Seasons* [Dec. 15, 1844, page 746] speaks of "Shem, who was Melchizedek."

   On the other hand, there is a case for their being two distinct personalities. Many persons believe D&C 84:14 is proof that there are perhaps several generations between Melchizedek and Noah. The scripture says, "Which Abraham received the priesthood from Melchizedek, who received it through the lineage of his fathers, even till Noah."

   If it does turn out that Shem and Melchizedek are the same person, this scripture should prove no stumbling block, because it could be interpreted to mean that priesthood authority commenced with Adam and came through the fathers, even till Noah, and then to Shem.[28]

THE MELCHIZEDEK PRIESTHOOD

"Having been approved of God, [Melchizedek] was ordained an high priest after the order of the covenant which God made with Enoch, it being after the order of the Son of God," which was passed from Enoch to Methuselah, then to Noah and Shem (JST, Genesis 14:27–28 [in the Bible appendix]).

"A revelation to Joseph Smith tells us why the higher priesthood [today] bears Melchizedek's name: It is 'because Melchizedek was such a great high priest. Before his day it was called *the Holy Priesthood, after the Order of the Son of God.* But out of respect or reverence to the name of the Supreme Being, to avoid the too frequent repetition of his name, they, the church, in ancient days, called that priesthood after Melchizedek' (D&C 107:2–4)."[29]

- **Hebrews 7:15, 17 Christ was similar to Melchizedek.** Elder Bruce R. McConkie explained: "The priesthood held by Melchizedek is the very priesthood promised [to] the Son of God during His mortal sojourn, which is to say that Christ was to be like unto Melchizedek."[30]
- **Hebrews 7:16 The Melchizedek Priesthood is the power of endless life** and lives because it administers the ordinances that bring endless posterity (see D&C 132:19–24).
- **JST, Hebrews 7:3 The Melchizedek Priesthood is "without descent."** "For this Melchizedek was ordained a priest after the order of the Son of God, which order was without father, without mother, without descent, having neither beginning of days, nor end of life."

  Elder Bruce R. McConkie remarked:

  > As compared to the Aaronic Priesthood, as administered in ancient Israel, the order of Melchizedek did not come "by descent from father and mother."[31] That is, the right to this higher priesthood was not inherited in the same way as was the case with the Levites and sons of Aaron. Righteousness was an absolute requisite for the conferral of the higher priesthood.[32]

  - **D&C 84:14, 17 The Melchizedek Priesthood is eternal—** "without beginning of days or end of years."

    The Prophet Joseph Smith declared, "The Priesthood is an everlasting principle, and existed with God from eternity, and will to eternity, without beginning of days or end of years [see JST, Hebrews 7:3 (in the Bible appendix)]."[33]
  - **Alma 13:8–9 The authority of Melchizedek Priesthood holders is also eternal.**
  - **JST, Hebrews 7:3 "And all those who are ordained unto this priesthood are [also] made like unto the Son of God,** abiding a priest continually." And, like Melchizedek, they can become priests and kings. The Prophet Joseph Smith said that holders of the fulness of this priesthood "are kings and priests of the Most High God, holding the keys of power and blessings."[34]
  - **Alma 13:1–5 Those who hold this priesthood were foreordained to do so.**

Elder Bruce R. McConkie wrote:

> Alma taught the great truth that every person who holds the Melchizedek Priesthood was foreordained to receive that high and holy order in the pre-existent councils of eternity. . . . Thus, he explains, Melchizedek Priesthood holders have been "prepared from the foundation of the world" for their high callings. The Lord has prepared them *"from eternity to all eternity, according to his foreknowledge of all things"* [Alma 13:5, 7].[35]

And the Prophet Joseph Smith stated:

> Every man who has a calling to minister to the inhabitants of the world was ordained to that very purpose in the Grand Council of heaven before this world was. I suppose that I was ordained to this very office in that Grand Council.[36]

MELCHIZEDEK'S CITY WAS TRANSLATED

"Although some Melchizedek traditions persisted in antiquity, it was left to the Restoration to bring back what the Lord has chosen to let us know about Melchizedek and his people."[37]

Melchizedek's Zion was eventually translated into heaven

The place over which Melchizedek presided was, according to the Book of Mormon "full of all manner of wickedness" (Alma 13:17). But Melchizedek, with faith and priesthood, "did preach repentance unto his people. And behold, they did repent; and Melchizedek did establish peace in the land in his days; therefore he was called the prince of peace" (Alma 13:18)."[38]

"While Abraham was in Canaan, engaged in the routines of life punctuated by the experiences that are recorded in the Bible, a great Zion community was flourishing and was eventually translated.... Abraham was to stay behind to become the father of a great nation."[39]

- **Hebrews 11:10, 16 Abraham wanted to join the celestial city of Zion,** Enoch's city, where Melchizedek had also gone with his people—the city of God, which other prophets also sought for (v. 16): "Enoch ... and his brethren ... were separated from the earth, and were received unto myself—a city reserved until a day of righteousness shall come—a day which was sought for by all holy men, and they found it not because of wickedness and abominations; and confessed they were strangers and pilgrims on the earth; but obtained a promise that they should find it and see it in their flesh" (D&C 45:11–14).

  "At the conclusion of the account of Melchizedek's meeting with Abraham, at Genesis 14:24, the Joseph Smith Translation adds more than 450 new words that summarize Melchizedek's career.[40] The following excerpts show some of this significant information revealed through the Prophet Joseph Smith:"[41]

  "Now Melchizedek was a man of faith, who wrought righteousness; and when a child he feared God, and stopped the mouths of lions, and quenched ... fire.

  "... He was ordained an high priest after the order of the covenant which God made with Enoch, it being after the order of the Son of God....

  "For God having sworn unto Enoch and unto his seed with an oath by himself; that every one being ordained after this order and calling should have power, by faith, to break mountains, to divide the seas, to dry up waters, to turn them out of their course; to put at defiance the armies of nations, to divide the earth, to break every band, to stand in the presence of God; to do all things according to his will, according to his command, [and to] subdue principalities and powers....

  "And men having this faith, coming up unto this order of God, were translated and taken up into heaven" [JST, Genesis 14:26–28, 30–32 (in the Bible appendix)].

"This last passage shows that even after the Flood, some faithful Saints were translated, just as others had been translated in earlier generations between the times of Enoch and Noah (see Moses 7:27). Melchizedek was 'a priest of this order.' As a righteous leader, 'he obtained peace in Salem, and was called the Prince of peace.' That he and his people were translated and joined the City of Enoch is evident in the passage that follows: 'And his people wrought righteousness, and obtained heaven, and sought for the city of Enoch which God had before taken' [JST, Genesis 14:33–34 (in the Bible appendix)]."[42]

"We need not wonder, then, why Melchizedek is such a mysterious person in the Bible. Like Enoch's city, Melchizedek's people were taken from the earth, seemingly without a trace, and thus left behind little historical evidence and apparently had no further influence on world events. Had they remained, presumably some of their history would have been preserved in the Bible."[43]

Notes

1. *Teachings of Presidents of the Church: Joseph Smith* (2007), 186.
2. Kent P. Jackson, *The Restored Gospel and the Book of Genesis* (2001), 111.
3. See Kent P. Jackson, *The Restored Gospel and the Book of Genesis,* 118–19.
4. Daniel H. Ludlow, *A Companion to Your Study of the Book of Mormon* (1976), 204.
5. "Some have suggested that Melchizedek's Salem was Jerusalem. This belief is based on two lines of reasoning: (a) a linguistic equation of *Rushalimum* and *Urushalim* (Jerusalem's names in the Middle and Late Bronze periods, respectively) with *Yerushalayim* (its name in biblical rimes), and (b) the use of Salem with reference to Jerusalem in Psalm 76:2. The linguistic equation is complicated and uncertain but possible. The Psalm reference is also not conclusive. In the language of Hebrew poetry, names are used metaphorically to show similarities in characteristics. In disparaging prophecies Jerusalem is called *Sodom* (Isaiah 1:10; Revelation 11:8), *Gomorrah* (Isaiah 1:10), and *Egypt* (Revelation 11:8). It would not be surprising to see it characterized more positively with a poetic reference to Melchizedek's community." (Kent P. Jackson, *The Restored Gospel and the Book of Genesis,* 125, note 20.)
6. See Isaiah 9:6, 2 Nephi 19:6; Joseph Smith Translation, Genesis 14:33 (in the Bible Appendix).
7. Kent P. Jackson, *The Restored Gospel and the Book of Genesis,* 122.

8. D. Kelly Ogden and Andrew C. Skinner, *New Testament Apostles Testify of Christ* (1998), 253, 254–55.

9. Joseph Smith, in *The Words of Joseph Smith: The Contemporary Accounts of the Nauvoo Discourses of the Prophet Joseph,* ed. Andrew F. Ehat and Lyndon W. Cook (1980), 246.

10. Kent P. Jackson, *The Restored Gospel and the Book of Genesis,* 122.

11. Kent P. Jackson, *The Restored Gospel and the Book of Genesis,* 122–23.

12. Bruce R. McConkie, *Mormon Doctrine,* 2nd ed. (1966), 475.

13. Bruce R. McConkie, *Mormon Doctrine,* 474.

14. Kent P. Jackson, *The Restored Gospel and the Book of Genesis,* 119, 120.

15. Joseph Smith, in *The Words of Joseph Smith: The Contemporary Accounts of the Nauvoo Discourses of the Prophet Joseph,* 246.

16. Joseph Smith, in *History of the Church,* 5:555.

17. D. Kelly Ogden and Andrew C. Skinner, *New Testament Apostles Testify of Christ,* 255.

18. Joseph Smith, in *The Words of Joseph Smith: The Contemporary Accounts of the Nauvoo Discourses of the Prophet Joseph,* 245.

19. Joseph Smith, in *The Words of Joseph Smith: The Contemporary Accounts of the Nauvoo Discourses of the Prophet Joseph,* 244.

20. Kent P. Jackson, *The Restored Gospel and the Book of Genesis,* 123.

21. Kent P. Jackson, *The Restored Gospel and the Book of Genesis,* 123–24.

22. Kent P. Jackson, *The Restored Gospel and the Book of Genesis,* 119.

23. Kent P. Jackson, *The Restored Gospel and the Book of Genesis,* 119.

24. Kent P. Jackson, *The Restored Gospel and the Book of Genesis,* 119, 121.

25. See D&C 138:41. See also Joseph F. Smith, *Gospel Doctrine,* 5th ed. (1939), 474.

26. See D&C 107:2; Hebrews 7:4; Alma 13:17; Genesis 14:18–20.

27. "When Abraham returned from the war, Shem, or, as he is sometimes called, Melchizedek, the king of righteousness, priest of the Most High God. . . ." (Louis Ginzberg, *The Legends of the Jews,* 6 vols. [1909], 1:233.) "Jewish tradition pronounces Melchizedek to be a survivor of the Deluge, the patriarch Shem." (William Smith, *Smith's Bible Dictionary,* rev. ed. [1948], 393.) "And Adonizedek king of Jerusalem, the same was Shem. . . ." (Book of Jasher 16:11.)

28. Alma E. Gygi, "Is It Possible That Shem and Melchizedek Are the Same Person?" *Ensign,* Nov. 1973, 15–16.

29. Kent P. Jackson, *The Restored Gospel and the Book of Genesis,* 123.

30. Bruce R. McConkie, *The Promised Messiah: The First Coming of Christ* (1978), 450.

31. *Teachings of Presidents of the Church: Joseph Smith,* 109.

32. Bruce R. McConkie, *Mormon Doctrine,* 478.

33. *Teachings of Presidents of the Church: Joseph Smith,* 104.

34. *Teachings of Presidents of the Church: Joseph Smith,* 109.

35. Bruce R. McConkie, *Mormon Doctrine,* 290–91.

36. *Teachings of Presidents of the Church: Joseph Smith,* 511.

37. Kent P. Jackson, *The Restored Gospel and the Book of Genesis,* 121. See also Ann N. Madsen, "Melchizedek, the Man and the Tradition" (M.A. thesis, Brigham Young University, 1975), 48–111.

38. Kent P. Jackson, *The Restored Gospel and the Book of Genesis,* 122.

39. Kent P. Jackson, *The Restored Gospel and the Book of Genesis,* 121.

40. See Joseph Smith Translation, Genesis 14:25–40 (in the Bible appendix).

41. Kent P. Jackson, *The Restored Gospel and the Book of Genesis,* 120.

42. Kent P. Jackson, *The Restored Gospel and the Book of Genesis,* 121.

43. Kent P. Jackson, *The Restored Gospel and the Book of Genesis,* 121.

CHAPTER 3

The Proposed Zion of Moses and Israel

(EXODUS 4–20; 25–29; 32–34; D&C 84)

"Another Enoch" (Moses) Arises among God's People

We come next to the Zion which the Lord proposed to establish with Moses and the children of Israel. Ever since the days of Melchizedek, there had not been another people so highly favored of the Lord. He called upon Moses to bring them out of captivity in Egypt and lead them to Mount Sinai, where they could become a Zion people.

Moses sought to make his people a Zion society

The story of Moses's call and of the Exodus from Egypt is one of the most profound examples of the lengths the Lord will go to in order to save and exalt His people. We will not rehearse here the entirety of Moses's mission nor the wanderings of the children of Israel in the desert. But we will summarize what the Lord did for them and the covenants He offered them.

The many miracles which accompanied the Israelites' exodus from Egypt and their sojourn in the desert were a clear indication that the Lord was willing to do for them what He had done for Enoch's and Melchizedek's people.

Miracles and Manifestations Given to the Israelites

1. **Signs from Jehovah**
   (Exodus 4:29–31)
   (Serpent from Staff, Healing Leprous Hand, Blood from Water)
2. **Plagues of Egypt**
   (Exodus 7–11)
   (Blood, Frogs, Lice, Flies, Plague, Boils, Hail, Fire, Locusts, Darkness, Death)
3. **The Passover**
   (Exodus 12:1–30)
   (Israel preserved from the deaths of Egypt's firstborn)
4. **The Exodus**
   (Exodus 12:31–51)
   (3 million slaves set free without conditions)
5. **Cloud/Pillar of Fire**.................................. (Exodus 13:21–22)
   (Israelites attended and directed by Jehovah Himself)
6. **Parting the Red Sea**.................................... (Exodus 14:1–31)
   (Israelites pass through on dry ground/Egyptians drowned)
7. **Marah Waters Healed**................................ (Exodus 15:23–27)
   (Moses purifies brackish water with a tree)
8. **Miracle of Quail**.. (Exodus 16:1–13)
   (God provides meat in the desert)
9. **Miracle of Manna**..................................... (Exodus 16:11–36)
   (A quart per person for 40 years - 3 million persons)
10. **Water from a Rock**...(Exodus 17:1–7)
    (Water gushes forth from the granite cliffs of Horeb)
11. **Delivered from Enemies**............................. (Exodus 17:8–16)
    (Israel prevails w/Moses raised hands; not one Israelite lost)

And now, beneath Mount Sinai, more manifestations were offered to them:

12. **Signs on Mount Sinai** .... (Exodus 19:1–25)
    (Great fire, smoke, earthquakes attest to Jehovah's presence)

13. **The Voice of Jehovah** .... (Exodus 20:1–22)
    (Ten Commandments given by Jehovah; all Israel hears it)

The power by which these things were done is the same as the power used by Enoch, who held back his people's enemies by the power of his priesthood. Moses proclaimed ten plagues upon Israel's oppressors. Enoch moved mountains and rivers (see Moses 7:13–17). Moses parted the Red Sea, brought water forth from a rock, and caused God to rain down manna from heaven to feed the children of Israel in the desert.

And there were more similarities. Both Enoch and Moses had a stuttering speech impediment and felt wholly inadequate in their callings (see Moses 6:31; JST, Exodus 6:30). It is clear that Moses admired Enoch and sought to be like him, since he went to great lengths to include the stories of Enoch and his Zion in the book of Moses.

Covenants Offered by God

1. **Protection/Purification** .... (Exodus 12:1–30)
   (Firstborn lamb's blood protects them from death and sin)

2. **Sanctification** .... (Exodus 13:1–10)
   (Firstborn of all to serve God; sanctify Israel)

3. **Physical Health** .... (Exodus 15:23–26)
   (No Egyptian diseases will be known among Israelites)

4. **Bread/Water from Heaven** .... (Exod. 16,17:1–7)
   (Fed without heavy labor and without fail)

5. **Protection from enemies** .... (Exodus 17:8–16)
   (Not one Israelite is lost; enemies destroyed)

And now, beneath Mount Sinai, God was ready to offer even greater covenants and blessings:

6. **Priesthood Blessings**....................................(Exodus 19:1–6)
   (Israel to be a kingdom of priests; a holy nation)

7. **Personal Witness**..(Exodus 19:7–25)
   (Israel will see and hear God personally)

8. **God's Laws Given** ....(Exodus 20:1–17)
   (A society governed by God and his laws)

9. **Temple Covenants**..(Exodus 25–29)
   (A temple to be built; Zion to be established)

10. **God's Presence** ....(Exodus 25–29)
    (The personal presence of God in Israel's midst)

The Proposed Covenant with Israel

Once they arrived at Mount Sinai, the Lord gave the children of Israel an invitation to become a Zion people.

- **Exodus 19:1–9 The Proposed Covenant.**

  — Israel covenanted with the Lord to become a holy people.

  — The Lord promised if they would be obedient, He would make them "a peculiar treasure, . . . a kingdom of priests, and an holy nation."

  This means that Israel would become the Lord's own special people or treasure, favored above all others and chosen to bear the priesthood and the gospel to all people (see Deuteronomy 7:6; 14:1–2; 1 Peter 2:9)

  These are the same promises given to Enoch's people (vv. 3–6) and they are the same conditions that will exist during the Millennium.

  — The requirement was obedience (v. 5).

  — Israel's answer: "We will!" (v. 8).

GOD DESCENDS UPON MOUNT SINAI

Three things were necessary for God to elevate the people of Israel to a "Zion" status:

- **Sanctification:** They would have to be sanctified—cleansed from their worldly ways (see D&C 84:23). Three days of sanctification were required.
- **Priesthood:** They would need to receive the Melchizedek Priest- hood (see Exodus 19:6)
- **A Temple:** They would need to construct a temple and receive its ordinances (see Exodus 25:8).

- **Exodus 19:16–25 As promised, the Lord descended upon Mount Sinai.** Great manifestations of power were seen on the mountain when this occurred.

THE TEN COMMANDMENTS

To understand what happened next we have to suspend our experience with Cecil B. DeMille's 1956 film *The Ten Commandments.* While some of what it shows is true, much of it is incorrect, and it gives no information whatsoever about the higher laws that God offered to the people.

The Israelites Hear God's Voice

Moses ascended the mountain alone. This was only the first of many trips up the mountain that he made, as the Lord gave instructions to His people. And the Ten Commandments were not the only things that God provided. Most importantly, they were declared by God's voice coming down from the mountain, with all Israel hearing it together.

The Ten Commandments Are Not the "Law of Moses"

The Ten Commandments are not the "lesser law" we often refer to. They are the laws of the everlasting gospel of Jesus Christ and have been given in every dispensation.

The Ten Commandments are found in three of the four standard works of the Church:

—	Old Testament	Exodus 20:1–26; Deut. 5:5–21
—	Book of Mormon	Mosiah 12:33–36; 13:12–24
—	New Testament	Matthew 5:17–37
—	Doctrine & Covenants	D&C 42:18–29; 59:5–16

President Joseph Fielding Smith said, "[The Ten Commandments] have not been abrogated; they have not been modified and are binding upon the people with all the force which accompanied them when first uttered."[1]

And Elder Mark E. Petersen wrote:

> The Ten Commandments . . . represent the basic law of the Almighty and have formed the underlying elements of civil and religious law ever since. They are fundamental to our relationships with God. They are an integral part of the restored gospel of the Lord Jesus Christ and are essential to our becoming perfect as our Father in Heaven is perfect. . . . Variations of these laws are given in the rules laid down in Leviticus and Deuteronomy as they are applied to specific matters, but generally they form the foundation for all proper human conduct.[2]

- The first four commandments show us our proper relationship to God.

  1. Thou shalt have no other gods before me.
  2. Thou shalt not make unto thee any graven image.
  3. Thou shalt not take the name of the Lord thy God in vain.
  4. Remember the Sabbath day to keep it holy.

- The fifth commandment establishes the importance of family and proper family relationships.

  5. Honor thy father and mother.

- The last five commandments regulate our relationships with others.

 6. Thou shalt not kill.
 7. Thou shalt not commit adultery.
 8. Thou shalt not steal.
 9. Thou shalt not bear false witness.
 10. Thou shalt not covet.

Israel's Reaction to Hearing God's Voice

The manifestations on Mount Sinai, and the voice of God speaking through the clouds in the hearing of all the people, proved to be too much for many of them.

The reaction now was: "We don't want this!" (see Exodus 20:19). They wanted Moses to talk to God for them and then bring them His word. Moses tried to calm their fears and said, "God is proving you." (v. 21).

GOD PROVIDES A GOVERNMENT TO ISRAEL

The "Laws" of Moses

We frequently refer to what said to Moses in Exodus 21–23 as "the law of Moses." But that is not correct. The law of Moses was given much later, long after the Ten Commandments had been given. Following the Ten Commandments, the Lord provided a set of civil laws (a government) by which they should be ruled. We should therefore refer to the commandments in this chapter as the "laws" of Moses.

"An eye for an eye"[3] is well known, but that is not all there was to these laws.

- **Exodus 23:1–8 Consider a few *details* of Mosaic justice:**
  - — This was not just a system of fierce retaliation and brutal punishment.
  - — The laws required a high degree of morality, justice, and righteousness and requirements to do good to one's neighbor.

— The death penalty was provided for murder, adultery, incest, homosexuality, bestiality, and kidnapping. But it was ***not required;*** it was ***allowed.*** Next of kin chose the punishment that would be applied.

— Mistreated slaves were set free.

— Theft required a two-fold restitution of damages.

— Interest on loans was not allowed .

— False witnesses were declared guilty of the **crime** about which they testified falsely.

The laws were written down and kept in the "book of the covenant" (v. 7). They were not written on stone.

- **Exodus 23:8–19 Feasts and festivals.** These would celebrate important events in God's dealings with Israel and help them to remember the many things He had done for them. We will not discuss them further here.

- **Exodus 23:20–31 God made five promises** if Israel would observe and keep these laws:

  — An angel of the Lord would lead them into the promised land (vv. 20–23).

  — They would be blessed with good health (vv. 24–25).

  — They and their flocks would be greatly multiplied (v. 26).

  — They would be successful in their fight against heathen nations (vv. 27–30).

  — They would ultimately inherit everything from the Red Sea to the Euphrates River (v. 31).

The Laws are Accepted by Covenant

- **Exodus 24:4–8** Israel covenanted to obey these new laws from God. We are told that all the people promised to keep the Lord's commandments (v. 7).

To signify this covenant, an offering was made and the blood of the animal was used to show the parties involved.

One-half of the blood was sprinkled on the altar. This represented God and His promises. The other half of the blood was sprinkled upon the people, signifying the promises they were making to the Lord.

GOD PROVIDES TEMPLE COVENANTS

The first step—sanctification—had now been achieved. And so Moses returned to the Holy Mount to receive the higher ordinances and covenants of the temple. This crucial event is not shown in DeMille's movie, and the world knows little or nothing concerning it. But it was at the heart of God's attempt to make of Israel a Zion people.

- **A Vision.** A great revelation was offered: God will come down in the sight of all the people and speak to Moses in their hearing. Seventy-three elders were taken a short distance up the mountain, where they saw Jehovah face to face (see Exodus 24:9–11). This great spiritual experience occurred as the Lord accepted their commitment.

  A similar event happened when the Lord appeared to the Nephites after His Resurrection (see 3 Nephi 11). And He has offered to do the same in our own day if we will sanctify ourselves and be obedient.

  The Prophet Joseph Smith said, "God hath not revealed anything to Joseph, but what He will make known unto the Twelve, and even the least Saint may know all things as fast as he is able to bear them."[4]

  Elder Bruce R. McConkie wrote:

  > As believing Saints it is our privilege . . . to see the Lord face to face; to talk with Him as a man speaketh with his friend; to have

His Person attend us from time to time; and to have Him manifest to us the Father. . . .

After the true Saints receive and enjoy the gift of the Holy Ghost; after they know how to attune themselves to the voice of the Spirit; after they mature spiritually so that they see visions, work miracles, and entertain angels; after they make their calling and election sure and prove themselves worthy of every trust—after all this and more—it becomes their right and privilege to see the Lord and commune with Him face to face. Revelations, visions, angelic visitations, the rending of the heavens, and appearances among men of the Lord Himself—all these things are for all of the faithful. They are not reserved for apostles and prophets only. God is no respecter of persons. They are not reserved for one age only, or for a select lineage or people. We are all our Father's children. All men are welcome.[5]

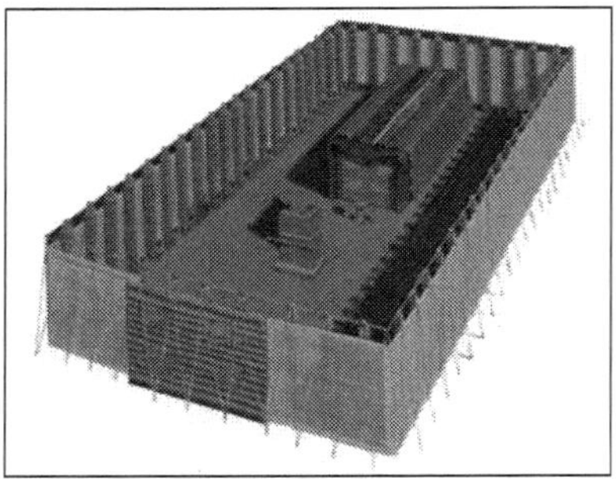

- **A Temple.** Instructions were given for building and operating the Tabernacle—a port- able temple.
- **Tables of stone** were promised, written with the finger of God (see Exodus 24:12). They will be written on both sides (Exodus 32:15).

Moses went back up the mountain, taking Joshua, Hur, and Aaron with him (see Exodus 24:13–15). But these three stayed further down the mountain while Moses continued on alone to the top. The purpose of this visit was to receive the "higher law," including the building of a portable temple—the Tabernacle—and the covenants associated with the Melchizedek Priesthood.

ISRAEL REJECTS GOD'S COVENANT

But a Zion society was not to be for Israel. They had been disobedient from the beginning, rebelling continuously in the desert and showing little inclination to actually change their lives and become a Zion people.

Disobedient from the Beginning

1. **Doubt and Fear** ....(Exodus 4–20)
   (Each miracle came in response to murmuring)
2. **Short Memories** .... (Exodus 4–20)
   (Each crisis was as though it was the first)
3. **Ingratitude/Disrespect** ....(Exodus 4–20)
   (Harsh talk and threats to stone Moses)
4. **Insincere Verbal Commitment** ....(Exodus 19:7–8)
   (A promise to obey God's covenants that was not kept)
5. **Disobedience** ....(Exodus 16; 19)
   (Gathering manna on the Sabbath; Going into the mountain)
6. **Childish Fear** .... (Exodus 20:18–22)
   (Refusing to hear God's voice; let Moses do it)

And even while receiving temple blessings and promises, they continued to rebel:

7. **Idolatry and Adultery**..Exodus 32
   (Return to the heathen cults & practices of Egypt; many die)
8. **The Lesser Law Is Given** ....Exodus 33
   (Survivors are given a lesser law to live)
9. **Lack of Faith**..Exodus 34
   (When Moses leaves for 40 days, they lose their faith again)

The Golden Calf

Moses was gone 40 days (nearly six weeks) (see Exodus 32:1–4). While waiting, the Israelites turned to idolatry—old and familiar practices they had learned in Egypt (see Exodus 32:1–9).

They made and worshipped a golden calf. This worship included nudity and adulterous public sexual intercourse as part of worshipping fertility—which the calf represented.

Thus, while the Lord was proposing the higher law and all of its blessings to Israel, they were turning away from Him and returning to the norms and practices of their former captors. God was angry and wanted to destroy them. He proposed raising up a people through Moses (see Exodus 32:10; Deuteronomy 9:14).

The Wicked Are Destroyed

Moses returned and found them engaged in gross sins (see Exodus 32:6, 17–20). Furious, he broke the tablets, knowing that he could not share such sacred things with so wicked a people. Three thousand of them were slain by earthquake and fire (see Exodus 32:26–29).

A New Set of Tablets

- **JST, Exodus 34:1–2** "And the Lord said unto Moses, Hew thee two other tables of stone, like unto the first, and I will write upon them also, the words of the law, according as they were written at the first on the tables which thou brakest; but it shall not be according to the first, for I will take away the priesthood out of their midst; therefore my holy order, and the ordinances thereof, shall not go before them; for my presence shall not go up in their midst, lest I destroy them.

"But I will give unto them the law as at the first, but it shall be after the law of a carnal commandment; for I have sworn in my wrath, that they shall not enter into my presence, into my rest, in the days of their pilgrimage. Therefore do as I have commanded thee, and be ready in the morning, and come up in the morning unto mount Sinai, and present thyself there to me, in the top of the mount."

ZION WAS LOST BY THE CHILDREN OF ISRAEL

The Lord Imposed Sanctions

Moses returned to the Holy Mount to plead with the Lord in Israel's behalf (see Exodus 32:30–34). The Lord agreed not to destroy them—if they would fully repent.

But the Lord would no longer lead the camp of Israel personally. They would receive only the ministering of an angel (an Aaronic Priesthood level of revelation) (see Exodus 33:2–4).

Moses pitched a temporary tabernacle outside the camp (see Exodus 33:7–10). This "tent" was not the Tabernacle described in Exodus 25–30. It was a tent belonging to Moses, which was made into a temporary sanctuary where the pillar of cloud came down upon it, and Jehovah talked with Moses.

It was there that the "lesser law" was provided (see Exodus 34:1).

What the Israelites Lost through Disobedience

The Lord had intended to dwell with Israel personally, as He did with Enoch's people and as He will do at the New Jerusalem (see Exodus 25:8; 29:43).

When the Lord originally spoke with Moses on Mount Sinai, He revealed a law that included the ordinances of the Melchizedek Priesthood (see D&C 84:19–23).

Because they forgot the Lord so quickly, He withdrew the Melchizedek Priesthood from them and revealed a lesser law—the law of Moses (see D&C 84:23–27; Joseph Smith Translation, Exodus 34:1–2; Mosiah 13:29–30).

What changes would we see in the Church today if the authority of the Melchizedek Priesthood were removed?

— Loss of the gift of the Holy Ghost
— Loss of spiritual blessings
— Loss of most temple ordinances, etc.

The Prophet Joseph Smith stated, "When God offers a blessing or knowledge to a man, and he refuses to receive it, he will be damned."[6]

When we consider what might have been for the children of Israel—a Zion similar to the ones of Enoch and Melchizedek—we can feel the depth of sorrow and disappointment that Moses must have felt. Unlike Enoch, whom he greatly loved and respected, he would not be able to fundamentally change his people into a Zion society.

Moses Himself Was Translated

The Israelites forfeited their opportunity to become a Zion people, and to be translated as the people of Enoch and of Melchizedek had done. But Moses had not forfeited this blessing. He himself was a Zion person, and he himself was translated at the end of his mission on earth.

"Moses ... had seen the promised land and now the time for his departure had come. Josephus describes the final scene as it appeared to those who were there. He says Moses 'dismissed the elders, and then, as he was embracing Eleazar and Joshua, and still speaking to them, a cloud suddenly stood over him and he vanished in a deep valley.'[7]"[8]

Elder Bruce R. McConkie wrote:

> The Old Testament account that Moses died and was buried by the hand of the Lord in an unknown grave is an error [see Deuteronomy 34:5–7]. It is true that he may have been "buried by the hand of the Lord," if that expression is a figure of speech which means that he was translated. But the Book of Mormon account, in recording that Alma "was taken up by the Spirit," says, "The scriptures saith the Lord took Moses unto himself; and we suppose that he has also received Alma in the spirit, unto himself" (Alma 45:18–19). It should be remembered that the Nephites had

the brass plates, and that they were the "scriptures" which gave the account of Moses being taken by way of translation.[9]

W. Cleon Skousen wrote:

> One of the most interesting things about the life of Moses is the way it ended. Unless they had been told, Joshua and Eleazar would never have guessed what actually happened. They saw Moses disappear in the cloud and for them this was the end of the matter. Therefore, when Joshua later wrote his comments on the death of Moses he assumed that the Lord had buried his great prophet in the valley beyond, so he said: "And he [the Lord] buried him in a valley in the land of Moab, over against Beth-peor." Nevertheless, in the very next sentence he frankly admits that this is purely a presumption on his part because "no man knoweth of his sepulchre unto this day" [Deuteronomy 34:6]. . . .
>
> This marked the end of a great historic epic in the annals of the race and, as the scripture declares, "There arose not a prophet since in Israel like unto Moses, whom the Lord knew face to face" [Deuteronomy 34:10].[10]

Notes

1. Joseph Fielding Smith, in Conference Report, Apr. 1943, 12.
2. Mark E. Petersen, *Moses: Man of Miracles* (1977), 110.
3. See Exodus 21:24; Leviticus 24:20; Deuteronomy 19:21; Matthew 5:38; 3 Nephi 12:38.
4. *Teachings of Presidents of the Church: Joseph Smith* (2007), 268.
5. Bruce R. McConkie, *The Promised Messiah: The First Coming of Christ* (1978), 571, 575.
6. *Teachings of Presidents of the Church: Joseph Smith* (2007), 265.
7. Josephus, *Antiquities of the Jews,* book 4, chapter 8, paragraph 48.
8. W. Cleon Skousen, *The Third Thousand Years,* rev. ed. (1997), 381.
9. Bruce R. McConkie, *Mormon Doctrine,* 2nd ed. (1966), 805.
10. W. Cleon Skousen, *The Third Thousand Years,* 382.

CHAPTER 4

The Zion of Early Christianity

(ACTS 2; 4–5)

Zion in the Early Christian Church

One of the great blessings of being a Zion people is the privilege of having the Lord dwell among you. And for 33 years, the Lord was among the people during His earthly ministry. The Savior proposed to make a covenant with the Jews, but they rejected both Him and His proposals. After He ascended into heaven, the Apostles sought to make the followers of Jesus Christ into a Zion society by turning to the Gentiles, who, at least temporarily, accepted the covenant.

Zion is defined in a number of ways, and some of these denote physical locations. Certainly Enoch's city and the New Jerusalem can be called Zion. But the Old Jerusalem and its Mount Zion, located west of the city, were also called Zion in the Old Testament. Thus, the people of Jesus's day literally dwelt in Zion.

Mount Zion in Jerusalem

More importantly, Zion is defined as a people—the pure in heart—and after the Savior departed some of the early Saints tried to live like a Zion people by observing the law of consecration.

Requirements to Establish Zion

In the previous chapter we identified three things that are necessary for the establishment of Zion and a Zion people:

— **Sanctification:** They would have to be sanctified—cleansed from their worldly ways (see D&C 84: 23). The Apostles sought to sanctify the people by having them live the celestial law of consecration.

— **Priesthood:** They would need to receive the Melchizedek Priesthood. This priesthood was conferred upon the Apostles by Jesus Christ Himself, and the Apostles then ordained others.

— **A Temple:** They already had a temple in their midst, and it was used by Christians and Jews alike. It would not remain among them for long, however, as it was taken away in A.D. 70 when the Romans destroyed it.

"All Things Common"

- **Acts 2:42–47 Under the Apostles' leadership, the Church unified and "had all things common"** (v. 44). They "sold their possessions and goods, and parted them to all men, as every man had need" (v. 45). "All things common" did not mean socialism—that everyone pooled all their resources and shared everything in common, all having equal amounts. It meant that every person and family had an equality according to their needs (see Acts 2:45; 4:32, 35; D&C 51:3).

  "The most striking thing about the law of the celestial kingdom as it operated among the [Church] was the economic equality that prevailed. The scriptures use the phrase 'all things common' to describe the condition"[1] (see Acts 4:32; see also Acts 2:44; 3 Nephi 26:19; 4 Nephi 1:3). "Some have speculated that the term *common* suggests a type of communalism or "Christian communism." This interpretation is in error."[2] "This was not a system of communal ownership. . . . Nor did it mean that each person had exactly the same amount of personal goods."[3] Indeed, the Prophet Joseph Smith spoke clearly against communal property systems. He attended a presentation on socialism in September 1843 at Nauvoo. His response was to declare that he *"did not believe the doctrine."*[4]

Later that month he reported: "I preached on the stand about one hour on the 2nd chapter of Acts, designing to show the folly of common stock [holding property in common]. In Nauvoo every one is steward over his own [property]."[5]

Under this celestial law, each stewardship is considered private property, and only the residues and surpluses consecrated for the storehouse become the "common property of the whole church" (D&C 82:18). It is referred to as the "common property" because each covenant member of the order had access to it, according to his just "wants" and "needs," including the need to improve his stewardship (see D&C 82:17–18).[6]

One Heart and One Soul

Barnabas

- **Acts 4:32–37 Most of "them that believed were of one heart and of one soul:** neither said any of them that ought of the things which he possessed was his own; but they had all things common" (v. 32). "Neither was there any among them that lacked: for as many as were possessors of lands or houses sold them, and brought the prices of the things that were sold" (v. 34). Among these was Barnabas, a Levite from the island of Cyprus, who "having land, sold it, and brought the money, and laid it at the apostles' feet" (v. 37). Distribution of these things "was made unto every man according as he had need" (v. 35). Barnabas served as a missionary companion to Paul (Acts 13–14), and was regarded as an Apostle (see Acts 14:4, 14).

Elder James E. Talmage wrote:

> No condition recorded of the early apostolic ministry expresses more forcefully the unity and devotion of the Church in those days than does the fact of the members establishing a system of common ownership of property (Acts 2:44, 46; 4:32–37; 6:1–4). One result of this community of interest in temporal things was a marked unity in spiritual matters; they 'were of one heart and of one soul.' Lacking nothing, they lived in contentment and godliness.[7]

Selfishness and Greed Arise

- **Acts 5:1–11 Ananias and Sapphira misuse sacred funds.** They pretended to consecrate in order to gain more, thus robbing God and the Saints for their own enrichment.

As members of the Church, Ananias and Sapphira made sacred covenants with the Lord in addition to their baptismal covenants. They covenanted to live the law of consecration as described in Acts 4:32–35. This order of things was the same as that practiced by the people of Enoch and the Book of Mormon society described in 4 Nephi, in which the people were of one heart and one mind, dwelt in righteousness, and had all things in common (compare Moses 7:18–19; Acts 4:32–35; 4 Nephi 1:15–17, 23–25). Their offense was much greater than simply lying.

As explained in our own dispensation, consecration is established by covenant. All who enter into the order do so with a "promise immutable and unchangeable" (D&C 104:2) to accept the law of consecration. The law of consecration is the law of the celestial kingdom, obedience to which would bring eternal exaltation and neglect of which would bring severe judgments.

RAPHAEL

Ananias lied and was struck dead

The placement of the story of Ananias and Sapphira

in Acts 5 is no accident—it comes immediately after the enumeration of the principal features of the law of consecration in Acts 4:32–35. It is meant to show what happens when certain higher laws of God's economy and social order, established by covenant, are deliberately transgressed.

The Temptation to Hold Back

In modern times, the Lord has set forth similar punishments for those who violate the higher covenants associated with the new and everlasting covenant. The punishment for willful violation of this higher law is found in Doctrine and Covenants 82:15– 21. There the Lord says violators are to "be delivered over to the buffetings of Satan" (D&C 82:21). From Doctrine and Covenants 132:26 we understand that the buffetings involve being "destroyed in the flesh," which is what happened to Ananias and Sapphira.

Elder Bruce R. McConkie wrote:

> In effect the lesson to learn from Ananias is that unrepentant liars will be damned. What, then, of the part tithepayer who tells his bishop the sum given the Church is a full tithing? Or of the immoral couple who, conspiring together, assert their purity in order to get a temple recommend? Or of Church members who deny sins of any sort which would keep them from receiving temple blessings, priesthood ordinations, or positions of leadership?[8]

Elder Neal A. Maxwell said:

> Ananias and Sapphira . . . "kept back" a portion instead of consecrating their all (Acts 5:1–11). Some would never *sell* Jesus for thirty pieces, but they would not *give* Him their all either! . . . We tend to think of consecration only in terms of property and money. But there are so many ways of keeping back part. One might be giving of money and time and yet hold back a significant portion of himself. One might share talents publicly yet privately retain a particular pride. One might hold back from kneeling before God's throne and yet bow to a particular gallery of peers. One might accept a Church calling but have his heart more set on maintaining a certain role in the world.[9]

President Marion G. Romney said:

> The Lord claims the earth as His, that it is not yours and mine to own and manage independently of Him. No matter how many stocks and bonds or how much land and other properties we possess, they are not wholly ours. They are the Lord's. He further says that He owns and gives to us all the blessings we have and that He makes us stewards over them, responsible to Him. He makes it clear that it is His purpose to provide for His Saints, but He requires that it be done in His way, which way, He explains, is for those who *have* to contribute to those who *have not.* Having made us stewards, He gives us our agency, however, and then lays down the condition that if we accept these blessings and refuse to contribute our share for the care of the poor, we shall go to—well, He tells us where we shall go.[10]

Our Attitude toward Others

CHRIST AND THE RICH YOUNG RULER,

The law of consecration is not just a temporal or economic program. It is also a spiritual law that helps Church members grow spiritually and prepare for eternal life (D&C 29:34–35). Living the law of consecration requires humility and a love of our fellow beings that is devoid of pride. Unrighteous pride is sometimes called the great sin of the spirit because it was the sin of Lucifer (see Isaiah 14:12–14). A Zion people do not exercise unrighteous pride.

Zion also requires charity. In the Book of Mormon we read of Alma's people who imparted "of their substance, every man according to that which he had, to the poor, and the needy, and the sick, and the afflicted." "They did not send away any who were naked, or that were hungry, or that were athirst, or that were sick, or that had not been nourished; and they did not set their hearts upon riches; therefore they were liberal to all, both old and young, both bond and free, both male and female, whether out of the church or in the church, having no respect to persons as to those who stood in need" (Alma 1:27, 30).

It is sad, but true, that some members of the early Christian Church were racists. Among Jewish members, the practice of consecration worked reasonably well, but prejudice against Gentile converts made it difficult to be "as one" as time went by. Although they were all now members of Christ's Church and kingdom, many held on to Mosaic notions of uncleanness, particularly with regard to circumcision. This division within the Church would eventually be its undoing.

Peter himself had difficulty meeting with Gentiles or eating the "unclean" food they ate. But the Lord told him to set aside such prejudice (see Acts 10:9–16). We are not immune to such things in our own dispensation. We may think that those who are in poverty are lazy or unworthy. Despite King Benjamin's counsel against such attitudes (see Mosiah 4:16– 19), some persist in judging and will not help others whom they despise. It is the exact opposite of the charitable spirit of consecration. And this problem proved to be the undoing of Zion in the early Church.

President Howard W. Hunter said:

> The world in which we live would benefit greatly if men and women everywhere would exercise the pure love of Christ, which is kind, meek, and lowly. It is without envy or pride. It is selfless because it seeks nothing in return. It does not countenance evil or ill will, nor rejoice in iniquity; it has no place for bigotry, hatred, or violence. It refuses to condone ridicule, vulgarity, abuse, or ostracism. It encourages diverse people to live together in Christian love regardless of religious belief, race, nationality, financial standing, education, or culture.
>
> The Savior has commanded us to love one another as He has loved us; to clothe ourselves "with the bond of charity" (D&C 88:125), as He so clothed Himself. We are called upon to purify our inner feelings, to change our hearts, to make our outward actions and appearance conform to what we say we believe and feel inside. We are to be true disciples of Christ.[11]

The Great Apostasy

Even while the Apostles were working to establish the Lord's kingdom on earth, the seeds of apostasy were already sprouting within the Church. Peter wrote that there were false teachers already among the people and that still others would come "who privily shall bring in damnable heresies, even denying the Lord that bought them, and bring upon themselves swift destruction" (2 Peter 2:1). Peter also predicted that "many shall follow their pernicious ways" (2 Peter 2:2).

Paul similarly testified that out of the congregation of believers would "men arise, speaking perverse things, to draw away disciples after them" (Acts 20:30). And he said concerning the Church: "The time will come when they will not endure sound doctrine; but after their own lusts shall they heap to themselves teachers, having itching ears; and they shall turn away their ears from the truth, and shall be turned unto fables" (2 Timothy 4:3–4).

Through the spirit of prophecy, the Apostles realized that an apostasy was not only inevitable but imminent, and so they did not perpetuate the Church by ordaining new Apostles. The existing Apostles were killed and revelation to guide the Lord's Church ceased, along with priesthood authority to lead it.

An Incomplete Zion

Thus we can see that although they made the attempt, the early Christian Saints did not establish Zion. The opportunity was there, and the Apostles sought to establish it, but the Church was too scattered around the Mediterranean region and too diverse in culture and sentiment to ever be able to unify themselves in the way required of a Zion people.

The temple, the priesthood, and the Church were taken off the earth, but not the people, who were not worthy of being translated. The Apostles died. Priesthood was lost. Loss of the Holy Spirit was evidenced by a gradual disappearance of spiritual gifts. Changes were made in church organization and government, and essential ordinances like baptism were modified. Sound doctrine did not endure, and the philosophies of the Greeks triumphed over truth.

Zion was lost.

Notes

1. Andrew C. Skinner, "The Course of Peace and Apostasy," in Kent P. Jackson, ed., *Studies in Scripture, Volume Eight: Alma 30 to Moroni* (1988), 223.
2. *Doctrine and Covenants Student Manual,* 2nd ed. (Church Educational System manual, 2001), 425.
3. Andrew C. Skinner, "The Course of Peace and Apostasy," 223.
4. Joseph Smith, in *History of the Church,* 6:33.
5. Joseph Smith, in *History of the Church,* 6:37–38.
6. See *Doctrine and Covenants Student Manual,* 425.
7. James E. Talmage, *Jesus the Christ,* 3rd ed. (1916), 718, note 3.
8. Bruce R. McConkie, *Doctrinal New Testament Commentary,* 3 vols. (1965–73), 2:58.
9. Neal A. Maxwell, "Settle This in Your Hearts," *Ensign,* Nov. 1992, 66.
10. Marion G. Romney, "Fundamental Welfare Services," *Ensign,* May 1979, 95–96.
11. *Teachings of Presidents of the Church: Howard W. Hunter* (2015), 263.

CHAPTER 5

The Zion of the Nephites

(4 NEPHI 1)

Jesus Christ Appears to the Nephites

Among the Nephites, there had been a number of prophecies of the coming of Christ to visit them. As early as the ministry of Nephi, he prophesied concerning it (2 Nephi 16:1, 9). And in 6 B.C., Samuel the Lamanite foretold not only His coming, but the time of His coming and the destructions that would precede it (see Helaman 14:20–27).

When that day arrived, the earth was convulsed with unprecedented destruction, including earthquakes, volcanoes, tornadoes, fierce lightning, landslides, mudflows, and floods. Many cities were burned and others were covered by landslides or by water (3 Nephi 8:5–19). This was followed by three days of impenetrable darkness while the earth continued to groan (3 Nephi 8:20–23).

Then, suddenly they heard a voice out of heaven. It was not a harsh voice nor a loud voice, but it was a still, small voice that penetrated to their core, causing their hearts to burn. The voice spoke a second time, but neither the first nor the second time did they understand what it was saying (see 3 Nephi 11:3–4).

The third time they heard the voice they understood it (see 3 Nephi 11:5–6). The voice said: "Behold my Beloved Son, in whom I am well pleased, in whom I have glorified my name—hear ye him" (3 Nephi 11:7). This was the voice of our Heavenly Father who was introducing His Son.

This event reminds us of the time when God spoke from the top of Mount Sinai to the children of Israel. The Israelites were frightened and told Moses to speak to God for them.

Then the Lord appeared face to face to 70 of their leaders on the lower reaches of the mount. All of this was done as part of the process of making them into a Zion people. The Nephites looked up and saw a Man clothed in a white robe descending out of heaven, who came down and stood among the people. They supposed He was an angel and did not dare to speak to Him (see 3 Nephi 11:8). But He stretched forth His hand and said: "Behold, I am Jesus Christ, whom the prophets testified shall come into the world" (3 Nephi 11:9–10).

There is plenty of historical evidence to support this account. Following are just two examples.

Ceasing of Idolatry

John L. Sorenson, in a 1955 paper entitled "A Chronological Ordering of the Mesoamerican Pre-Classic," dates to about A.D. 50 a sudden and total change in the culture of Mesoamerica:

> What now appears to be one of the most unprecedented religious events in Mesoamerica's long history can be detected in the late pre-Classic [time of Christ] in connection with [a] sharp, sudden change [in] aspects of culture. The modification is evidenced most clearly by the widespread abandonment of the time-honored figurine cult. This drastic step occurred simultaneously over a wide area . . . [and] corresponds in time to the abandonment of the long-traditional incense-burner forms of highland Guatemala. . . . [There are] indications of a puritanical religious spirit [of early and undefiled Christianity] which alone could account for the [change].[1]

A Gospel of Righteousness and Peace

The Padre Torquemada, who arrived in Mexico from Spain about the middle of the sixteenth century [ca. A.D. 1550], wrote of Mexico's Messiah:

> He was perfect in *moral virtues* and they say that He is alive and that He is to return. He never wanted nor permitted sacrifices of blood. . . . He very efficiently prohibited and forbade wars, robberies, and deaths and other harm they inflicted on each other. . . . He was very chaste and very honest, and very moderate. . . . When they took an oath or said, "By our Lord," it was understood they referred to Quetzalcoatl. . . . The lordship of Quetzalcoatl was gentle, and He asked of them in service but light things as distinguished from painful things, and He taught them those things which were virtuous, prohibiting them those things which were evil, noxious, and harmful, . . . teaching them also to hate evil things.[2]

Zion Is Established in America

Following the appearance and preaching of the Savior in A.D. 34, the people in America lived in continual peace and happiness. There was no contention among them (see 4 Nephi 1:15–16). There were no envyings, nor strifes, nor tumults, nor whoredoms, nor lyings, nor murder, nor any manner of lusts (see 4 Nephi 1:16). They had all things in common (see 4 Nephi 1:3). This was a period of time when Zion existed in the hearts of the people and in the land. They could be likened to the people of the City of Enoch who were taken up into heaven after 365 years because they had continued always in righteousness (see Moses 7).

Requirements to Establish Zion

In the previous two chapters we identified three things that are necessary for the establishment of Zion and a Zion people:

— **Sanctification:** They would have to be sanctified—cleansed from their worldly ways (D&C 84:23). When Jesus appeared among the Nephites, He came following great destructions that removed the unrighteous from among them. Those that were left were not perfect, but they were the humble believers in Jesus Christ. They were worthy enough to have the personal presence of the Savior among them, which is also the privilege of any Zion people. Thus was met the first of the requirements for a Zion people: sanctification.

— **Priesthood:** They would need to have the Melchizedek Priesthood. President Joseph Fielding Smith said: "There were no Levites who accompanied Lehi to the Western Hemisphere. Under these conditions the Nephites officiated by virtue of the Melchizedek Priesthood from the days of Lehi to the days of the appearance of our Savior among them."[3]

— **A Temple:** TheNephites built several temples over time. Nephi built one in the land of Nephi after the Nephites separated from the Lamanites (2 Nephi 5:16). There was another temple at Zarahemla, from which King Benjamin gave his sermon on Christlike living (Mosiah 2:1, 5–6). And finally, there was a temple in the land of Bountiful, to which the surviving Nephites gathered after the great destructions on this continent (3 Nephi 11: 1–10). This was the temple where the Savior appeared to them.

© J. BRICKEY, USED BY PERMISSION

Nephi built a temple in the Land of Nephi

An Unshakable Witness

How did this happen? What caused such righteousness and unity to be established? And why did it last 200 years? The answer lies in the testimonies of the people.

CHRIST IN AMERICA, © JOSEPH BRICKEY. USED BY PERMISSION.

- **3 Nephi 10:18–19 Those who survived both saw and touched the risen Lord.** Both Nephites and Lamanites received this privilege (v. 18). Christ showed His body unto them and ministered unto them (v. 19).
- **3 Nephi 11:12–15 Jesus invited everyone in the crowd to come forth individually and touch His resurrected body.** We are later told that there were 2,500 people in the multitude (see 3 Nephi 17:25). If each person had only 30 seconds with Him, to have 2,500 of them do so would have taken nearly 21 hours!

This was a highly personal and individual experience—putting your finger into the wounds of His hands and His feet and thrusting your hand into the hole in His side—personally handling the body of the Master.

Why did Jesus offer such an intimate personal experience to each of them individually? It was a personal and tangible witness that they would never forget, and which would lead them to be a Zion people for nearly 200 years.

President Joseph Fielding Smith said, "[The Lord] showed these wounds to the Nephites when He visited with them with [this] purpose in view, to convince them of His identity, and give to them a witness of His suffering."[4]

Unto the Third and Fourth Generation

The scriptures speak frequently of the third and fourth generations following some great event. The "iniquity of the fathers" seems to continue in their posterity until three or four generations of time (see Exodus 20:5). And righteousness also seems to last through those same generations. Why?

Elder H. Verlan Andersen said:

> When the Lord appeared, He established one unified society in which there was no sin, no crime, and no wars. These conditions continued to prevail in some areas for around three hundred years [see 4 Nephi 1:15–16]. What would one not give to live in a society like that? . . . How were those races able to live as a celestial society for so long? We might also ask, How will it be possible during the Millennium for the people to remain righteous for almost a thousand years? The answer seems to be the same in both cases, and I believe that it consists in this: Parents teaching their children the gospel, and doing so especially during that early period of their lives when they cannot be tempted.[5]

We can understand that anyone who has physically touched the Savior and His wounds would have a sure witness that cannot be shaken. That's the first generation. These people, in turn, can bear solemn witness to their children of what they saw and heard, and their children are not very likely to doubt them, especially when an entire generation of adults is all saying the same thing. That's the second generation. These same people can testify to their grand children, with similar results. That's the third generation.

However, by the time of the arrival of the fourth generation—the great-grandchildren of the original witnesses—that initial generation is likely to have died. There is nobody left who can look you in the eyes and say, "I know, because I saw Him and I touched Him, and I saw Him return into heaven." The fourth generation must rely on the hearsay of those who have heard the original witnesses' testimonies. And this uncertainty only increases as further generations come and go.

Zion among the Nephites

After the Lord's departure, the disciples of Jesus formed a Church in all of the surrounding lands (v. 1). Many who had not seen the Savior were taught concerning Him, repented, and received the Holy Ghost. By the end of the third year, "the people were all converted unto the Lord" (v. 2) and the unity of the people caused Zion to be established among them.

- **4 Nephi 1:2, 13 "Every man did deal justly."** There were no contentions or disputations, and peace prevailed.

  President Brigham Young said:

  > We need to learn, practice, study, know, and understand how angels live with each other. When this community comes to the point to be perfectly honest and upright, you will never find a poor person; none will lack, all will have sufficient. Every man, woman, and child will have all they need just as soon as they all become honest. When the majority of the community are dishonest, it maketh the honest portion poor, for the dishonest serve and enrich themselves at their expense.[6]

- **4 Nephi 1:3 "They had all things in common,"** so there were no rich or poor, and no slaves because they had all been "made free" by the teachings of the gospel.
- **4 Nephi 1:4–5, 13 Many miracles were performed** beginning in the fourth year and continuing for nearly 100 more.
- **4 Nephi 1:6–9 The people greatly prospered over the next 11 years,** rebuilding many of the cities that had been destroyed at the time of Christ's coming.
- **4 Nephi 1:10–11 They "multiplied exceedingly fast,"** and were a "fair and delightsome people."
- **4 Nephi 1:14 After 100 years, many of them had passed away,** including all of the twelve disciples except the Three Nephites who were translated.
- **4 Nephi 1: 15–17 There were "no manner of -ites,"** and because there were no divisions among the people, there was no contention, no crime, and no wickedness.

President Russell M. Nelson said:

> Throughout the world, . . . strident voices are engaged in divisive disputation and name-calling. Often demeaning nicknames are added to—or even substituted for—given names. Unfortunately, terms of derision obscure the true identity of children of the covenant. . . . When the Nephites were truly righteous, they avoided divisive nicknames. . . . "There were no . . . Lamanites, nor any manner of - ites; but they were in one, the children of Christ, and heirs to the kingdom of God" [4 Nephi 1:17]. That lesson from history suggests that we also delete from our personal vocabularies names that segregate.[7]

- **4 Nephi 1:16 "There could not be a happier people."** President George Q. Cannon said:

> Whence comes your enjoyment? Whence come the glorious feelings that you have when you feel the best? Do they come from the outside? Do external circumstances produce real happiness of the kind that I describe? Doubtless, they contribute to happiness; but the purest joy, the greatest happiness, that which is most heavenly proceeds from within. A man must carry the principles of happiness and the love of God in his own breast, or he will not be happy. It is not true enjoyment when it comes from any other source. Not from without, therefore, must we expect happiness and exaltation, but from within. Deity is within us, and its development brings happiness and joy inexpressible.[8]

- **4 Nephi 1:18–20 The first generation had passed away after 110 years,** including the prophet Nephi. At that point, his son Amos continued to keep the record of the people, which he did for the next 84 years until he died.

From Zion to Total Wickedness

- **4 Nephi 1:20 The first divisions among the people started after 194 years.** After so many years of peace and righteousness, one might suppose that nothing could disturb their Zion society. But as he always does, Satan crept into the hearts of the people and "lull[ed] them away into carnal security, . . . and [led] them away carefully down to hell" (2 Nephi 28:21). A small part of the people revolted from the Church, and began to call themselves Lamanites.

Ruins of their richly adorned buildings

- **4 Nephi 1:22 "The second generation had all passed away save it were a few."**
- **4 Nephi 1:23–25 By A.D. 201 the people became exceedingly rich** because of their prosperity in Christ (v. 23), and they began to be lifted up in pride, such as the wearing of costly apparel and other fine things of the world (vv. 24–25).

President George Q. Cannon said:

> When the principles of the gospel were practiced among the [Nephites], they were equal to a very great extent; but when they began to violate the principles of the gospel, their inequality manifested itself. Some were lifted up in pride, some looked with scorn upon their poor brethren and sisters. Classifications arose in society which had their origin not in virtue, not in holiness, not in purity, not in any superiority arising from intelligence, but because some were richer than others, some could dress better than others, some could have better surroundings than others, doubtless dwelt in finer houses, better furnished, and they were better clad, and had probably finer and nicer food. . . .
>
> There is something in the human heart of that character that when human beings are prospering they are apt to be lifted up in pride and to forget the cause or the source of their prosperity; they are apt to forget God, who is the fountain of all their blessings, and to give glory to themselves. . . . God has sent us here and given unto us a mission on the earth, not to accumulate riches, not to become worldly-minded, not to pile up the things of this world. . . . The

happiness of a people does not consist in the abundance of worldly things.[9]

- **4 Nephi 1:25–26 By A.D. 210 the law of consecration ceased** and they began to be divided into classes.
- **4 Nephi 1:26–34 Other churches appeared which dissented from and persecuted the true Church of Christ.** Ministers of these churches began to teach what the people wanted to hear in their unrighteousness (vv. 27–28), and they were paid for their false preaching (v. 26). They despised the miracles and gifts of the true Church, and cast the Three Nephites into prisons (which could not hold them because the Lord set them free). The Three Nephites were also cast into furnaces of fire and dens of beasts, but they came forth without harm (vv. 29–33).
- **4 Nephi 1:35–39 By A.D. 230 there became a great division among all the people.** There were the Nephites, who were true believers in Christ, and the Lamanites, who rejected the gospel entirely (vv. 35–38). The Lamanites were now teaching their children to not believe that which was good and to hate those who were good (vv. 38–39).
- **4 Nephi 1:40 By A.D. 244 the wicked far exceeded the people of God.**
- **4 Nephi 1:41–43 In A.D. 260, the secret combinations of Gadianton appeared** among the wicked part of the people and their richly adorned churches (vv. 41–42).
- **4 Nephi 1:40–45 By A.D. 300 the Nephites had became exceedingly proud because of their riches.** They were as vain and as wicked as the Lamanites.
- **4 Nephi 1:46 The Gadianton robbers overran the land** because there were none to oppose their wickedness.

Wars Begin

In A.D. 322 the wars between the wicked Lamanites and the wicked Nephites began (see Mormon 1:8–11), with many resulting deaths. The war stopped for four years, but unrighteousness did not.

The people were so wicked that the Three Nephites were taken away by A.D. 326. The people were so wicked that the prophet Mormon was forbidden to preach to them (see Mormon 1:17).

Mormon became the leader of the Nephite armies, but even with his righteous leadership, they lost badly. Mormon was encouraged when they began to repent of their iniquity and to mourn, but their repentance was not unto God, whom they cursed (see Mormon 1:9–14).

From A.D. 345 to A.D. 349 the wars continued. From A.D. 350 to A.D. 360 there was peace, but in A.D. 360 the Lamanites came again with all their might against the Nephites (see Mormon 3:4–7). When the Nephites would win a battle they would boast of their strength and wanted to seek revenge (see Mormon 3:9–10). Mormon refused to lead them now, but stood by, as the Lord commanded, and witnessed their great destruction (see Mormon 3:16).

For the next 15 years, until A.D. 375, the battles continued. The Nephites and Lamanites had both hardened their hearts to the point that they delighted in the shedding of blood (see Mormon 4:10–11). The anger between the Nephites and the Lamanites was so strong that they had no fear of death and they thirsted after blood and revenge continually (see Moroni 9:5).

Captured women and children were offered us as sacrifices to their idol gods (see Mormon 4:14, 21). The Lamanites fed the captured Nephite women upon the flesh of their husbands, and the children upon the flesh of their fathers (see Moroni 9:7–8). The Nephites were equally depraved as they raped, tortured, and then devoured the flesh of the captive daughters of the Lamanites as a token of bravery (see Moroni 9:9–10). The people were without order or mercy, their depravity and perversion so strong and brutal that they delighted in everything except that which was good (see Moroni 9:16–20).

The Nephites Are Destroyed

The Nephites were finally defeated in one great battle in 385. Millions died in a matter of days. Those who escaped were hunted down and killed by the Lamanites, including the prophet Mormon (see Mormon 8:2).

The Lamanites Become Dark and Loathsome

The Lamanites continued to war among themselves and the whole face of the land was one continual round of murder and bloodshed (see Mormon 8:8). This was still the case when the Europeans came to America and found multiple warring tribes of Native Americans. In Mexico and Central and South America the Incas and Aztecs and others were practicing human sacrifices and worshipping idols. There was no common language or common history among them. They had lost all knowledge of their original heritage, and also had no remaining vestige of their glorious Zion society.

Dr. Hugh W. Nibley wrote:

> Mormon and Moroni supply the epilogue to the Book of Mormon, the son drawing freely on his father's notes and letters. The picture that these two paint of their world, which in their minds has a significant resemblance to our own, is one of unrelieved gloom. The situation is unbelievably bad and, in view of the way things are going, quite without hope. The scenes of horror and violence, culminating in the sickening escalation of atrocities by Lamanites and Nephites in the 9th chapter of Mormon, need no news-photographs to make their message convincing to the modern world. The Nephites, like the great heroes of tragedy—Oedipus, Macbeth, Achilles—as they approach their end, are hopelessly trapped by a desperate mentality in which the suppressed awareness of their own sins finds paranoid expression in a mad, ungovernable hatred of others: "They have lost their love, one towards another; and they thirst after blood and revenge continually" (Moroni 9:5). Their awful guilt leaps out in their instant resentment of any criticism of themselves: "When I speak the word of God with sharpness they tremble and anger against me" (Moroni 9:4).

They have reached that point of suicidal defiance which the Greeks called *Atę,* the point of no return, when the sinner with a sort of fatal fascination does everything that is most calculated to hasten his own removal from the scene—he is finished, and now all that remains is to get him out of the way: "O my beloved son, how can a people like this, that are without civilization . . . expect that God will stay his hand?" (Moroni 9:11, 14).

Nephite civilization was thus not extinguished at Cumorah. It had already ceased to exist for some time before the final house-cleaning. War had become the order of the day, "and every heart was hardened" (Mormon 4:11), with the military requisitioning the necessities of life and leaving the noncombatants "to faint by the way and die" (Moroni 9:16). "O the depravity of my people!" cries Mormon, and he tells us in what this depravity consists:

"They are without order and without mercy, . . . they have become strong in their perversion; and they are alike brutal, sparing none, neither young nor old, . . . and the suffering of our women and our children upon all the face of this land doth exceed everything. . . . Thou knowest that they are without principle and past feeling. . . . I cannot recommend them unto God lest he should smite me" (Moroni 9:18–21). Here then is the real calamity that befell the Nephites in all its tragic horror—and there is no mention whatever of enemy action or of anyone belonging to the wrong party: the ultimate catastrophe is not that people are struck down, but that they should be found in any circumstances whatever "without order and without mercy, . . . without principle and past feeling."[10]

Notes

1. Bruce W. Warren and Thomas Stuart Ferguson, *The Messiah in Ancient America* (1987), 31–32.
2. Bruce W. Warren and Thomas Stuart Ferguson, *The Messiah in Ancient America,* 19–20.
3. Joseph Fielding Smith, *Answers to Gospel Questions,* comp. Joseph Fielding Smith Jr., 5 vols. (1957–66), 1:124.

4. Joseph Fielding Smith, *Doctrines of Salvation,* comp. Bruce R. McConkie, 3 vols. (1954–56), 2:292.
5. H. Verlan Andersen, "Bring Up Your Children in Light and Truth," *Ensign,* Nov. 1991, 80.
6. *Teachings of Presidents of the Church: Brigham Young* (1997), 180.
7. Russell M. Nelson, "Children of the Covenant," *Ensign,* May 1995, 34.
8. George Q. Cannon, in *Gospel Truth: Discourses and Writings of George Q. Cannon,* sel. Jerreld L. Newquist, 2 vols. in 1 (1987), 78.
9. George Q. Cannon, "Discourse," *Deseret News,* June 15, 1881, 306.
10. Hugh W. Nibley, *Since Cumorah,* ed. John W. Welch, 2nd ed. (1981), 399–400.

Section Two

Zion In The Last Dispensation

Chp	Chapter Title	Page

STAGES OF DEVELOPMENT FOR ZION

(D&C 58:1–7, 44–45; 105)

In this section of the book, we will discuss the command that the Lord has given us to establish Zion in these last days. This is the final dispensation and so the Zion that we must build will usher in the Millennium, and must last until the end of it. There is no room for failure.

Elder Bruce R. McConkie said:

> The gathering of Israel and the establishment of Zion in the latter days is divided into three periods or phases. The first phase

> is past; we are now living in the second phase; and the third lies ahead. . . .
>
> Phase I—From the First Vision, the setting up of the kingdom on April 6, 1830, and the coming of Moses on April 3, 1836, to the secure establishment of the Church in the United States and Canada, a period of about 125 years.
>
> Phase II—From the creation of stakes of Zion in overseas areas, beginning in the 1950s, to the Second Coming of the Son of Man, a period of unknown duration.
>
> Phase III—From our Lord's Second Coming until the kingdom is perfected and the knowledge of God covers the earth as the waters cover the sea, and from then until the end of the Millennium, a period of 1,000 years.[1]

We can readily see that we are currently in Phase II of the process. We do not know how long this phase will last. But we have made solemn covenants to sacrifice and consecrate whatever is necessary for the building up of the Kingdom and the establishment of Zion.

Elder McConkie also said:

> As of now, the Lord has laid upon us the responsibility to lay the foundation for that which is to be. We have been commissioned to prepare a people for the Second Coming of the Son of Man. We have been called to preach the gospel to every nation and kindred and tongue and people. We have been commanded to lay the foundations of Zion and to get all things ready for the return of Him who shall again crown the Holy City with His presence and glory. . . .
>
> Stakes of Zion are . . . being organized at the ends of the earth. . . . A stake of Zion is a part of Zion. You cannot create a stake of Zion without creating a part of Zion. Zion is the pure in heart; we gain purity of heart by baptism and by obedience. A stake has geographical boundaries. To create a stake is like founding a City of Holiness. Every stake on earth is the gathering place for the lost sheep of Israel who live in its area.

The gathering place for Peruvians is in the stakes of Zion in Peru, or in the places which soon will become stakes. The gathering place for Chileans is in Chile; for Bolivians it is in Bolivia; for Koreans it is in Korea; and so it goes through all the length and breadth of the earth. Scattered Israel in every nation is called to gather to the fold of Christ, to the stakes of Zion, as such are established in their nations. . . .

That is to say—Israel shall be gathered one by one, family by family, unto the stakes of Zion established in all parts of the earth so that the whole earth shall be blessed with the fruits of the gospel.

This then is the counsel of the Brethren: Build up Zion, but build it up in the area where God has given you birth and nationality. Build it up where He has given you citizenship, family, and friends. Zion is here in South America and the Saints who comprise this part of Zion are and should be a leavening influence for good in all these nations.

And know this: God will bless that nation which so orders its affairs as to further His work.[2]

Notes

1. Bruce R. McConkie, "Come: Let Israel Build Zion," *Ensign,* May 1977, 115.
2. Bruce R. McConkie, "Come: Let Israel Build Zion," 116, 118.

CHAPTER 6

Restoration and the Call to Build Zion

(JOHN 1; ACTS 20; 2 THES. 2; 2 TIM. 4; 1 NEPHI 13; MORMON 1; D&C 1; 5; 98; 101; 105; JOSEPH SMITH—HISTORY)

INTRODUCTION

The Messiah Ben Joseph

YOUNG JOSEPH, ©WALTER RANE, USED BY PERMISSION

The disciples in Jesus's day knew all about the coming prophet of the Restoration—known as the Messiah ben Joseph—who would gather Israel together prior to the coming of the Messiah ben David to reign on earth. This great prophet, a descendant of the tribe of Joseph, was especially important to the Samaritans (partly descended from Joseph), and was a sore subject for the Jews, who despised the Samaritans, considering them to be unworthy half-breeds.

- **John 1:19–21 Jewish leaders ask John the Baptist, "Art thou that prophet?"** Troubled by his rising popularity, mighty preaching, and baptisms, the leaders of the Jews sent priests to ask John the Baptist, "Who art thou?" (v. 19). There were many who had pretended to be the Messiah over the years, but John made it clear: "I am not the Christ" (v. 20). Well then, who? "Art thou Elias?"—meaning Elijah, who they knew would return prior to the advent of the Messiah. John said, "I am not." There was only one other possibility if he was not the Christ and not Elijah. They asked, "Art thou that prophet?"—meaning the prophet descended from Joseph who would also come before the Messiah. And John said again, "No" (v. 21).

- **The important role of the Messiah ben Joseph.** W. Cleon Skousen wrote:

> From the most ancient times, Jewish tradition has proclaimed that a great servant of God from the House of Joseph would come in the latter days to prepare the way for the coming of Shilo, the Great Messiah.[1] In fact, so profound was the respect of the rabbis for this "Joseph" that they began calling him, "Messiah ben Joseph," and called their Shilo [coming Savior], "Messiah ben David." Literally translated, these appellations mean, "The anointed One, son of Joseph," and "The anointed One, son of David." A comprehensive study of this mysterious "Messiah ben Joseph" was made by Dr. Joseph Klausner, Professor Emeritus of Hebrew literature and Jewish history at the Hebrew University in Jerusalem. Dr. Klausner . . . put down the basic attributes which Jewish tradition variously ascribed to him [the Messiah ben Joseph].[2]

Skousen summarized the characteristics of Messiah ben Joseph listed by Dr. Klausner as follows:[3]

- He will rise up shortly before the coming of Shilo, the great Messiah ben David.
- He will be a descendant of Joseph through Ephraim.
- His mission will commence about the time the prophet Elijah comes as promised in Malachi 4:5–6.
- In preparing mankind for the coming of Shilo, Messiah ben Joseph will enter into a great contest with the anti-Christ forces.
- In the heat of this contest with the anti-Christ, Messiah ben Joseph will be killed.

Dr. Klausner's list of the Samaritan version of the Messiah ben Joseph tradition states that:[4]

- He would be a descendant of Joseph through Ephraim (a "son of Ephraim").

- They called him Teal, meaning "a restorer," "he who returns," or, according to others, "he who causes to return."
- He would call the people to repentance and bring back better days for Israel.
- This Joseph of the latter day "will restore everywhere the true Law to its former validity and convert all peoples, *especially the Jews,* to the Samaritan [Ephraimite] religion."

The Greatness of the Prophet Joseph Smith

President Brigham Young taught:

The Prophet Joseph Smith

> It was decreed in the counsels of eternity, long before the foundations of the earth were laid, that he, Joseph Smith, should be the man, in the last dispensation of this world, to bring forth the word of God to the people, and receive the fulness of the keys and power of the Priesthood of the Son of God. The Lord had His eyes upon him, and upon his father, and upon his father's father, and upon their progenitors clear back to Abraham, and from Abraham to the Flood, from the Flood to Enoch, and from Enoch to Adam. He has watched that family and that blood as it has circulated from its fountain to the birth of that man. He was foreordained in eternity to preside over this last dispensation [see 2 Nephi 3:6–15].[5]

- **D&C 5:7–10 The Lord declared that this generation (dispensation) would have His words through Joseph Smith.** The Lord said that many would not believe Joseph's words, just as they had not believed Him when He was on earth (v. 7). This was true, He said, even "if it were possible that you should show them all these things which I have committed unto you" (v. 7). But because of their unbelief He would not permit Joseph to show them everything that he had been shown;

these would be made known only unto "future generations" (vv. 8–9). In the meantime, the Lord said, "This generation shall have my word through you" (v. 10).

As a dispensational prophet called to restore knowledge of all previous dispensations to the earth, the Prophet Joseph Smith knew much more than he was able to tell us. He said in a discourse at Nauvoo in April 1843:

> It is my meditation all the day, and more than my meat and drink, to know how I shall make the Saints of God comprehend the visions that roll like an overflowing surge before my mind. Oh! how I would delight to bring before you things which you never thought of! But poverty and the cares of the world prevent. But I am glad I have the privilege of communicating to you some things which, if grasped closely, will be a help to you when earthquakes bellow, the clouds gather, the lightnings flash, and the storms are ready to burst upon you like peals of thunder.[6]

On another occasion the Prophet lamented that he could not tell all he knew: "Would to God, brethren, I could tell you who I am! Would to God I could tell you what I know! But you would call it blasphemy, and there are men upon this stand who would want to take my life. . . . If the Church knew all the commandments, one-half they would reject through prejudice and ignorance. . . . When God offers a blessing, or knowledge to a man, and he refuses to receive it, he will be damned."[7]

THE APOSTASY AND RENAISSANCE

The Great Apostasy

After Jesus's Ascension, His Apostles presided over the Church. But soon persecution, divisions, and apostasy increased, and within a few decades, there was a falling away from the true Church, as the Apostles had prophesied.

- **Acts 20:28–30 Paul said "the flock" (Church) would not be spared from apostasy.** He counseled Church leaders to "take heed" and to "feed the church of God" (v. 28), because "after my [Paul's] departing shall grievous wolves enter in among you, not sparing the flock" (v. 29). And even among Church leaders themselves "shall men arise, speaking perverse things [false doctrines], to draw away disciples after them" (v. 30).

- **JST, 2 Thessalonians 2:1–3 Paul said the Second Coming of Christ would not occur until after "a falling away first."** There were already in his day false doctrines circulating that the Second Coming was at hand (vv. 1–2). He ad- monished Church members to not be deceived or "soon shaken in mind, or be troubled by letter, except ye receive it from us; neither by spirit, nor by word, as that the day of Christ [Second Coming] is at hand" (v. 2). Note the reference to false letters being sent to congregations in the name of Paul. He said, "Let no man deceive you by any means; for there shall come a falling away [apostasy, defection[8]] first" (v. 3).

Paul warned of a coming apostasy

- **2 Timothy 4:3–4 Paul said the Church would "not endure sound doctrine."** He warned Timothy that congregations of the Church would "heap to themselves teachers, having itching ears" (a figure of speech meaning teachers willing to teach whatever listeners wanted to hear) (v. 3). "And they shall turn away their ears from the truth, and shall be turned unto fables" (v. 4).

A recent book, *The Inevitable Apostasy and the Promised Restoration,* by Elder Tad R. Callister,[9] provides a comprehensive explanation of the Great Apostasy—in my opinion the best since Elder James E. Talmage's *The Great Apostasy,*[10] and much easier to read. Observations by Church leaders of the time are among the many hundreds of evidences cited by Callister that the predictions of the Apostles were literally fulfilled. He also cites dozens of modern non-Mormon scholars who verify the reality and effects of the Great Apostasy. I recommend this excellent book to anyone who wishes to understand what happened to the original Church of Jesus Christ.

One scholar remarked that both before and after the deaths of the Apostles, "the heresies . . . came in, like locusts, to devour the harvests of the Gospel."[11]

Greek philosophy overtook the Church

Persecution from the Romans, perversion from sexual rites adopted from the pagans, and the silent, slow, but deadly influx of Greek philosophy all took their toll. Will Durant observed that "Christianity did not destroy paganism; it adopted it. The Greek mind, dying, came to a transmigrated life in the theology and liturgy of the Church. . . . The Greek mysteries passed down into the impressive mystery of the Mass. . . . Christianity was the last great creation of the ancient pagan world."[12] And William Manchester noted that "Christianity was in turn infiltrated, and to a considerable extent subverted, by the paganism it was supposed to destroy."[13]

As a result of these forces, the Great Apostasy occurred. President Spencer W. Kimball elaborated, "When the light of [the first century A.D.] went out, the darkness was impenetrable, the heavens were sealed, and the 'dark ages' moved in. The thickness of this spiritual darkness was not unlike that physical darkness in Nephite history when 'neither candles, neither torches; neither could there be fire kindled with their fine and exceedingly dry wood' (3 Nephi 8:21). The spiritual vapor of darkness was impenetrable, and centuries were to pass with hardly the dim uncertain light of a candle to break its austere darkness."[14] And "so the world entered that long night of apostasy, the Dark Ages. The church, no longer sanctioned by God, exercised an oppressive tyranny on the minds of men and shackled them with chains of false traditions. Truth was turned to superstition, joy to despair, and worship to ritual."[15]

And Elder Bruce R. McConkie expounded:

> When the gospel sun went down almost two millennia ago, when the priesthood was taken away and a dreary dusk descended in the congregations that once had known light, when light and truth no longer shone forth from heaven, and when those on earth no

> longer were taught and directed by apostles and prophets, then spiritual darkness reigned. Darkness covered the earth and gross darkness the minds of the people (see Isaiah 60:2). The dark ages had their beginning, and the light of heaven no longer dwelt in the hearts of those who professed to worship [God].[16]

There were many consequences of the Great Apostasy:[17]

- — There was no longer priesthood authority on the earth.
- — There were no longer apostles and prophets on the earth.
- — Essential knowledge about the nature of God was lost.
- — The doctrines of the gospel were corrupted.
- — Sacred ordinances, such as baptism, were changed.
- — The original Church became divided into discordant sects.
- — The darkness of the Great Apostasy lasted many centuries.

- **D&C 1:15–16 The Lord's evaluation of the Great Apostasy.** "For they have strayed from mine ordinances, and have broken mine everlasting covenant; they seek not the Lord to establish his righteousness, but every man walketh in his own way, and after the image of his own god, . . . in the likeness of the world, and whose substance is that of an idol, which waxeth old and shall perish in Babylon."
- **Mormon 1:13–14 Mormon described the effects of apostasy upon the Nephites.** "But wickedness did prevail upon the face of the whole land, insomuch that the Lord did take away his beloved disciples, and the work of miracles and of healing did cease because of the iniquity of the people. And there were no gifts from the Lord, and the Holy Ghost did not come upon any, because of their wickedness and unbelief."

Preparing the Way for the Restoration[18]

The darkness of the Apostasy lasted many centuries. However, God foresaw the Apostasy and planned for the Restoration. Beginning in the 14th century, the Lord inspired the social, educational, religious, economic, and governmental conditions under which He could more easily restore the gospel through Joseph Smith.[19]

- **The Renaissance** was a rebirth of learning, especially in literature, art, and science. Inventions such as the printing press came forth. The

Renaissance was no chance occurrence, but rather "a development predetermined in the Mind of God to illumine the benighted minds of men in preparation for the restoration of the gospel of Jesus Christ, which was appointed to be accomplished some centuries later."[20]

- **The Reformation** began when John Wycliffe, Martin Luther, John Calvin, and other reformers challenged the practices and teachings of existing churches, perceiving that these churches had strayed from the teachings of Christ. Through their protests, the reformers created a religious climate in which men could inquire freely concerning doctrine and truth, and God could restore His priesthood authority.

- **Discovery of the Americas.** America—the land promised to the posterity of Joseph in Egypt—was colonized by religious people and eventually became an independent nation (see 1 Nephi 13:12–19).

  — **1 Nephi 13:12 Columbus was led by the Spirit to the Americas.** Nephi saw in vision "a man among the Gentiles, who was separated from the seed of my brethren [in the Americas] by the many waters; and I beheld the Spirit of God, that it came down and wrought upon the man; and he went forth upon the many waters, even unto the seed of my brethren, who were in the promised land."

Christopher Columbus

Columbus himself said, "Who can doubt that this fire was not merely mine, but also of the Holy Spirit who encouraged me with a radiance of marvelous illumination from His sacred Holy Scriptures, . . . urging me to press forward? . . . With a hand that could be felt, the Lord opened my mind to the fact that it would be possible . . . , and He opened my will to desire to accomplish the project. . . . The Lord purposed that there should be something clearly miraculous in this matter of the voyage to the Indies."[21]

Columbus saw his voyages as a fulfillment of a divine plan for his life—and for the soon-to-come Second Coming of Christ. As he put it in 1500: "Of the new Heaven and Earth which our Lord has made, and as St. John writes in the Apocalypse [see Revelation 21:1], after He had told of it by the mouth of Isaiah, He made me the *messenger* for it and showed me where to find it."[22] Columbus also cited various scriptures that he believed validated his mission: John 10:16—"And other sheep I have that are not of this fold: them also I must bring. And they shall hear my voice: and there shall be one fold and one shepherd."[23] And Isaiah 60:9— "For, the islands wait for me, and the ships of the sea in the beginning: that I may bring thy sons from afar, their silver and their gold with them, to the name of the Lord thy God and to the Holy One of Israel, because he hath glorified thee."[24]

THOMAS DALZIEL, PUBLIC DOMAIN

— **1 Nephi 13:13–16 The Pilgrims and others came to and were prospered in the Americas.** Nephi said, "I beheld the Spirit of God, that it wrought upon other Gentiles; and they went forth out of captivity, upon the many waters" (v. 13). Eventually there were "multitudes of the Gentiles upon the land of promise; and I beheld the wrath of God, that it was upon the seed of my brethren; and they were scattered before the Gentiles and were smitten" (v. 14). These Gentiles "did prosper and obtain the land for their inheritance. . . . They were white, and exceedingly fair and beautiful. . . . [They] did humble themselves before the Lord; and the power of the Lord was with them" (vv. 15–16).

"Certain dissenters among the Puritans, Roger Williams chief among them, argued that there ought to be a clear distinction between church and state and that no particular religion ought to be imposed upon the citizens. He also taught that all churches had fallen away from the true apostolic succession. Williams was banished from Massachusetts in 1635, and within a few years, he and others with similar ideas succeeded in obtaining a charter to establish the colony of Rhode Island, which allowed total toleration of all religions."[25]

- **Independence of the United States of America.** The land had to be independent of all other nations in order to protect its inhabitants against the tyranny of false creeds and oppressive kings of that time.

  — **1 Nephi 13:17–19 The Gentiles upon the promised land were protected against all other nations that sought to destroy them.** The Lord protected these Gentiles when "their mother Gentiles were gathered together upon the waters, and upon the land also, to battle against them. . . . The power of God was with them, and . . . the wrath of God was upon all those that were gathered together against them to battle," so that "the Gentiles that had gone out of captivity were delivered by the power of God out of the hands of all other nations."

- **The Constitution of the United States** was established, guaranteeing the religious freedom that would be necessary for the Restoration. The Prophet Joseph Smith testified: "The Constitution of the United States is a glorious standard; it is founded in the wisdom of God. It is a heavenly banner; it is to all those who are privileged with the sweets of liberty, like the cooling shades and refreshing waters of a great rock in a thirsty and weary land."[26]

HOWARD CHANDLER CHRISTY, 1940

The founders of the United States were inspired

— **D&C 101:77–80 The founders of the nation were inspired of God.** The Lord declared that "the laws and constitution of the people, which I have suffered to be established,... should be maintained for the rights and protection of all flesh, according to just and holy principles; that every man may act in doctrine and principle..., according to the moral agency which I have given unto him, that every man may be accountable for his own sins in the day of judgment" (vv. 77–78).

The Lord continued, "It is not right that any man should be in bondage one to another. And for this purpose have I established the Constitution of this land, by the hands of wise men whom I raised up unto this very purpose, and redeemed the land by the shedding of blood" (vv. 79–80). Thus, "God inspired the earlier explorers and colonizers of America and the framers of the Constitution of the United States to develop a land and governing principles to which the gospel could be restored."[27]

— **D&C 98:4–10 The Saints are to support the constitutional law of the land.** There were deep feelings of resentment among the Saints that their constitutional rights to freedom, property, and religion had been trampled on by mobs in Missouri. And the United States government had done nothing to restore these rights. But the Lord counseled the Saints to do whatsoever He commanded them concerning the laws of the land (v. 4).

God justifies the "constitutional law of the land" (v. 6), which was inspired to support and maintain the freedoms and rights of mankind (v. 5). And He will justify us when we befriend the Constitution (v. 6). Anything more or anything less than the rights enumerated in the Constitution "cometh of evil" (v. 7). And under this glorious document, "I, the Lord God, make you free,... and the law also maketh you free" (v. 8).

"Nevertheless, when the wicked rule the people mourn" (v. 9). "Wherefore, honest men and wise men should be sought for diligently, and good men and wise men ye should observe to uphold"; and any other kind of leader would result in "evil" (v. 10).

In a day when some denigrate or minimize the principles of the Constitution and deny heavenly influence in its framing, it is well to remember how the founding of the United States fits into God's overall plan to save His children. As the cradle for the Restoration, the protector of the Church's assets, leaders, and missionaries, and the blessed land promised to the posterity of Joseph and Ephraim, it is the most blessed place on earth, and regardless of our individual nationalities, we should have special reverence for its role.

THE PROMISED RESTORATION BEGINS

A Call to Build Zion

The conditions were now set for the Restoration to begin. Just 18 years after the establishment of the Constitution, the Prophet Joseph Smith was born. And about 25 years later the call to build Zion began.

Dr. Hugh W. Nibley wrote:

> The first commandment given to the Saints in this last dispensation, delivered at Harmony, Pennsylvania, in April of 1829, before the formal incorporation of the Church, was an ominous warning: "Seek not for riches but for wisdom" (D&C 6:7)—all in one brief mandate that does not allow compromise. Why start out on such a negative note? The Lord knew well that the great obstacle to the work would be what it always had been in the past. The warning is repeated throughout the Doctrine and Covenants and the Book of Mormon again and again. The positive and negative are here side by side and back to back, making it clear, as the scriptures often do, that the two quests are mutually exclusive—you cannot go after both, you cannot serve both God and Mammon, even if you should be foolish enough to try.[28]

The progression of this commandment was steady and clear. In November 1831, at Hiram, Ohio, the Lord warned again: "They also seek not earnestly the riches of eternity, but their eyes are full of greediness" (D&C 68:31). The Saints are not to be "idlers" seeking for riches, but they are to "labor for Zion; for if they labor for money they shall perish"! (2 Nephi 26:31).[29]

At the next general conference (1832), the law of consecration was introduced clearly and explicitly (see D&C 82), with some anticipation of strong resistance (see D&C 82:21). The Lord declared that by living this law "the church may stand independent above all other creatures beneath the celestial world" (D&C 78:14). "And Zion cannot be built up unless it is by the principles of the law of the celestial kingdom; otherwise I cannot receive her unto myself" (D&C 105:5).[30]

In the October conference of 1831, the Prophet reminded the Saints "that God had often sealed up the heavens because of covetousness in the Church, . . . and except the Church receive the fulness of the Scriptures . . . they would yet fall."[31] Covetousness, the desire to be rich, was the one thing that could wreck the establishment of a latter-day Zion.[32]

GATHERING TO MISSOURI

The idea of ultimately gathering to a New Jerusalem "on the borders by the Lamanites" was known to the Saints even before they gathered to Ohio. Those who were paying attention to the revelations knew that Kirtland was a temporary stop along the way. It is useful to consider the following revelations, which started coming while the Saints were still in New York and which continued for nearly a year in both Kirtland and Missouri:

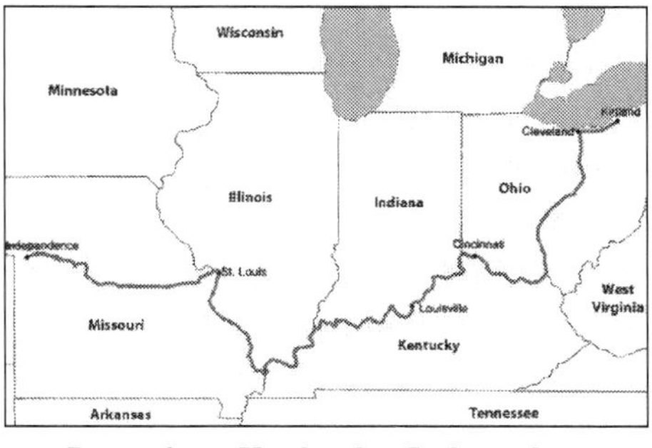

Route from Kirtland to Independence

A Chronology of Revelations Concerning Missouri[33]

— Sept. 1830	**D&C 28:9 The city of Zion will be "on the borders by the Lamanites"**—the precise location would be revealed later.
— Sept./Oct. 1830	**D&C 30:5–6; 32:1–3 The Lord calls four missionaries to preach to the Lamanites**—the first Church members to actually go to Missouri.
— Feb. 9, 1831	**D&C 42:62 The Lord promises to reveal the location of the New Jerusalem** in His own due time.
— June 6, 1831	**D&C 52:2–5, 42–43 The Lord calls Joseph Smith, Sidney Rigdon, and others to go to Missouri.** The Lord promised to consecrate Missouri as the land of their inheritance.
— June 10, 1831	**D&C 54:8 The Lord tells the Colesville Saints to continue on to Missouri.** The Colesville Saints had come from Colesville, New York. Despite persecution and several forced migrations, they tended to remain together for many years, from New York to Ohio and on to Missouri.
— July 20, 1831	**D&C 57:1–3 The city of Zion will be in Jackson County, Missouri, with Independence as the center place.** A temple will be built in Independence.
— July/Aug. 1831	**D&C 57:4–7; 58:52–58 The Saints are to purchase lands and receive inheritances in Missouri,** but in an orderly way and not in haste. **The Lord extends a number of important callings in Missouri.** At Kirtland, Ohio, in February 1831, Edward Partridge was called to be the first bishop of the Church (see D&C 41:9). After arriving in Missouri, Bishop Partridge became bishop of the Saints in Missouri and

received from the Lord the command to "stand in the office to which I have appointed him, and divide unto the saints their inheritance, even as I have commanded; and also those whom he has appointed to assist him" (D&C 57:7). Sidney Gilbert was to establish a store (see D&C 57:8–10). William W. Phelps was to be a printer (see D&C 57:11). And Oliver Cowdery was to edit publications (see D&C 57:13).

— Aug. 1, 1831

D&C 58:7 Those who were "honored in laying the foundation" of Zion included members of the Colesville Branch and others who had arrived in Jackson County.

D&C 58:1–7, 44–45 The establishment of Zion as a city and a people did not occur immediately after the Saints' arrival in Jackson County. Much hard work lay ahead, and Zion would not be redeemed until after "many years" (v. 44). Knowing this helped the Saints to remain faithful through the coming difficulties in Missouri and elsewhere. The Lord's people must be tried in all things to become worthy of Zion (see D&C 136:31).

— Aug. 2, 1831

The Prophet Joseph Smith recorded: "I assisted the Colesville branch of the Church to lay the first log, for a house, as a foundation of Zion in Kaw township, twelve miles west of Independence [in what is now Kansas City, Missouri]. The log was carried and placed by twelve men, in honor of the twelve tribes of Israel. At the same time, through prayer, the land of Zion was consecrated and dedicated by Elder Sidney Rigdon for the gathering of the Saints. It was a season of joy to those present, and afforded a glimpse of the future, which time will yet unfold to the satisfaction of the faithful."[34]

Aug. 3, 1831 **The Prophet Joseph Smith dedicated the spot for the temple in Zion,** a little west of Independence, Missouri.[35]

- **D&C 97:10–16 A house (temple) is to be built in Zion** in which the pure in heart "shall see God" (v. 16). It was to be constructed "like unto the pattern which I have given you" (v. 10)—the plans for which look similar to those used for the Kirtland Temple. The temple was to be "built speedily, by the tithing of my people. Behold, this is the tithing and the sacrifice which I, the Lord, require at their hands, that there may be a house built unto me for the salvation of Zion" (vv. 11–12).

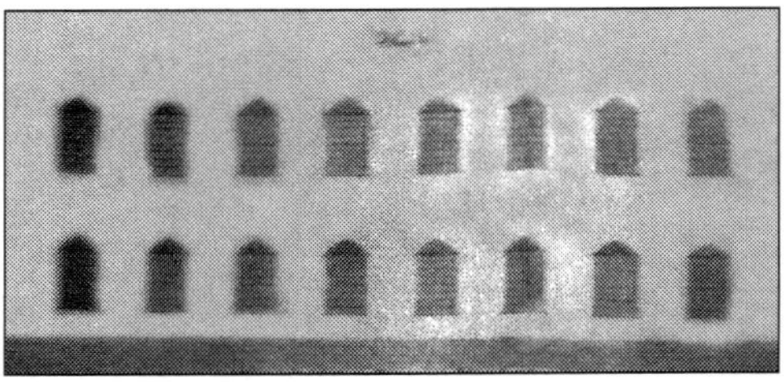

Drawing of the temple in Zion

The purpose of the temple was fourfold:

(1) "A place of thanksgiving for all saints" (v. 13).

(2) "A place of instruction for all those who are called to the work of the ministry" (v. 13).

(3) "That they may be perfected in the understanding of their ministry" (v. 14).

(4) That they may be instructed "in theory, in principle, . . . in doctrine, in all things pertaining to the kingdom of God on the earth" (v. 14).

- **D&C 97:15–17 "Suffer [no] unclean thing to come into it."** As a literal House of the Lord, He promised that His glory would rest upon it and His presence would be there, "for I will come into it" (vv. 15–16). This is true of all temples built and dedicated unto the Lord, so long as we "do not suffer any unclean thing to come into it, that it be not defiled" (v. 15). "But if it be defiled I will not come into it, and my glory shall not be there; for I will not come into unholy temples" (v. 17).

- **D&C 97:18–20 Zion will become "very glorious" and "very great."** The promise of the Lord concerning Zion is sure: "Behold, if Zion do these things she shall prosper, and spread herself and become very glorious, very great, and very terrible. And the nations of the earth shall honor her, and shall say: Surely Zion is the city of our God, and surely Zion cannot fall, neither be moved out of her place, for God is there, and the hand of the Lord is there; and he hath sworn by the power of his might to be her salvation and her high tower."

WHAT IS ZION?

- **The word *Zion* has several meanings:**[36]
  - Zion is "the pure in heart" (D&C 97:21). "Zion is not only a location but a condition as well. The Lord declares that a person worthy of Zion is one who is 'pure in heart.'"[37] Hyrum Smith characterized Zion as "the honest and pure in heart that will h[e] arken to the everlasting covenant."[38]
  - Zion is the Church and its stakes (see D&C 82:14).
  - Zion is the city of Enoch (see Moses 7:19).
  - Zion is the Old Jerusalem (see 2 Samuel 5:6–7; 1 Kings 8:1).
  - Zion is the New Jerusalem (see D&C 45:66–67; D&C 57:1–2; Articles of Faith 1:10).
  - Zion is the eventual dwelling place of those who are exalted (see Hebrews 12:22–23).
- **Requirements for the establishment of Zion:**[39]
  - Zion must arise, fill the earth, and increase in beauty and holiness (see D&C 82:14–15).
  - We must become unified as a people (see D&C 38:27; Moses 7:18).
  - We must be an obedient people (see D&C 64:34–35; 105:3, 5–6).
  - We must care for the poor and needy among us (see D&C 105:3).
  - We must teach one another and learn our duties more perfectly (see D&C 105:10).
  - We must build temples and receive temple blessings (see D&C 97:10–16).

— We must strive to be pure in heart (see D&C 97:21).

— We must preach the gospel to the world (see D&C 133:8–9).

The establishment of Zion on the earth again was one of the primary reasons for the Restoration. The call to establish Zion came early to the Church, and it continues to this day.

Notes

1. See Joseph Klausner, *The Messianic Idea in Israel* (1955). Chapter 9 of Dr. Klausner's book is devoted exclusively to this subject.
2. W. Cleon Skousen, *The Third Thousand Years,* rev. ed. (1997), 128–29.
3. W. Cleon Skousen, *The Third Thousand Years,* 129.
4. See W. Cleon Skousen, *The Third Thousand Years,* 129–30.
5. *Teachings of Presidents of the Church: Brigham Young* (1997), 96.
6. Joseph Smith, in *History of the Church,* 5:362.
7. Joseph Smith, in Orson F. Whitney, *Life of Heber C. Kimball* (1945), 322, 323.
8. See 2 Thessalonians 2:3, footnote *b.*
9. Tad R. Callister, *The Inevitable Apostasy and the Promised Restoration* (2006).
10. James E. Talmage, *The Great Apostasy* (1909).
11. A. Cleveland Coxe, in Alexander Roberts and James Donaldson, eds., *The Ante-Nicene Fathers,* 10 vols. (1885; reprinted 1980–85), 1:309.
12. Will Durant, *The Story of Civilization,* vol. 3, *Caesar and Christ* (1944), 595.
13. William Manchester, *A World Lit Only by Fire: The Medieval Mind and the Renaissance: Portrait of an Age* (1992), 11.
14. *The Teachings of Spencer W. Kimball,* ed. Edward L. Kimball (1982), 424.
15. *The Teachings of Ezra Taft Benson* (1988), 85.
16. Bruce R. McConkie, "The Morning Breaks; the Shadows Flee," *Ensign,* May 1978, 12.
17. See "Lesson 3: 'I Had Seen a Vision,'" *Doctrine and Covenants and Church History Gospel Doctrine Teacher's Manual* (1999), 12.
18. The contents of this section are adapted from "Lesson 3: 'I Had Seen a Vision,'" *Doctrine and Covenants and Church History Gospel Doctrine Teacher's Manual,* 12.

19. See Bruce R. McConkie, *Mormon Doctrine,* 2nd ed. (1966), 717.
20. James E. Talmage, *Jesus the Christ,* 3rd ed. (1916), 749.
21. *The Libro de las profecías of Christopher Columbus,* trans. Delno C. West and August Kling (1991), 105, 107.
22. *The Libro de las profecías of Christopher Columbus,* 60.
23. *The Libro de las profecías of Christopher Columbus,* 229.
24. *The Libro de las profecías of Christopher Columbus,* 179.
25. *Church History in the Fulness of Times,* 2nd ed. (Church Educational System student manual, 2003), 10.
26. Joseph Smith, in *History of the Church,* 3:304.
27. M. Russell Ballard, "Restored Truth," *Ensign,* Nov. 1994, 66.
28. Hugh W. Nibley, *Approaching Zion,* ed. Don E. Norton (1989), 343.
29. See Hugh W. Nibley, *Approaching Zion,* 343.
30. See Hugh W. Nibley, *Approaching Zion,* 343–44.
31. Joseph Smith, in "Minutes, 25–26 October 1831," p. 13, The Joseph Smith Papers, accessed August 9, 2017, http://www.josephsmithpapers.org/ paper-summary/ minutes-25-26-october-1831/4
32. See Hugh W. Nibley, *Approaching Zion,* 344.
33. Adapted from "Lesson 12: 'The Gathering of My People,'" *Doctrine and Covenants and Church History Gospel Doctrine Teacher's Manual* (1999), 65–66.
34. *Teachings of Presidents of the Church: Joseph Smith* (2007), 184.
35. See *Teachings of Presidents of the Church: Joseph Smith,* 184. See also *History of the Church,* 1:199.
36. Adapted from "Lesson 46: 'Zion—The Pure in Heart,'" *Doctrine and Covenants and Church History Gospel Doctrine Teacher's Manual,* 267.
37. "Section 97: 'This Is Zion—the Pure in Heart,'" 230.
38. Hyrum Smith, in *History of the Church,* 6:320.
39. Adapted from "Lesson 46: 'Zion—The Pure in Heart,'" 268–69.

CHAPTER 7

Gathering a Zion People

(GEN. 48–49; DEUT. 33; ISA. 5; 10–11; 13–14; 35; 48–49; 51; 58; 61; JER. 3; 16; 23–24; 30–31; 33; 50; 1 NE. 22; 2 NE. 9; 29; 3 NE. 21; D&C 1; 29; 43; 66; 86; 110; 113; 133; MOSES 7)

Before the events of the Second Coming can occur, the Lord must gather His people into the kingdom of God, which is the Church. Many prophets have spoken concerning this great gathering, which is underway even at this time and will continue until the Lord's coming. The following events have occurred or will occur in our time:

Wheat gathered in bundles

— **D&C 110:11** Moses committed the keys of the gathering of Israel from the four parts of the earth to Joseph Smith and Oliver Cowdery in the Kirtland Temple. These keys give the Church the power and authority to organize the gathering and leading of the ten tribes back from the north.

— **D&C 133:7–40** All men are commanded to flee from Babylon, come to Zion, and prepare for the Lord's Second Coming. Christ will stand on Mount Zion, the continents will become one land, and the lost ten tribes will return. The gospel revealed through Joseph Smith is to be preached in all the world.

— **D&C 43:28–30** The Lord urges us to labor in His vineyard, gathering Israel for the last time before His Second Coming ushers in the Millennium.

— **Isaiah 11:10–12; 2 Nephi 21:10–12** The Lord will set up an ensign for the nations and gather scattered Israel home from the four corners of the earth.

— **2 Nephi 29:12–14** The scattered people of Israel will gather together in one, and will bring their scriptures with them.

— **3 Nephi 21:26–29** God will prepare the nations to hear the gospel message, and His servants will then teach and gather them, not in haste, but with order.

— **D&C 29:7–11** Scattered Israel will be gathered to Zion upon the American continent to escape the desolation that will be poured out upon the wicked, who are ripening iniquity and who, if they do not repent, will be burned at Christ's Second Coming.

— **Moses 7:62** Righteousness and truth will sweep the earth to help the honest in heart gather to the New Jerusalem, where a great temple of the Lord will be built.

President Joseph Fielding Smith spoke concerning the house of Israel today:

> *Every person who embraces the gospel becomes of the house of Israel.* In other words, they become members of the *chosen lineage,* or Abraham's children through Isaac and Jacob unto whom the promises were made.[1]

And President Spencer W. Kimball declared:

> Now, the gathering of Israel consists of joining the true Church and their coming to a knowledge of the true God. . . . Any person, therefore, who has accepted the restored gospel, and who now seeks to worship the Lord in his own tongue and with the Saints in the nations where he lives, has complied with the law of the gathering of Israel and is heir to all of the blessings promised the Saints in these last days.[2]

ISAIAH'S PROPHECIES OF THE GATHERING

An Ensign Will Be Lifted Up in the Last Days

- **Isaiah 5:25–30; 2 Nephi 15:25–30 Israel will be gathered in haste—with means not known in Isaiah's day.** Although the Lord would permit great destruction and death in Judah's streets, yet His hand was still offered to her inhabitants in peace if they would take it (v. 25). And eventually, in the latter days, He will gather them again in peace.

  He will "lift up an ensign to the nations from far, and will hiss unto them from the end of the earth: and, behold, they shall come with speed swiftly" (v. 26). An *ensign* or *banner* is a military symbol designating a gathering place or rallying point. To "hiss" is a figure of speech from Isaiah's day meaning to signal (such as with a whistle)—to summon others to pay attention and to come. The place where the banner will be raised and the whistle blown will be "from the end of the earth"—literally halfway around the world from where Isaiah prophesied (v. 26). And the Lord's people will come by means and with speed that must have seemed miraculous to Isaiah as he witnessed it (vv. 26–29).

  Elder LeGrand Richards wrote:

> In fixing the time of the great gathering, Isaiah seemed to indicate that it would take place in the day of the railroad train and the airplane: [See Isaiah 5:26–29; 2 Nephi 15:26–29.] Since there were neither trains nor airplanes in that day, Isaiah could hardly have mentioned them by name. However, he seems to have described them in unmistakable words. How better could "their horses' hoofs be counted like flint, and their wheels like a whirlwind" than in the modern train? How better could "their roaring . . . be like a lion" than in the roar of the airplane? Trains and airplanes do not stop for night. Therefore,

Hooves of steel like a whirlwind and the roar of a lion

was not Isaiah justified in saying: "none shall slumber nor sleep; neither shall the girdle of their loins be loosed, nor the latchet of their shoes be broken"? With this manner of transportation the Lord can really "hiss unto them from the end of the earth," that "they shall come with speed swiftly." Indicating that Isaiah must have foreseen the airplane, he stated: "Who are these that fly as a cloud, and as the doves to their windows?" (Isaiah 60:8).[3]

All of this will occur in a day when the earth will be encompassed by the "roaring of the sea"—a well-known symbol of chaos and evil in Isaiah's day. It will come in a day when, upon the earth, there will be "darkness and sorrow" (v. 30).

The Restoration of Scattered Israel

- **Isaiah 10:23–25; 2 Nephi 20:23–25 Israel will be consumed by the Assyrians.** Isaiah prophesied, "The Lord God of hosts shall make a consumption[4] . . . in the midst of all the land" (v. 23). This consumption will occur under the hand of the Assyrians, who will "smite thee with a rod, and . . . lift up [their] staff against thee, after the manner of Egypt"[5] (v. 24). But the Lord comforts them with the knowledge that after "a very little while," their "indignation shall cease" as a result of "their [the Assyrians'] destruction" (v. 25). Not long thereafter, the children of Israel (the northern ten tribes) were set free and wandered northward toward Europe and the steppes of northern Asia.

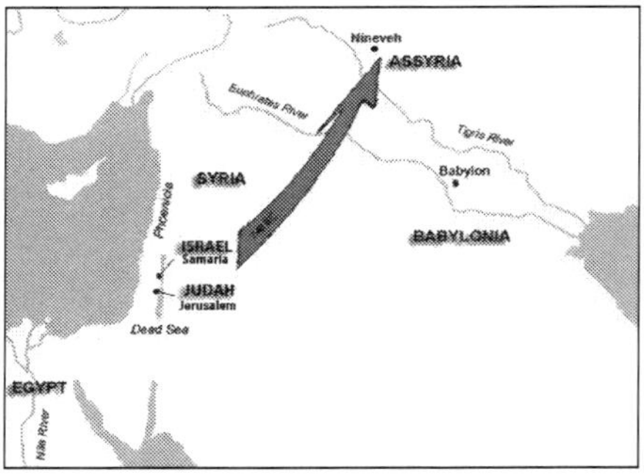

Israel was taken captive into Assyria

- **Isaiah 10:20–22; 2 Nephi 20:20–22 A remnant of Israel will return to God and will "overflow with righteousness."** The remnant of Israel that manages to escape from their long captivity and dispersion "shall no more again stay [rely] upon him that smote them; but shall stay [rely] upon the Lord, the Holy One of Israel, in truth" (v. 20). This will occur when they "return . . . unto the mighty God" (v. 21). Although in that day the descendants of Israel shall be as numerous as the "sand of the sea," only "a remnant of them shall return," but they will "overflow with righteousness" (v. 22).

This scripture provides a five-point formula for salvation: seeing, hearing, understanding, returning or repenting, and being healed.[6] This is the process converts go through as they first see (become aware of) the kingdom of God, then hear its message, come to understand its importance, and repent and are baptized for the remission of sins. Finally, they are healed from their lost condition.

A Gathering of Both Israel and Judah

- **Isaiah 11:11–12; 2 Nephi 21:11–12 The Lord will gather His chosen people "the second time" from "the four corners of the earth."** Their first captivity was in Egypt, from which they were gathered by Moses. The second time will be from among all the nations of the earth, even stretching to "the islands of the sea" (a figure of speech meaning the "ends of the earth") (v. 11).

  The place names in this scripture—Assyria (Syria), Egypt, Pathros (upper Egypt), Cush (Ethiopia), Elam (Iran), Shinar (Iraq), and Hamath (lower Syria and Lebanon)—are both literal and symbolic. These are nations and places that surround Israel and are today some of her most bitter enemies, yet the gospel message will apparently penetrate them before the Lord comes. After naming them, Isaiah adds "the four corners of the earth" (v. 12) to the list, suggesting that the gathering will be worldwide and not just local.

- **Isaiah 11:12; 2 Nephi 21:12 Two different groups—Israel and Judah—will be gathered.** The Lord will do this by setting up an "ensign" (a royal metaphor for a place of gathering) "for the nations." And He will gather both the "outcasts of Israel" and the "dispersed of Judah" to their places of inheritance in both the Old World and the New World (v. 12).

  Elder LeGrand Richards elaborated:

  > From this scripture [Isaiah 11:10–12; 2 Nephi 21:10–12] . . . we learn that three important events were to transpire: (1) He shall set up an ensign for the nations; (2) He shall assemble the outcasts of

> Israel; (3) He shall gather together the dispersed of Judah from the four corners of the earth. It is clear there are to be two gathering places—one for Israel and one for Judah.[7]

- **Isaiah 11:14; 2 Nephi 21:14 The role of the Gentiles in the gathering of Israel.** Isaiah said that the gathered souls of Israel and Judah "shall fly upon the shoulders of the Philistines toward the west." This dualistic prophecy not only predicts the gathering of the children of Edom, Moab, and Ammon into the land of Israel to the west of them, but also the gathering of all the hosts of Israel from around the world to the Western Hemisphere, where the Church's headquarters and New Jerusalem would be established.

  Elder Orson F. Whitney remarked:

  > Seven hundred years before the birth of the Savior, the prophet Isaiah, looking down the vista of time, saw the latter-day gathering of the scattered house of Israel, and said concerning them: "They shall fly upon the shoulders of the Philistines toward the west." We recognize the fulfillment of that prophecy in the founding of this Church by Joseph Smith, a lineal descendant of Abraham, Isaac, and Jacob, who thus lifted the ensign for the gathering of their descendants from their long dispersion among the nations. But a part of the fulfillment rests with the Gentiles. Their steamships, their railroads, their means of rapid transit and communication—these are "the shoulders of the Philistines," upon which the children of Ephraim have been and are being brought to the West, to the land of Zion, where the New Jerusalem is to rise, where the pure in heart will assemble, and the necessary preparation be made for the coming of the Lord in His glory. God works outside as well as inside His Church, and uses big things and little things for the accomplishment of His purposes.[8]

- **Isaiah 13:1–5; 2 Nephi 23:1–5 God will gather His "sanctified ones . . . from the end of heaven."** "From the end of heaven" (v. 5) means "from a far country." Latter-day Israel will be "a great people . . . of nations gathered together" (v. 4).

- **Isaiah 14:1–3; 2 Nephi 24:1–3 Israel will be gathered to "their own land . . . the land of the Lord."** The children of Israel will be gathered to "their own land," and "strangers" (non-Israelite converts) shall be joined with them (v. 1). Isaiah makes a distinction here about where the ten tribes of Israel will gather, as opposed to Judah. They will be gathered "to their place . . . from far . . . to their lands of promise," where the house of Israel shall possess "the land of the Lord" (2 Nephi 24:2). It is interesting that the "land of the Lord" is designated as the place of gathering for the lost ten tribes.

Elder George Reynolds and Janne M. Sjodahl observed that the word *America* was probably coined after indigenous American words like *Amerique* or *Marca.* These words consist of three parts: (1) *A,* which is the same as the Hebrew *the;* (2) *malek,* or *malick,* which means king; and (3) *i* or *iah,* which means Jehovah. Put together, then, the name means "The King of Jehovah." The main difference between the Book of Mormon name Amaleki and the modern name America is that there is an *R* in place of the *L.* But that can be explained by the fact that some Native American dialects lack six letters in the Spanish alphabet, one of which is *L.*

R, they tell us, takes its place, as it does with *Peru* for *Pelu.* They believe—and quote sources which support the idea—that *America* is the accepted form of the old Indian names *Americ* or *Amerique,* and not, as generally taught in our schools, in glorification of the map maker Amerigo Vespucci. "If this view is correct," they tell us, "*America* is, both in form and meaning, identical with the Book of Mormon names, *Amaleki* and *Amalickiah,* the meaning of which is, 'The King of Jehovah,' and, as applied to the country, 'The Land of the King of Jehovah'; that is to say, in other words, *The Land of Zion.*"[9]

It makes sense that the latter-day tribes of Israel will be gathered to the land of the King Jehovah, which is the land of Zion.

Metaphors of Israel's Scattering and Gathering

- **Isaiah 48:3, 5–8; 1 Nephi 20: 3, 5–8 God's foreknowledge of the children of Israel's fate.** "I have declared the former things from the beginning," said the Lord, "and they went forth out of my mouth, and I shewed them; I did them suddenly, and they came to pass" (v. 3). The Lord declared these things unto the children of Israel before they came to pass "lest thou shouldest say, Mine idol hath done them, and my graven image, and my molten image, hath commanded them" (v. 5). Also, because He did not want them to claim after the fact that they already knew them, the Lord declared "new things . . . , even hidden things, and thou didst not know them" (vv. 6–7). The Lord knew their treacherous hearts and left them without excuse by means of His prophecies concerning their future (v. 8).

- **Isaiah 48:4; 1 Nephi 20:4 The Lord calls apostate Israel stiffnecked and hardheaded.** "I knew that thou art obstinate, and thy neck is an iron sinew, and thy brow brass." Isaiah uses two metaphors in this scripture:

— "Thy neck is an iron sinew."	means "You are stiffnecked."
— "Thy brow [is] brass."	means "You are hardheaded."
Hence, the Lord is saying:	*"You are stiffnecked, and you are hardheaded."*

- **Isaiah 48:9–11; 1 Nephi 20:9–11 Israel will become chosen through "the furnace of affliction."** The Lord could have chosen to destroy the Israelites, as He had done to their predecessors in the land of Canaan. However, He said, "For my name's sake will I defer mine anger, and for my praise will I refrain for thee, that I cut thee not off" (v. 9). Instead, He will "refine . . . thee, but not with silver; I have chosen thee in the furnace of affliction" (v. 10). This is a way of saying that He will purify them like silver is purified in a furnace. By this process, the Lord will prevent His name (and His people) from being polluted (v. 11).

- **Isaiah 48:18–19; 1 Nephi 20:18–19 The Lord reminds the Israelites of the blessings they might have enjoyed had they had chosen to obey Him.** "O that thou hadst hearkened to my commandments! then had thy peace been as a river, and thy righteousness as the waves of the sea: thy seed also had been as the sand, and the offspring of thy bowels like the gravel thereof." Isaiah uses both similes and figures of speech in this scripture:

— Peace "as a river" means peace that is deep and continuous.

— Righteousness "as the waves of the sea" means strong and continuous righteousness.

— Seed "as the sand" means seed as numerous as grains of sand upon the seashore.

Hence this scripture means: "O that you had hearkened to my commandments—then would your peace have been *deep and continuous,* and your righteousness *strong and continuous.* Your seed also would have been *as numerous as grains of sand upon the seashore.*"

The Mission of the Latter-day Saints

- **Isaiah 49:2; 1 Nephi 21:2 The polished shaft hidden in the shadow of the Lord's hand.** Isaiah uses some more figures of speech in this verse:

— "Mouth like a sharp sword" is a simile that compares the Lord's mouth to a sword, suggesting that what He says cuts like a knife through error and obstacles.

— Hiding Israel in "the shadow of his hand" is a figure of speech that means the Lord has covered Israel with His hand so nobody can see her (see D&C 86:8–9).

— The metaphor of a "polished shaft" (arrow) hidden in the Lord's "quiver" (a bag that hold arrows) compares Israel to a secret weapon.

Hence this means: "And what I say shall cut through all obstacles; I will hide my people Israel from sight until the latter days, and they will be my secret weapon in the gathering of Israel, by which I will be glorified."

— **D&C 86:8–9** Clarifies the meaning of a "hidden" people. "Therefore, thus saith the Lord unto you, with whom the priesthood hath continued through the lineage of your fathers—for ye are lawful heirs, according to the flesh, and have been hid from the world with Christ in God."

Joseph Smith identified himself as one of the Lord's polished shafts:

> I am like a huge, rough stone rolling down from a high mountain; and the only polishing I get is when some corner gets rubbed off by coming in contact with something else, striking

with accelerated force against religious bigotry, priestcraft, lawyer-craft, doctor-craft, lying editors, suborned judges and jurors, and the authority of perjured executives, backed by mobs, blasphemers, licentious and corrupt men and women—all hell knocking off a corner here and a corner there. Thus I will become a smooth and polished shaft in the quiver of the Almighty, who will give me dominion over all and every one of them, when their refuge of lies shall fail, and their hiding place shall be destroyed, while these smooth-polished stones with which I come in contact become marred.[10]

The Prophet Joseph Smith

Dr. Monte S. Nyman commented:

> The arrow shaft is polished that it might fly truer and faster, and the shaft that is polished is generally reserved for one's most important shot. The last dispensation, when all things are gathered in one, is the Lord's most important "shot," so He saved His "polished shaft" for this latter-day work. Joseph [Smith] was called to give this generation the word of God (see D&C 5:10), which recalls also the sharp sword analogy mentioned in verse 2 [of Isaiah 49 and 1 Nephi 21].[11]

And the Prophet Joseph Smith taught:

> Every man who has a calling to minister to the inhabitants of the world was ordained to that very purpose in the Grand Council of heaven before this world was. I suppose that I was ordained to this very office in that Grand Council. It is the testimony that I want that I am God's servant, and this people His people.[12]

- **Isaiah 49:3–13; 1 Nephi 21:3–13 Latter-day Israel will be a light unto the Gentiles and to the spirits in prison.** In figurative language, the Lord has a conversation with latter-day Israel in these verses. The Lord begins by saying, "Thou art my servant, O Israel, in whom I will be glorified" (v. 3). Israel responds that she has "laboured in vain" to gather her children but takes solace in the Lord's promise that "though Israel be not gathered, yet shall I be glorious in the eyes of the Lord, and my God shall be my strength" (vv. 4–5).

The Lord then says, "It is a light thing that thou shouldest be my servant to raise up the tribes of Jacob, and to restore the preserved of Israel" (v. 6). "It is a light thing" is a figure of speech meaning "It is not enough." The Lord is saying that gathering Israel is not enough—that He "will also give [Israel] for a light to the Gentiles, that [Israel] mayest be [His] salvation unto the end of the earth" (v. 6). As a result of this gathering of Gentiles, "kings shall see and arise, princes also shall worship, because of the Lord that is faithful" (v. 7).

The Lord then lists others who will be gathered, including those who inhabit the "isles of the sea" (1 Nephi 21:8), which is a figure of speech meaning "far-flung places" (see Isaiah 49:1; 1 Nephi 21:1). Also, the gathering will include "the prisoners" to whom it will be said: "Go forth; to them that are in darkness, Shew yourselves" (v. 9). This has multiple meanings, one of which is a reference to missionary work that will be done among the dead in spirit prison. In a subsequent verse, the Lord makes mention of His "mountains" and His "highways," both of which are metaphors for temples (v. 11). And finally, the Lord says that those who are gathered "shall come from far: and, lo, these from the north and from the west; and these from the land of Sinim" (v. 12). This gathering will be permanent, because those who are gathered "shall be smitten no more; for the Lord hath comforted his people, and will have mercy upon his afflicted" (1 Nephi 21:13).

- **Isaiah 49:14–23; 1 Nephi 21:14–23 Metaphors of the gathering.** The Lord uses a series of metaphors and figures of speech to describe what the gathering of Israel will be like in the last days.

  — **Attentive mother metaphor.** In verse 15 the Lord asks if mothers can forget their nursing children while they are feeding at their breasts. Perhaps. But the Lord will not forget us.

  — **Attentive Savior metaphor.** In verse 16 Christ says He has "graven [us] upon the palms of [His] hands"—a figure of speech about making it impossible to forget, but also a metaphor for the Lord's Crucifixion. Will He forget what He did for us? No, He won't.

Christ also mentions in verse 16 our "walls"—a metaphor for our circumstances—that are continually before (within the view of) Him.

— **Growing family metaphor.** Verse 20 reads, "The place is too strait[13] for me: give place to me"—a figure of speech meaning so many people will come during the gathering of Israel that it will seem too crowded. Verse 21 reads, "Who hath begotten me these . . . where [have] they been?"—a figure of speech for "Where in the world did all these people come from?"

— **Nurturing parents metaphor.** In verse 22 we read how the Lord will set up His "standard"—a military flag or ensign that is raised to indicate where soldiers should gather. Verse 22 also tells of the Gentiles who will carry the Israelites "upon their shoulders"—a figure of speech meaning "help you get there." Verse 23 describes the Gentiles as "nursing fathers" and "nursing mothers" unto Israel—a metaphor for nurturing parents protecting a young child.

President Spencer W. Kimball saw a partial fulfillment of these verses in the Church's modern missionary efforts with the Lamanites. Also, in 1917, Great Britain established a protectorate in Jerusalem administered by a Jew—the first Jewish government there since A.D. 70. Moreover, in 1947, the United Nations, including the then-Soviet Union and many other countries now hostile to Israel, voted to partition Palestine and create a Jewish state in the land for the first time in nearly two thousand years.

JEREMIAH'S PROPHECIES OF THE GATHERING

- **Jeremiah 3:12–14 "One of a city" and "two of a family" will return to the Lord.** Even in the midst of terrible wickedness, the Lord's message through Jeremiah was one of hope for redemption: "Return, thou backsliding Israel, saith the Lord; and I will not cause mine anger to fall upon you: for I am merciful, saith the Lord, and I will not keep anger for ever" (v. 12).

  All He asked was that they "acknowledge thine iniquity, that thou hast transgressed against the Lord thy God, and . . . have not obeyed my voice" (v. 13). "Turn, O backsliding children, . . . for I am married unto you: and I will take you one of a city, and two of a family, and I will bring you to Zion" (v. 14).

President Spencer W. Kimball reflected:

PRISCILLA AND AMOS CHASE IN NAUVOO

> In my youth I used to wonder how the world could be converted to the gospel when it was to go to "one of a city, and two of a family" (Jeremiah 3:14), but as I came to understand the gospel more clearly, the matter seems quite clear. My grandfather came out of the world only a hundred and forty-four years ago, as one of a family, and today there are possibly eight or ten thousand or more of his direct posterity, most of whom were born in the Church and many of whom are faithful. . . . I am sure that the veil is thin. My grandfather, being one of a family, searched all his life to get together his genealogical records; and when he died in 1868, he had been unsuccessful in establishing his line back more than the second generation beyond him. I am sure that most of my family members feel the same as I do—that there was a thin veil between him and the earth after he had gone to the other side and that which he was unable to do as a mortal he perhaps was able to do after he had gone into eternity. . . . The Spirit of Elijah [is] at work on the other side and . . . our grandfather [has] been able to inspire men on this side to search out these records; and as a result, two large volumes are in my possession, with about seventeen thousand names. "One of a city, and two of a family" may yet accomplish the great objective.[14]

- **Jeremiah 3:16–19 The children of Israel will multiply and be blessed in their homeland.** "Ye [shall be] multiplied and increased in the land, in those days," the Lord promised (v. 16). And "at that time they shall call Jerusalem the throne of the Lord; and all the nations shall be gathered unto it, to the name of the Lord, to Jerusalem" (v.

17). Also, "in those days the house of Judah shall walk with the house of Israel, and they shall come together out of the land of the north to the land that I have given for an inheritance unto your fathers" (v. 18). All this will be made possible because the children of Israel in the last days "shalt call me, My father; and shalt not turn away from me" (v. 19).

— **D&C 133:26–35 (See also Isaiah 35:1, 6–10.)** A modern-day explanation of how these things will occur. "Their prophets shall hear his voice, and shall no longer stay themselves; and they shall smite the rocks, and the ice shall flow down at their presence. And an highway shall be cast up in the midst of the great deep" (vv. 26–27). Their enemies will fall before them (v. 28).

C. C. A. CHRISTENSEN

Isaiah saw the pioneers coming into the parched Salt Lake Valley

Where will they go? "In the barren deserts there shall come forth pools of living water; and the parched ground shall no longer be a thirsty land" (v. 29). "And they shall bring forth their rich treasures unto the children of Ephraim, my servants" (v. 30). "And the boundaries of the everlasting hills shall tremble at their presence" (v. 31).

This appears to be a prophecy of their gathering to The Church of Jesus Christ of Latter-day Saints and to its temples. "And there shall they fall down and be crowned with glory, even in Zion, by the hands of the servants of the Lord, even the children of Ephraim" (v. 32). There, they will be "filled with songs of everlasting joy" (v. 33). They will receive the rich eternal blessings of membership in the restored Church and of the temple under the administration of "the head of Ephraim and his fellows" (v. 34).

Judah will also be gathered to the Old Jerusalem. "And they also of the tribe of Judah, after their pain, shall be sanctified in holiness before the Lord, to dwell in his presence day and night, forever and ever" (v. 35).

Priesthood Leaders and Missionaries

- **Jeremiah 23:3–4 The "shepherds . . . which shall feed them" are righteous priesthood leaders** who, unlike the priests and prophets of Jeremiah's time, lead their people to do good and obey the Lord. "I will gather the remnant of my flock out of all countries whither I have driven them, and will bring them again to their folds; and they shall be fruitful and increase," promised the Lord (v. 3). "And I will set up shepherds over them which shall feed them: and they shall fear no more, nor be dismayed, neither shall they be lacking, saith the Lord" (v. 4).

- **Jeremiah 16:16 Missionaries ("fishers" and "hunters") will perform a great gathering of Israel.** "Behold, I will send for many fishers, saith the Lord, and they shall fish them; and after will I send for many hunters, and they shall hunt them from every mountain, and from every hill, and out of the holes of the rocks." They will search for the honest in heart on every continent, in every nation, in every city, town, and village, until "this gospel shall be preached unto every nation, and kindred, and tongue, and people" (D&C 133:37).

The Lord described the Apostles of His day as "fishers of men" (see Matthew 4:18–19), and Elder LeGrand Richards tells us concerning these verses:

The Lord calls fishers of men

> Jeremiah saw the day when the Lord would do this very thing, when He would call for many fishers and many hunters, "and they shall hunt them from every mountain, and from every hill, and out of the holes of the rocks" (Jeremiah 16:16). Where do you find those fishers and hunters that we read about in this great prophecy of Jeremiah? They are these 14,000 missionaries of this Church [as of 1971], and those who have preceded them from the time that the Prophet Joseph Smith received the truth and

> sent the messengers out to share it with the world. Thus have they gone out, fishing and hunting, and gathering them from the hills and the mountains, and the holes in the rocks. I think that is more literal than some of us think![15]

Moreover, Elder Richards noted:

> It is evident that the Lord has made bare His arm to fulfill His promise made by the Prophet Jeremiah with respect to the gathering of Israel in the latter days. The prophet indicated that the Lord would send fishers and hunters to "hunt them from every mountain, and from every hill, and out of the holes in the rocks," showing how completely He would fulfill His promise, that after Israel was sifted among the nations, "yet shall not the least grain fall upon the earth" (Amos 9:8–9).
>
> In the establishment of The Church of Jesus Christ of Latter- day Saints upon the earth in these latter days, the Lord has provided therein a great missionary program, through which a great many male members of the Church give two years or more of their lives, at their own expense, to preach the message of the restored gospel to all the inhabitants of the earth. . . . These are the "fishers" and "hunters" the Lord promised to send [see Jeremiah 16:16].[16]

Elder Bruce R. McConkie stated:

> The gathering of Israel consists of receiving the truth, gaining again a true knowledge of the Redeemer, and coming back into the true fold of the Good Shepherd. In the language of the Book of Mormon, it consists of being "restored to the true church and fold of God," and then being "gathered" and "established" in various "lands of promise" (2 Nephi 9:2).[17]

And President Spencer W. Kimball taught:

> A great group of people left the Old World at the time of the Tower of Babel. Another great group left the Old World [in] 600 B.C. And since the coming of Columbus to America, there have been numerous groups that have come to America from the Old World. The Lord had that in hand and watched it. He said through Nephi, "The house of Israel [sooner or later will] be scattered upon all the face of the earth" (1 Nephi 22:3). And now He says, "I will

gather the remnant of my flock out of all countries whither I have driven them" (Jeremiah 23:3).

The gathering of Israel is now in progress. Hundreds of thousands of people have been baptized into the Church. Millions more will join the Church. And this is the way that we will gather Israel. The English people will gather in England. The Japanese people will gather in the Orient. The Brazilian people will gather in Brazil. So that important element of the world history is already being accomplished.

It is to be done by missionary work. It is your responsibility to attend to this missionary work.[18]

A Gathering of Both Israel and Judah

- **Jeremiah 30:1–3 Israel and Judah will be restored to their own lands.** The Lord commanded Jeremiah to "write . . . all the words that I have spoken unto thee in a book" (vv. 1–2) so that they could be preserved until the latter days. In that day, the Lord said, "I will bring again the captivity of my people Israel and Judah, . . . and I will cause them to return to the land that I gave to their fathers, and they shall possess it" (v. 3).

This is a dualistic prophecy, fulfilled by three separate events:

— The return of the Jews after 70 years of captivity in Babylon.

— The restoration of the Jews to their homeland in the last days.

— The return of the lost ten tribes from the lands of the north.

President Ezra Taft Benson said:

This miracle of the return of the Jews was to be one of the events to precede Christ's Second Coming, and the scriptures are very clear with reference to this fact. Isaiah said that they shall gather "the dispersed of Judah from the four corners of the earth" [Isaiah 11:12] and "set them in their own land"

[Isaiah 14:1], that they will "build the old waste" [Isaiah 58:12], and "repair the waste cities" [Isaiah 61:4]. Jeremiah, who predicted so clearly their dispersion, also states that the Lord will "cause them to return to the land that I gave to their fathers, and they shall possess it," and "build them, as at the first" (Jeremiah 30:3; 33:7).[19]

- **Jeremiah 30:8 Israel and Judah will break their yoke of oppression.** "For it shall come to pass in that day, saith the Lord of hosts, that I will break his yoke from off thy neck, and will burst thy bonds, and strangers shall no more serve themselves of [you]."[20]

  This is another dualistic prophecy, fulfilled by at least two events:

  — The breaking of the yoke of oppression of Nebuchadnezzar with the return of the Jews to their homeland 70 years after their captivity.

  — **D&C 113:9–10** These "yokes" and "bonds" were also explained by the Prophet Joseph Smith: "What are we to understand by Zion loosing herself from the bands of her neck; 2d verse?" (v. 9). "We are to understand that the scattered remnants are exhorted to return to the Lord from whence they have fallen; which if they do, the promise of the Lord is that he will speak to them, or give them revelation. See the 6th, 7th, and 8th verses. The bands of her neck are the curses of God upon her, or the remnants of Israel in their scattered condition among the Gentiles" (v. 10).

- **Jeremiah 30:5–7 There will be a time of distress and punishment first.** The Lord promises "a voice of trembling, of fear, and not of peace" (v. 5). Then He describes men in so much distress that it is as if they "travail with child . . . with his hands on his loins, as a woman in travail, and all faces are turned into paleness" (v. 6). Those days will be unforgettable, "great, so that none is like it: it is even the time of Jacob's trouble," but the promise is that, through it all, Jacob (Israel) "shall be saved out of it" (v. 7).

  This is yet another dualistic prophecy, fulfilled by at least two events:

  — The destruction of Israel and Judah when they went into captivity.

  — The great destructions just prior to the Second Coming of the Lord.

- **Jeremiah 30:16–17, 23–24 Israel's enemies will be destroyed.** The Lord promises: "They [the Babylonians] that devour thee shall be devoured" (by the Medes and Persians). The Assyrians were destroyed by the Babylonians; the Babylonians were destroyed by the Medes and Persians; the Egyptians and Persians were destroyed by the Greeks. All these nations have now vanished, but the Jews still exist as a distinct people. The persecutors and destroyers of the Lord's people will be punished and destroyed by "the whirlwind of the Lord [that will] go . . . forth with fury, a continuing whirlwind: [and] it shall fall with pain upon the head of the wicked" (v. 23). It will not stop until it has been fully accomplished (v. 24).

- **Jeremiah 30:18–22 Israel will be gathered in from her long dispersion.** To "bring again the captivity of Jacob's tents" means to bring them back to their homelands. There, the Lord will have mercy on their homes and allow them to rebuild their city "upon her own heap" (v. 18). This is clearly a reference to their returning from their captivity in Babylon and the rebuilding of the Old Jerusalem.

  But the prophecy is also symbolic of the latter-day gathering, when the children of Israel will also have "thanksgiving and the voice of them that make merry," will be multiplied ("not [a] few"), and glorified (v. 19). "Their congregation shall be established before me, and I will punish all that oppress them," the Lord promises (v. 20). They will have their own nobles and governors, not ones appointed by foreign rulers (v. 21). And these leaders will be righteous—"engaged his heart to approach unto me" (v. 21). "And ye shall be my people, and I will be your God" (v. 22).

- **Jeremiah 30:23–24 "In the latter days ye shall consider it."** In the latter days Israel will be the Lord's people, and He will be their God. All of her enemies will have been destroyed. And only then, in the last days, after these promises have been realized, can one fully understand what Jeremiah was saying.

- **Jeremiah 24:1–7 Judah will be established again, never to be plucked up.** This message was symbolically delivered to Jeremiah in the vision of the two baskets of figs. "One basket had very good figs, even like the figs that are first ripe: and the other basket had very naughty[21] figs, which could not be eaten, they were so bad" (v. 2).

The "good figs" represented the children of Judah who had been sent away and humbled, and would then be restored (vv. 3–5). "For I will set mine eyes upon them for good, and I will bring them again to this land: and I will build them, and not pull them down; and I will plant them, and not pluck them up. And I will give them an heart to know me, that I am the Lord: and they shall be my people, and I will be their God: for they shall return unto me with their whole heart" (vv. 6–7).

Jeremiah saw two baskets of figs

THEBIBLEREVIVAL.COM, #13

This prophecy clearly does not refer to the return of the Jews from Babylon, because it includes the promise that they will never be plucked up again. As a matter of history, we know that they were, indeed, again plucked up, destroyed, and scattered—this time by the Romans in A.D. 70—following the ministry of our Lord Jesus Christ. We can only conclude, therefore, that this prophecy has mainly to do with the final gathering of the Jews in the last days.

- **Jeremiah 50:19–20 Both Israel and Judah will be forgiven and restored.** This is speaking of the latter days, because Israel never was "[brought] again to his habitation" in Old Testament days. Those ten tribes were scattered all over the earth, and they remain there today. But the promise is that Israel will be gathered, "and he shall feed on Carmel and Bashan, and his soul shall be satisfied upon mount Ephraim and Gilead" (v. 19). "In those days, and in that time, saith the Lord, the iniquity of Israel shall be sought for, and there shall be none; and the sins of Judah, and they shall not be found: for I will pardon them whom I reserve" (v. 20).
- **Jeremiah 50:33–34 The Lord will redeem both the "children of Israel" and "the children of Judah."** Both nations had been severely chastised. "All that took them captives held them fast; they refused to let them go" (v. 33). But "their Redeemer is strong; the Lord of hosts is

his name: he shall throughly plead their cause, that he may give rest to the land, and disquiet the inhabitants of Babylon" (v. 34).

- **Jeremiah 31:1–5 Jehovah will again be the God of all the tribes (families) of Israel.** In the latter days, "I [will] be the God of all the families of Israel, and they shall be my people," the Lord proclaimed (v. 1). His people, "which were left of the sword" (descendants of those who survived their destruction and captivity), will find "grace in the wilderness," where the Lord will "cause him to rest" (v. 2). The Lord has been appearing to the prophets of Israel since days of old, promising, "I have loved thee with an everlasting love: therefore with loving kindness have I drawn thee"[22] (v. 3). "Again I will build thee, and . . . thou shalt again be adorned with thy tabrets, and shalt go forth in the dances of them that make merry. Thou shalt yet plant vines upon the mountains of Samaria" (vv. 4–5).

- **Jeremiah 31:6–7 Ephraim, as the firstborn with priesthood rights, will gather Israel.** "For there shall be a day," the Lord promised, "that the watchmen upon the mount Ephraim shall cry, Arise ye, and let us go up to Zion unto the Lord our God" (v. 6). These "watchmen" are righteous latter-day prophets (see Ezekiel 3:16–21). They will "publish" (say) to all the "chief" (great) nations, "Sing with gladness for Jacob, and shout" because the Lord will now "save [His] people, the remnant of Israel" (v. 7).

- **Jeremiah 31:8 Israel will gather from the north country and from the coasts (ends) of the earth.** Among them will be "the blind and the lame, the woman with child and her that travaileth with child together," amounting to "a great company" of people that "shall return thither" (v. 8). Note that the Lord does not say they will gather "hither" (where Jeremiah is speaking), but "thither" (somewhere else that has been designated).

- **Jeremiah 31:9 Ephraim is the Lord's birthright people.** "For I am a father to Israel, and Ephraim is my firstborn," He said. Thus, Ephraim was entitled to a double portion of inheritance, as all firstborn sons were in Israel. And both Jacob and Moses made special note of the blessed land that Ephraim would inhabit in the last days.

— **Gen. 49:22–26** **Deut. 33:13–17** Joseph was to be given a new and bounteous land in the "utmost bound of the everlasting hills," where his birthright son, Ephraim, would be responsible for gathering and saving all the other tribes of Israel.

President Joseph Fielding Smith explained:

> Ephraim was blessed with the *birthright* in Israel,[23] and in this dispensation he has been called to stand at the *head* to bless the other tribes of Israel.[24] . . . It is essential in this dispensation that Ephraim stand in his place at the head, exercising the birthright in Israel which was given to him by direct revelation. Therefore, *Ephraim must be gathered first to prepare the way*, through the gospel and the priesthood, for the rest of the tribes of Israel when the time comes for them to be gathered to Zion. The great majority of those who have come into the Church are Ephraimites. It is the exception to find one of any other tribe, unless it is of Manasseh.[25]

- **Jeremiah 31:9 The gathering will be difficult and will require sacrifice.** "They shall come with weeping, and with supplications," the Lord said. Yet He will "lead them: I will cause them to walk by the rivers of waters in a straight way, wherein they shall not stumble."
- **Jeremiah 16:19 They will have paid the price of their fathers' sins.** For thousands of years, the descendants of the children of Israel have been scattered over the earth. Their descendants have been hated, persecuted, cast out, and killed. And now, as they gather from among the nations, these "Gentiles" (converts from among the Gentile nations) will say, "Surely our fathers have inherited lies, vanity, and things wherein there is no profit" (v. 19). They had worshipped gods made with their own hands "and they are no gods" (v. 20).

They will have paid the price of their fathers' sins.

— **Jeremiah 31:27–30** A proverb in Israel acknowledged this by saying, "The fathers have eaten a sour grape, and the children's teeth are set on edge." The bitterness of the fathers passes to their posterity.

— **Exodus 20:5–6** The Lord told Moses that children do, in fact, inherit consequences of parental behavior. "I . . . visit . . . the iniquity of the fathers upon the children unto the third and fourth generation of them that hate me; and shew . . . mercy unto thousands of them that love me, and keep my commandments."

— **D&C 68:25** Children may suffer in this life because of the neglect and sins of their parents. But ultimately, the parents will be held accountable for it. "And again, inasmuch as parents have children in Zion, or in any of her stakes which are organized, that teach them not to understand the doctrine of repentance, faith in Christ the Son of the living God, and of baptism and the gift of the Holy Ghost by the laying on of the hands, when eight years old, the sin be upon the heads of the parents."

— **Jeremiah 31:15 Rachel weeping for her children.** "Thus saith the Lord; A voice was heard in Ramah, lamentation, and bitter weeping; Rachel weeping for her children refused to be comforted for her children, because they were not."

"These words are embroidered in Hebrew on the covering of Rachel's tomb, which is located between modern Jerusalem and Bethlehem."[26]

A scene from the Holocaust

They are also quoted by Matthew (2:18) in describing the sorrow in Judah over the slaughter of the male infants in Bethlehem by Herod after the birth of Christ. Our mother Rachel must indeed sorrow over the waywardness of her children in Jeremiah's day and their suffering ever since. Anciently, in Christ's day, and in our own day, they have been mercilessly slaughtered by their enemies.

- **Jeremiah 31:10–16 "They shall not sorrow any more at all."** These verses describe the great joy and happiness that will accompany the return of Israel—abundance (v. 12), rejoicing (v. 13), and the end of sorrow (vv. 15–16).

A NEW AND EVERLASTING COVENANT

- **Jeremiah 31:31–34 A "new" covenant will be restored.** "Behold, the days come, saith the Lord, that I will make a new covenant with the house of Israel, and with the house of Judah" (v. 31). This will not be the same covenant He made with their fathers, "which . . . covenant they brake" (v. 32). It will be a new covenant, in the last days, when the Lord will "put my law in their inward parts, and write it in their hearts; and will be their God, and they shall be my people" (v. 33). This is the full gospel of Jesus Christ, with its higher laws and individual responsibilities. "And they shall teach no more every man his neighbour, and every man his brother, saying, Know the Lord: for they shall all know me, from the least of them unto the greatest of them, saith the Lord; for I will forgive their iniquity, and I will remember their sin no more" (v. 34).

  The Prophet Joseph Smith said:

  > This covenant has never been established with the house of Israel, nor with the house of Judah, for it requires two parties to make a covenant, and those two parties must be agreed, or no covenant can be made. Christ, in the days of His flesh, proposed to make a covenant with them, but they rejected Him and His proposals, and in consequence thereof, they were broken off, and no covenant was made with them at that time. But their unbelief has not rendered the promise of God of none effect: no, for there was another day limited in David, which was the day of His power; and then His peo-ple, Israel, should be a willing people—and He would write His law in their hearts, and print it in their thoughts; their sins and their iniquities He would remember no more. . . .
  >
  > I will proceed to tell you what the Lord requires of all people, high and low, rich and poor, male and female, ministers and people, professors of religion and non-professors, in order that they may enjoy the Holy Spirit of God to a fulness and escape the judgments of God, which are almost ready to burst upon the nations of the earth. Repent of all your sins, and be baptized in water for the remission of them, in the name of the Father, and of the Son, and of the Holy Ghost, and receive the ordinance of the laying on of

the hands of him who is ordained and sealed unto this power, that ye may receive the Holy Spirit of God; and this is according to the Holy Scriptures . . . and the only way that man can enter into the celestial kingdom. These are the requirements of the new covenant.[27]

— **D&C 1:17–23 The Restoration includes the reestab- lishment of God's covenant with Israel.** The Lord lists here the reasons for calling the Prophet Joseph Smith and restoring His Church in its fulness:

- "[That] weak things of the world shall come forth and break down the mighty" (v. 19).
- "That every man might speak in the name of God the Lord, even the Savior" (v. 20).
- "That faith also might increase in the earth" (v. 21).
- "That mine everlasting covenant might be established" (v. 22).
- "That the fulness of my gospel might be proclaimed by the weak and the simple unto the ends of the world, and before kings and rulers" (v. 23).

— **D&C 66:2** "Verily I say unto you, blessed are you for receiving mine everlasting covenant, even the fulness of my gospel, sent forth unto the children of men, that they might have life and be made partakers of the glories which are to be revealed in the last days, as it was written by the prophets and apostles in days of old."

This "new and everlasting covenant" embraces the whole gospel, including the covenants of baptism, priesthood, and eternal marriage, each of which is properly called a new and everlasting covenant.[28]

- **Jeremiah 31:35–37 Neither the ordinances nor the covenant will ever depart again from the earth.** The Lord can do all things. He gave us the sun, the moon, and the stars for light, and He divides the sea when needed (v. 35). Surely, then, He can keep this promise concerning the gospel in the latter days:

"If those ordinances depart from before me, saith the Lord, then the seed of Israel also shall cease from being a nation before me for ever" (v. 36). And since He had already promised that His priesthood and ordinances would never again depart from the earth, this statement is just another way of saying it will never happen.

- **Jeremiah 33:6–14 Happiness and joy will be restored to Jerusalem.** Among the blessings promised to them are health, revelation, peace, and truth (v. 6). Their captivity will end, "and I will cleanse them from all their iniquity, whereby they have sinned against me; and I will pardon all their iniquities" (vv. 7–8). Then His people will become "to me a name of joy, a praise and an honour before all the nations of the earth, which shall hear all the good that I do unto them: and they shall fear and tremble for all the goodness and for all the prosperity that I procure unto it" (v. 9).

  In those streets that were left "desolate, without man, and without inhabitant, and without beast" because of the captivity will be heard "the voice of joy, and the voice of gladness, the voice of the bridegroom, and the voice of the bride, the voice of them that shall say, Praise the Lord of hosts: for the Lord is good" (vv. 10–11). Shepherds will again "caus[e] their flocks to lie down" in cities of the mountains, cities of the vale, cities of the south, in the land of Benjamin, and in Jerusalem (vv. 12–13).

  Concerning Zion, Isaiah promised:

  > "The redeemed of the Lord shall return, and come with singing unto Zion; and everlasting joy and holiness shall be upon their heads; they shall obtain gladness and joy; sorrow and mourning shall flee away" *(2 Nephi 8:11; compare Isaiah 51:11).*
  >
  > The long days of Israel's dispersal will be over.

Notes

1. Joseph Fielding Smith, *Doctrines of Salvation,* comp. Bruce R. McConkie, 3 vols. (1954–56), 3:246.
2. *The Teachings of Spencer W. Kimball,* ed. Edward L. Kimball (1982), 439.

3. LeGrand Richards, *Israel! Do You Know?* (1954), 182.
4. That is, cause the decreed destruction (Isaiah 10:23, footnote *a*).
5. That is, as the Egyptians did in earlier times (Isaiah 10:24, footnote *b*).
6. See Avraham Gileadi, "Isaiah: Four Latter-day Keys to an Ancient Book," in Monte S. Nyman, ed., *Isaiah and the Prophets: Inspired Voices from the Old Testament* (1984), 132.
7. LeGrand Richards, *A Marvelous Work and a Wonder* (1976), 202.
8. Orson F. Whitney, in Conference Report, Oct. 1919, 69.
9. See George Reynolds and Janne M. Sjodahl, *Commentary on the Book of Mormon,* edited and arranged by Philip C. Reynolds, 7 vols. (1955–61), 2:323, 328–31.
10. Joseph Smith, in *History of the Church,* 5:401.
11. Monte S. Nyman, *"Great Are the Words of Isaiah"* (1980), 177.
12. *Teachings of Presidents of the Church: Joseph Smith* (2007), 511.
13. Or tight or narrow (Isaiah 49:20, footnote *a*).
14. Spencer W. Kimball, Regional Representatives' Seminar, Apr. 5, 1976; quoted in Daniel H. Ludlow, *A Companion to Your Study of the Old Testament* (1981), 316–17.
15. LeGrand Richards, "In the Mountain of the Lord's House," *Ensign,* June 1971, 98–99.
16. LeGrand Richards, *Israel! Do You Know?* 175.
17. Bruce R. McConkie, "Come: Let Israel Build Zion," *Ensign,* May 1977, 117.
18. Spencer W. Kimball, in Conference Report, São Paulo Brazil Area Conference, Feb.–Mar. 1975, 73.
19. Ezra Taft Benson, in Conference Report, Apr. 1950, 75.
20. Or enslave, or exploit [you] (Jeremiah 30:8, footnote *b*).
21. Hebrew: bad or corrupted (Jeremiah 24:2, footnote *b*).
22. That is, to me (Jeremiah 31:3, footnote *d*).
23. See Genesis 48:5–22; Jeremiah 31:9.
24. See Doctrine and Covenants 133:30–34.
25. Joseph Fielding Smith, *Doctrines of Salvation,* 3:247, 252.
26. Daniel H. Ludlow, *A Companion to Your Study of the Old Testament,* 325.
27. Joseph Smith, in *History of the Church,* 1:313, 314–15.
28. See Joseph Fielding Smith, *Church History and Modern Revelation,* 2 vols. (1953), 2:354–56. See also Doctrine and Covenants 39:11; 22:1–4; 132:4.

CHAPTER 8

Parables of the Latter-day Kingdom

(MATTHEW 25)

INTRODUCTION

The Nature of Parables

The word *parable* comes from the Greek word *parabole,* which means "placing beside" or "together," a comparison, an illustration of one subject by another. A parable is an earthly story with a heavenly message. It is a "divine truth . . . presented by comparison with material things."[1]

PAOLO VERONESE, CA. 1585

Elder James E. Talmage wrote:

> [Parables are] designed to convey some great spiritual truth. . . . [A parable is] a brief narrative or descriptive allegory founded on real scenes or events such as occur in nature and human life, and usually with a moral or religious application.[2]

Elder Talmage also wrote:

> Let it not be forgotten that a parable is but a sketch, not a picture finished in detail; and that the expressed or implied similitude in parabolic teaching cannot logically and consistently be carried beyond the limits of the illustrative story. . . . The parable is to

> be studied in the spirit of its purpose; and strained inferences or extensions are unwarranted. A strong metaphor, a striking simile, or any other expressive figure of speech, is of service only when rationally applied; if carried beyond the bounds of reasonable intent, the best of such may become meaningless or even absurd.[3]

Thus, we must use caution in interpreting parables, making sure we do not expand the meaning of a parable beyond what the Savior intended. The safest course is to:

— Always interpret parables in the simplest terms, not in the most complex.

— If provided, always use the interpretation given by the Savior or His prophets.

— Interpret the parable's meaning within the context in which it was given.

The Prophet Joseph Smith instructed:

> I have a key by which I understand the scriptures. I [i]nquire, what was the question which drew out the answer, or caused Jesus to utter the parable? . . . To ascertain its meaning, we must dig up the root and ascertain what it was that drew the saying out of Jesus.[4]

In other words, look at the reason why the parable was given in the first place in order to understand the meaning of the story itself.

The Doctrine and Covenants is a valuable resource for understanding parables, as it relates and interprets a number of parables from the New Testament.

—	D&C 35:16; 45:36–38	The fig tree.
—	D&C 45:56–57; 63:54	The ten virgins.
—	D&C 86:1–7; 101:64–67	The wheat and the tares.
—	D&C 101:81–91	The importuning widow and the unjust judge.

We will use some of these latter-day scriptures to better understand the parables discussed in this chapter.

THREE PARABLES ABOUT THE LAST DAYS

Having just finished relating His prophecies concerning the future of Jerusalem and the last days, Jesus then shared three parables with His disciples that all had to do with the Church in the last days. While these were given to His earliest disciples, they are primarily about us in our latter-day dispensation. We would do well to consider them carefully.

The Parable of the Ten Virgins

19th-century Jewish wedding ceremony

The parable of the ten virgins is based on Jewish wedding customs in Jesus's day. Traditionally, the bridegroom and his friends escorted the bride from her home to the home of the bridegroom. Along the way, the friends of the bride waited to join them. When they arrived at the bridegroom's home, they went inside for the wedding. These weddings usually took place in the evening, so those waiting for the bride and bridegroom carried small lamps fueled by oil.

PROVIDENCE LITHOGRAPH CO., 1906, #38

- **Matthew 25:1–13 A parable about the readiness of Church members to be summoned to the marriage feast at the end of the world.** Speaking of the Church in the latter days, the Lord spoke the parable of the ten virgins, saying, "The kingdom of heaven [shall] be likened unto ten virgins, which took their lamps, and went forth to meet the bride-groom. And five of them were wise, and five were foolish" (vv. 1–2). Thus, we may conclude that one-half of the members of the Church will be unwise and ill-prepared when the Lord comes.

The five virgins that were foolish "took their lamps, [but] took no oil with them" (v. 3). The five wise virgins "took oil in their vessels with their lamps" (v. 4). Then, as they all waited for "the bridegroom" to come, "they all slumbered and slept" (v. 5).

Finally, "at midnight there was a cry made, Behold, the bridegroom cometh; go ye out to meet him" (v. 6). The great day had come, and "all those virgins arose, and trimmed their lamps" (v. 7). But the unwise could not light their lamps because they lacked sufficient oil by that time. They said to the wise, "Give us of your oil; for our lamps are gone out [are going out[5]]. But the wise answered, saying, Not so; lest there be not enough for us and you: but go ye . . . to them that sell, and buy for yourselves" (vv. 8–9).

While the five foolish virgins were out trying to obtain oil, "the bridegroom came; and they that were ready went in with him to the marriage: and the door was shut [locked[6]]" (v. 10). It was too late for the foolish virgins; they had missed His coming. They knocked on the door and cried out, "Lord, Lord, open to us. But he answered and said, Verily[7] I say unto you, I know you not" (vv. 11–12). "Watch therefore," Jesus said to His disciples, "for ye know neither the day nor the hour wherein the Son of man cometh" (v. 13).

A. BIDA, 1874

— **D&C 45:56–59** provides a modern-day interpretation of this parable. The Lord says that "they that are wise and have received the truth, and have taken the Holy Spirit for their guide, and have not been deceived—verily I say unto you, they shall not be hewn down and cast into the fire, but shall abide the day" (v. 57). Thus, the "oil" is spiritual preparation. And if they are found worthy at the time of the Lord's coming, "the earth shall be given unto them for an inheritance; and they shall multiply and wax strong, and their children shall grow up without sin unto salvation. For the

> Lord shall be in their midst, and his glory shall be upon them, and he will be their king and their lawgiver" (vv. 58–59).

President Spencer W. Kimball taught:

> I believe that the Ten Virgins represent the people of the Church of Jesus Christ and not the rank and file of the world. All of the virgins, wise and foolish, had accepted the invitation to the wedding supper; they had knowledge of the program and had been warned of the important day to come. They were not the Gentiles or the heathens or the pagans, nor were they necessarily corrupt and reprobate, but they were knowing people who were foolishly unprepared for the vital happenings that were to affect their eternal lives.
>
> They had the saving, exalting gospel, but it had not been made the center of their lives. They knew the way but gave only a small measure of loyalty and devotion. I ask you: What value is a car without an engine, a cup without water, a table without food, a lamp without oil?
>
> Rushing for their lamps to light their way through the blackness, half of them found them empty. They had cheated themselves. They were fools, these five unprepared virgins. Apparently, the bridegroom had tarried for reasons that were sufficient and good. Time had passed, and He had not come. They had heard of His coming for so long, so many times, that the statement seemingly became meaningless to them. Would He ever come? So long had it been since they began expecting Him that they were rationalizing that He would never appear. Perhaps it was a myth.
>
> Hundreds of thousands of us today are in this position. Confidence has been dulled and patience worn thin. It is so hard to wait and be prepared always. But we cannot allow ourselves to slumber. The Lord has given us this parable as a special warning.[8]

And President Wilford Woodruff observed:

> The parable of the ten virgins is intended to represent the Second Coming of the Son of Man, the coming of the Bridegroom to meet the bride, the Church . . . ; and I expect that the Savior was about right when He said, in reference to the members of the

Church, that five of them were wise and five were foolish; . . . if He finds one-half of those professing to be members of His Church prepared for salvation, it will be as many as can be expected, judging by the course that many are pursuing.[9]

— **D&C 45:56–59 How and when the wise virgins will be blessed.** President Kimball continued: "In the parable, oil can be purchased at the market. In our lives the oil of preparedness is accumulated drop by drop in righteous living. Attendance at sacrament meetings adds oil to our lamps, drop by drop over the years. Fasting, family prayer, home teaching, control of bodily appetites, preaching the gospel, studying the scriptures—each act of dedication and obedience is a drop added to our store. Deeds of kindness, payment of offerings and tithes, chaste thoughts and actions, marriage in the covenant for eternity—these, too, contribute importantly to the oil with which we can at midnight refuel our exhausted lamps."[10]

The Parable of the Talents

- **Matthew 25:14–30** In New Testament times, a talent was a sum of money.[11] Jesus used the image of a talent to represent a sacred trust upon which a servant was expected to improve. He told the story of "a man travelling into a far country, who called his own servants, and delivered unto them his goods. And unto one he gave five talents, to another two, and to another one; to every man according to his several ability; and straightway took his journey" (vv. 14– 15). Note that the amount entrusted to each servant was determined by each person's abilities. Unto whom much was given, much was expected in return. Unto others, less was entrusted and less was expected, although everyone was expected to make the most of whatever they had been given.

  The man who "received the five talents went and traded with the same, and made them other five talents. And likewise he that had received two, he also gained other two. But he that had received one went and digged in the earth, and hid his lord's money" (vv. 16–18). To each of the first two servants, who had doubled their inheritance through wise choices, the Lord promised an entry into "the joy of thy lord" (vv. 19–23).

Last of all came the man to whom only one talent had been entrusted. He said to his lord, "I knew thee that thou art an hard [strict[12]] man, reaping where thou hast not sown, and gathering where thou hast not strawed: and I was afraid, and went and hid thy talent in the earth: lo, there thou hast that

THE HOLMAN BIBLE, 1890, #59

is thine" (vv. 24–25). There are two problems with this response: (1) the man had made no effort to improve upon his trust, and (2) he sought to blame his lord for his failure. Neither was acceptable.

His lord condemned him, calling him "wicked and slothful" (v. 26). He knew his lord expected him to put his talent to good use and to improve upon it so that at his lord's coming, "[the lord] should have received [his] own with usury [interest]" (v. 27). He commanded, "Take therefore the talent from him, and give it unto him which hath ten talents. For unto every one that hath shall be given, and he shall have abundance: but from him that hath not shall be taken away even that which he hath. And cast ye the unprofitable servant into outer darkness: there shall be weeping and gnashing of teeth" (vv. 28–30).

In this parable, the man traveling to a far country represents the Lord. The servants represent each of us. The talents represent gifts and abilities given to us from God. Even though we have differing talents, we are all expected to serve with all diligence. Note that the amount entrusted and the amount earned were not the point. Each who made the most of his trust was given the same reward. Only he who had buried his talent was condemned. And because he had neglected his stewardship, it was taken from him and given to another who could be trusted.

— **D&C 46:11–12 Every person has been given at least one gift from God; some gifts are more visible than others.** "For all have not every gift given unto them; for there are many gifts, and to every man is given a gift by the Spirit of God. To some is given one, and to some is given another, that all may be profited thereby." We should note the reason for these gifts is so that "all may be profited thereby." We are given our gifts so we can share them with others. When we come together in our ward and stake congregations, all of the gifts of the Spirit are present. Nobody has all of them, but by meeting with and blessing each other with our gifts we *all* can receive the benefit of *all* the gifts of God.

The Parable of the Sheep and the Goats

Jesus will divide sheep from goats

- **Matthew 25:31–46 We will be judged by how we have served our fellow men.** Jesus compared the Second Coming and the Final Judgment to the division of sheep and goats. "When the Son of man shall come in his glory, and all the holy angels with him, then shall he sit upon the throne of his glory: and before him shall be gathered all nations: and shall separate them one from another, as a shepherd divideth his sheep from the goats: and he shall set the sheep on his right hand, but the goats on the left" (vv. 31–33).

The "sheep" who are found on the Lord's right hand will be told, "Come, ye blessed of my Father, inherit the kingdom prepared for you from the foundation of the world" (v. 34). And how will they get there on His right hand? He will answer, "I was an hungred, and ye gave me meat: I was thirsty, and ye gave me drink: I was a stranger, and ye took me in: naked, and ye clothed me: I was sick, and ye visited [took care of, cared for[13]] me: I was in prison, and ye came unto me" (vv. 35–36). And how will they have done these things unto the Lord? He will answer, "Inasmuch as ye have done it unto one of the least of these my brethren, ye have done it unto me" (vv. 37–40).

To the "goats" on the Lord's left hand, He will say, "Depart from me, ye cursed, into everlasting fire, prepared for the devil and his angels" (v.

41). And why? Because "I was an hungred, and ye gave me no meat: I was thirsty, and ye gave me no drink: I was a stranger, and ye took me not in: naked, and ye clothed me not: sick, and in prison, and ye visited me not" (vv. 42–43). And when they protest, asking when they failed to do these things for the Lord, He will answer, "Inas- much as ye did it not to one of the least of these, ye did it not to me" (vv. 44–45). And these—those who have neglected their fellow beings—"shall go away into everlasting punishment: but the righteous into life eternal" (v. 46).

Elder Marion D. Hanks said:

> Jesus taught His followers the parable of the sheep and the goats, representing the judgment to come, in which He clearly identified those who will inherit "life eternal" and those who will "go away into everlasting punishment" (Matthew 25:46). The key difference was that those who should inherit the kingdom with Him had developed the habit of helping, had experienced the joy of giving, and the satisfaction of serving—they had responded to the needs of the hungry, thirsty, homeless, the naked, the sick, and those in prison. . . . Nothing would seem more clear than the high premium the Savior put upon selfless service to others as an indispensable element of Christian conduct and of salvation.[14]

Notes:

1. See Bible Dictionary in the Latter-day Saint edition of the King James Version of the Bible, "Parables."
2. James E. Talmage, *Jesus the Christ,* 3rd ed. (1916), 298, 304.
3. James E. Talmage, *Jesus the Christ,* 285–86.
4. Joseph Smith, in *History of the Church,* 5:261.
5. See Matthew 25:8, footnote *a.*
6. See Matthew 25:10, footnote *b.*
7. Compare Joseph Smith Translation, Matthew 25:11 (in Matthew 25:12, footnote *a*).
8. Spencer W. Kimball, *Faith Precedes the Miracle* (1972), 253–54.
9. *Teachings of Presidents of the Church: Wilford Woodruff* (2004), 256.

10. Spencer W. Kimball, *Faith Precedes the Miracle,* 256.

11. See Bible Dictionary in the Latter-day Saint edition of the King James Version of the Bible, "Money."

12. See Matthew 25:24, footnote *a*.

13. See Matthew 25:36, footnote *a*.

14. Marion D. Hanks, "The Royal Law," *Ensign,* May 1992, 9.

CHAPTER 9

The Law of Consecration

(D&C 19; 29; 42; 51; 56; 58; 64; 70; 72; 78; 82–83; 92; 97; 104–105; PSALM 24; ACTS 2; 4; MOSES 7)

A ZION PEOPLE MUST CONSECRATE

In February 1831, soon after the Saints began to gather to Kirtland, Ohio, the Lord revealed that they should begin to live the law of consecration. This is consistent with what the Lord has done in every dispensation where He has gathered together a group of chosen people. He immediately offers to them the opportunity to become a Zion people.

He did this with Enoch's people, and they accepted His offer and were translated.[1] He did it again with Melchizedek's people with the same result—they were translated.[2] He tried it with the children of Israel at Mount Sinai, but they rejected His offer and brought upon themselves the restrictive society of the Mosaic Law.[3] He tried it among the Nephites after His visit to them, and it worked for about 200 years (four generations), then fell apart.[4]

JOHN MARTIN, 1841

A Zion people must live this law

Now, in February 1831, the Lord was attempting to unite the Latter-day Saints as a Zion people. And as in previous dispensations, there were mixed results.

The Kirtland bishop's storehouse

- **D&C 78:3 The need for order in consecration.** In March 1832, the Lord revealed that there must be an organization to regulate and administer the law of consecration among His people. The system cannot function properly in an informal or chaotic context.

- **D&C 78:3–4 Establishing storehouses for the poor.** In this revelation, received at Kirtland, Ohio, in March 1832, the Lord commanded the Saints to establish bishops' storehouses both in Kirtland and in Missouri (v. 3).

  This procedure of storing goods "for the poor of my people" was to be "a permanent and everlasting establishment and order unto my church, to advance the cause, which ye have espoused, to the salvation of man, and to the glory of your Father who is in heaven" (vv. 3–4). Ever since that day, the Church has spent enormous amounts of time and money to build and maintain such storehouses. They have become the center of the Church's humanitarian and welfare efforts around the world.

- **D&C 78:5–7 The law of consecration's purpose.** The storehouse was one part of the law of consecration. This law was established "that you may be equal in the bonds of heavenly things, yea, and earthly things also, for the obtaining of heavenly things. For if ye are not equal in earthly things ye cannot be equal in obtaining heavenly things; for if you will that I give unto you a place in the celestial world, you must prepare yourselves by doing the things which I have commanded you and required of you."

- **D&C 78:17–18 We are "little children" in our understanding of heavenly things.** Speaking to the early Saints, who were all converts to the Church and understood little of its functions and destiny, the Lord gently reminded them, "Ye are little children, and ye have not as yet understood how great blessings the Father hath in his own hands and prepared for you; and ye cannot bear all things now; nevertheless, be of good cheer, for I will lead you along. The kingdom is yours and the blessings thereof are yours, and the riches of eternity are yours."

- **D&C 78:19–22 The faithful will inherit all things.** "He who receiveth all things with thankfulness shall be made glorious; and the things of this earth shall be added unto him, even an hundred fold, yea, more" (v. 19). The Lord has prepared all things for us before He takes us home to dwell with Him (v. 20). Those who dwell in His celestial kingdom are referred to as "the church of the Firstborn," and they will be "take[n] . . . up in a cloud, and appoint[ed] every man his portion" (v. 21). And the portion that has been reserved for "a faithful and wise steward" is "all things" that the Father has. We will receive this inheritance as joint-heirs with Jesus Christ.

Why Consecration Is Required of Saints

In April 1832, while the Prophet Joseph Smith was in Missouri, the Lord further explained why consecration is required of the Saints. They needed to be more unified and less competitive with each other. Also, if they were to become a Zion people, greater things were required of them.

- **D&C 82:1–4, 7 Where much is given, much is required.** There was need for greater unity between the leadership in Zion and the leaders at Kirtland. The Lord reminded the Brethren that "inasmuch as you have forgiven one another your trespasses, even so I, the Lord, forgive you" (v. 1). He also said that "there are those among you who have sinned exceedingly; yea, even all of you have sinned; but verily I say unto you, beware from henceforth, and refrain from sin, lest sore judgments fall upon your heads" (v. 2).

  A greater standard is expected of a Zion people. "For of him unto whom much is given much is required; and he who sins against the greater light shall receive the greater condemnation" (v. 3). These were the ordained ministers of Christ's Church, and they were receiving revelations from the Lord. But "inasmuch as ye keep not my sayings, which I give unto you, ye become transgressors; and justice and judgment are the penalty which is affixed unto my law" (v. If they would repent of their sins, "the Lord . . . will not lay any sin to your charge; go your ways and sin no more; but unto that soul who sinneth shall the former sins return, saith the Lord your God" (v. 7).

- **D&C 82:9–10 "I, the Lord, am bound when ye do what I say."** Because the Lord does all that He does with us by way of covenant, we can literally "bind" the Lord to bless us if we keep His commandments. "I give unto you directions how you may act before me, that it may turn to you for your salvation," He said (v. 9). "I, the Lord, am bound when ye do what I say; but when ye do not what I say, ye have no promise" (v. 10).

- **D&C 82:14 Zion must increase in beauty and holiness.** "Her borders must be enlarged; her stakes must be strengthened; yea, verily I say unto you, Zion must arise and put on her beautiful garments." The Church at that time was small and isolated. But the Lord declared that it would grow and spread, and its worthy members "put on [their] beautiful garments" as they receive temple ordinances and covenants. We see this prophecy being fulfilled today as millions of people have joined the Church and 150-plus temples dot the earth. And we are told that this is only the beginning.

- **D&C 82:15, 17 "You are to be equal."** The Lord required His early Latter-day Saints to "bind [them]selves by this covenant, . . . according to the laws of the Lord. . . . You are to be equal" (vv. 15, 17). They were to receive "properties" as "stewardships, every man according to his wants and his needs, inasmuch as his wants are just" (v. 17).

THE UNITED ORDER

- **D&C 92:1–2 The united order.** In March 1833, the Lord organized the system of consecration into what He called the "united order."

- **D&C 104:78–86 Further instructions on the united order.** One year later, in April 1834, the Church and the Prophet found themselves in serious debt.

  The Lord said the following about the Church's debts and the need for consecration in order to pay them:

  — **The Lord wants those in the united order to pay all their debts.** "Humble yourselves before me," He said, and then they can "obtain this blessing by your diligence and humility and the prayer of faith" (vv. 78–79).

— **He will "soften the hearts" of their debtors** until such time as He can "send means unto you for your deliverance" (v. 80). He tells Joseph Smith to write to his debtors in New York "according to that which shall be dictated by my Spirit," and if he does this "it shall be taken away out of their minds to bring affliction upon you" (v. 81).

— **He will deliver them "this once out of [their] [financial] bondage"** so long as they "are humble and faithful and call upon [His] name" (vv. 82–83).

— **He gave them permission to borrow money** "by hundreds, or thousands, even until you shall loan [borrow] enough to deliver yourself from bondage" (v. 84). In order to do this, they may "pledge the properties which I have put into your hands, this once," but only if it is done by "common consent or otherwise, as it shall seem good unto you" (v. 85).

— **The ultimate solution is to live the law of consecration** ("do the things which I have laid before you, according to my commandments"). He reminds them that "all these things are mine, and ye are my stewards, and the master will not suffer his house to be broken up" (v. 86).

THE EARLY SAINTS FAILED TO CONSECRATE

This concept was not well understood by the Saints, let alone their enemies. The law of consecration was the doctrine that seems to have fired some mobsters to action, especially those who were former Church members who felt that the Prophet was trying to rob them of their inheritance. They justified their actions as a defense of private property. Other factors included their simple greed and jealousy.

- **D&C 105:4–5 By June 1834, the Saints were still not living this law.** The Lord said they were "not united according to the union required by the law of the celestial kingdom" (v. 4). The Lord made it clear that

"Zion cannot be built up unless it is by the principles of the law of the celestial kingdom; otherwise I cannot receive her unto myself" (v. 5).

- **D&C 105:34 The law of consecration was temporarily suspended in June 1834** until the time of Zion's future redemption. There were several reasons why the Lord suspended it:
  - **The Lord both gives and revokes His commandments** as needed (see D&C 56:4).
  - **The Lord's promises are conditioned upon obedience** (see D&C 58:31–33). The Lord always keeps His part of the covenants He makes with us. The problem is that men are not obedient. "I command and men obey not," He said, and therefore "I revoke and they receive not the blessing" (v. 32). But then, like selfish children, "they say in their hearts: This is not the work of the Lord, for his promises are not fulfilled" (v. 33). They fail to see the connection between keeping their covenants and receiving the blessings attached to those covenants.
  - **The Saints then in Missouri were not living the law of consecration nor keeping the commandments** (see D&C 105:2–4). They were guilty of adultery, dishonesty, and division, in addition to not living the law of consecration.
  - **Because of this the Saints "must needs be chastened until they learn obedience,** if it must needs be, by the things which they suffer" (D&C 105:6).
  - **The result was that they were driven out of the center place of Zion** (Jackson County, Missouri) by their enemies. The Saints were simply not worthy of Zion.

Disobedience and Greed in Kirtland

At Kirtland, Ohio, the failure of consecration was based mostly on greed. No sooner had the Lord introduced this celestial principle than Satan countered with a serious blow.

In the Kirtland Temple during the "days of Pentecost," great signs and wonders were shown, including the appearance of angels, tongues of flaming fire, and even the Lord Jesus Christ. The Saints were united like never before or since, and many expected the Second Coming of our Lord to be imminent. But they were not yet a Zion people and were not willing to live the law of consecration.

The Prophet Joseph Smith prophesied of their weakness:

> Soon after the [Kirtland Temple] was finished, . . . Joseph [Smith] had a vision which lasted until he besought the Lord to take it from him, for it showed him things which were very painful for him to contemplate. But it returned immediately and remained before his eyes until near the middle of the forenoon. . . . [The following day] he preached as he was accustomed to do, [and the following is a part of his remarks:]
>
> "[Brethren, I am rejoiced to see you, and I have no doubt, but that you are glad to see me.] We are now nearly as happy as we can be on earth, for we have accomplished more than we had any reason to anticipate when we began. Our lovely and beautiful house is finished, and the Lord has acknowledged it by pouring out His Spirit upon us here and revealing to us much concerning His purposes in regard to the work which He is about to perform. Furthermore, we have plenty of everything necessary to our comfort and convenience, and judging from appearances, one would not suppose that anything could occur that would break up our friendship for each other or distress us in the least.
>
> "But, brethren, beware, for I tell you in the name of the Lord that there is an evil in this very congregation, which, if it is not repented of, will result in making one-third of you who are here this day so much my enemies that you will have a desire to take my life; and you even would do so, if God permitted the deed.
>
> "But, brethren, I call upon you now to repent, while there is room for repentance, and cease all your hardness and turn from those principles of dishonesty and death which you are harboring in

your bosoms, before it is eternally too late, for there is yet room for repentance."

He continued to labor in this way with them, appealing to them in the most feeling and solemn manner, until the exertion of his mind and the fatigue of speaking quite exhausted him, and he sat down, leaving almost everyone in the house in tears. The following week was much given to surmises and speculations as to who would be the traitors and why they should be so.[5]

What was this great evil in their hearts? Greed and selfish- ness. The Prophet Joseph Smith wrote:

> The spirit of speculation in lands and property of all kinds, which was so prevalent throughout the whole nation, was taking deep root in the Church. As the fruits of this spirit, evil surmisings, fault finding, disunion, dissension, and apostasy followed in quick succession, and it seemed as though all the powers of earth and hell were combining their influence in an especial manner to overthrow the Church at once, and make a final end. . . . The enemy abroad, and apostates in our midst, united in their schemes, flour and provisions were turned towards other markets, and many became disaffected toward me as though I were the sole cause of those very evils I was most strenuously striving against.[6]

President Heber C. Kimball tells how, returning from his mission to the East,

> . . . We were very much grieved on our arrival in Kirtland, to see the spirit of speculation that was prevailing in the Church. Trade and traffic seemed to engross the time and attention of the Saints. When we left Kirtland a city lot was worth about $150; but on our return, to our astonishment, the same lot was said to be worth from $500 to $1000. . . . In fact everything in the place seemed to be moving in great prosperity, and all seemed determined to become rich. . . . This appearance of prosperity led many of the Saints to believe that the time had arrived for the Lord to enrich them with the treasures of the earth, and believing so, it stimulated them to great exertions.[7]

This was the very self-justification for profiteering against which they had been warned in the beginning. They believed that anything that would improve their temporal situation was justified, no matter whom it might harm, including the newly arrived and poor Saints.

"Then came the crash of 1837, brought on by those same shrewd, hardheaded businessmen."[8] "During this time," President Kimball recalled, "I had many days of sorrow and mourning, for my heart sickened to see the awful extent that things were getting to."[9] Many apostatized and "also entered into combinations to obtain wealth by fraud and every means that was evil."[10]

Later, President Kimball returned to Kirtland again after a mission to England. Elder Orson F. Whitney noted some of the changes that took place in Kirtland while President Kimball was in England:

> The Church had suffered terribly from the ravages of apostasy.... The Ohio mobbings, the Missouri persecutions, the martyrdom, the exodus, nor all that Zion's cause has suffered since, have imperiled it half so much as when mammon and the love of God strove for supremacy in the hearts of His people.[11]

This apostasy from the principles of Zion destroyed the Church in Kirtland. Anyone who would not lift up his heel against the Prophet put his life in danger, including Brigham Young. The righteous had to flee to Missouri for safety.

Wickedness and Greed in Missouri

Their destination, Far West, Missouri, quickly became a boomtown. In the midst of all the buying and selling of farms and the construction of buildings, the Saints were again overcome by the spirit of financial speculation. Apparently, they had learned very little from their experience in Kirtland.

The Prophet stood on the framework of a schoolhouse under construction and made another disturbing prophecy:

> Brethren, we are gathering to this beautiful land, to build up "Zion."... But since I have been here I perceive the spirit of selfishness. Covetousness ... exists in the hearts of the Saints....

> Here are those who begin to spread out buying up all the land they are able to do, to the exclusion of the poorer ones who are not so much blessed with this world's goods, thinking to lay foundation for themselves only, looking to their own individual families and those who are to follow them. . . . Now I want to tell you that Zion cannot be built up in any such way. . . . Speculative schemes are being introduced [and] this is the way of the world—Babylon indeed—and I tell you in the name of the God of Israel, if there is not repentance . . . and a turning from such ungodliness, covetousness, and self-will, you will be broken up and scattered from this choice land to the four winds of Heaven.[12]

President Brigham Young explained how the Saints excused themselves from the requirements of consecration:

> When the revelation . . . was given in 1838, I was present. . . . The brethren wished me to go among the churches and find out what surplus property the people had, with which to forward the building of the temple we were commencing at Far West. I accordingly went from place to place through the country. Before I started, I asked Brother Joseph, "Who shall be the judge of what is surplus property?" Said he, "Let them be the judges themselves, for I care not if they do not give a single dime."[13]

This is an important principle of consecration. It is entirely a free-will offering. Nobody is forced to comply. "As in [ancient] Israel, the amount of the free-will offering was left entirely up to the giver, since it was he who was being tested. The offering was required but the amount was up to him. The results, Brigham Young reports of his journey, were laughable—nobody had any surplus property!"[14]

Members of the Church needed to understand that living solely for themselves and ignoring the law of consecration was *not* acceptable to the Lord. No Zion people have ever been established without living this law. But time and time again, in the early days of this Church, the Saints kept returning to the principles of Babylon. The Saints in Missouri failed to repent and were indeed driven out of the state.

Worldliness in Nauvoo

Arriving at Nauvoo in a humbled condition, some Saints did not take long to return to the ways of Babylon. Speculation in land—the vice that had already taken them in a snare at Kirtland and in Missouri—raised again its ugly head.

Alarmed, the Prophet Joseph Smith spoke out strenuously against such evil practices: "If there are any among you who aspire after their own aggrandizement, and seek their own opulence, while their brethren are groaning in poverty, . . . they cannot be benefited by the intercession of the Holy Spirit."[15]

The Prophet continued:

> Organization of large [organizations] upon common stock principles . . . opens such a dreadful field for the avaricious, the indolent, and the corrupt hearted to prey upon the innocent and virtuous and honest. . . . [They are] aspiring men . . . who [have] not the substance of godliness about them.[16] Every man who is . . . covetous . . . will be taken in a snare.[17]
>
> Now, in this world, mankind are naturally selfish, ambitious, and striving to excel one above another. . . . Some seek to excel. And this was the case with Lucifer when he fell.[18]
>
> The greatest temporal and spiritual blessings which always flow from faithfulness and concerted effort, never [come from] individual exertion or enterprise.[19] Party feelings, separate interests, [and] exclusive designs should be lost sight of in the one common cause, in the interest of the whole [see 1 Corinthians 12:21, 26].[20]

As Dr. Hugh W. Nibley observed, "It was Far West all over again."[21] On June 18, 1842, in a grove near the Nauvoo Temple, "Joseph, the prophet, arose and spoke in great plainness upon the corruption and wickedness of John C. Bennett. He also prophesied that if the merchants of the city and the rich did not open their hearts and contribute to the poor they would be cursed by the hand of God and cut off from the land of the living."[22] But his warnings were to no avail because "the people in those days, . . . like Israel of old associated . . . worldly success . . . with [righteousness], and [worldly] misfortunes with their ideas of wrong."[23] In other words, if you are rich, you are righteous.

By the time the Saints were expelled from Nauvoo, President Brigham Young stated that "the Saints were becoming slothful and covetous, and would spend their means upon fine houses for themselves before they would put it into a House of the Lord."[24] "Through the selfishness of some, which is idolatry, through their covetousness, which is the same, and the lustful desire of their minds, they were cast out and driven from their homes."[25]

Better Success in Utah

Crossing the Plains to Utah brought the Saints to their senses, and, according to President Heber C. Kimball, the famine that afflicted them in 1848 was averted only "by the exercise of the highest wisdom and the broadest charity, and the partial observance of the principle of the United Order, which the Saints had before sought to introduce, and still have it in their mission to establish. The people were put upon rations, all sharing the same, like members of one great family."[26]

Elder Matthias F. Cowley noted that the Saints even gave freely of their scarce grain to the hungry Pawnee Indians. "The spirit begotten by such an act of generosity opened the hearts of the Saints . . . and fitted them more perfectly for the worship of God."[27]

Elder Cowley also observed:

> The design of President Young [in Utah] was that no speculation in lands by the brethren should be allowed whereby the first comers should enrich themselves at the expense of their brethren who should follow. . . . This arrangement prevented any one man from holding a large tract [of land] near the city, and by so doing prevented speculation by the individual to the detriment of the whole community. . . . In other words, the interest of the whole was to be uppermost in the mind of each man, and the spirit of greed and avarice seldom asserted itself on the part of those noble founders of Utah's great commonwealth.[28]

"The question of consecration was presented [in conference of April 1854]. President Heber C. Kimball said, 'I want all I have to be secured in the Kingdom of God.' They knew the dangers and temptations of wealth, the selfishness which it begets, as well as its destruction of brotherly love."[29]

"The main thing Brother Brigham insisted on in their new home was that they get over the illusion of personal economic independence."[30] But it was short-lived. By 1851, he was saddened by the sight of so many of the Saints running to California chiefly after the God of this world, and he was unable to address them.[31]

"Why not . . . day by day watch and chasten yourselves?" he asked the Saints. . . . Instead of that,

> everyone "becomes so absorbed in their improvement and increase, that he forgets why he came here, [and] that the hands upon the Public Works need food to sustain life, that after all he is only a steward at most. . . . While another, still more culpable in that he produces nothing, strives to amass wealth, and build up a name by becoming a mere trader, and far too often a shaving trader, and of course he too is soon fully imbued with the ruling passion of selfishness."[32]

What about Today?

We might well ask ourselves if we are any different today. It is easy to see how easily the earlier Saints fell into worldliness at the expense of establishing Zion. But we are just as prone to be greedy and selfish.

Looking down the years, President Brigham Young said in 1857:

> I am more afraid of covetousness in our Elders than I am of the hordes of hell. Have we men out now of that class? I believe so. I am afraid of such spirits, for they are more powerful and injurious to this people than all hell outside of our borders. All our enemies in the United States or in the world, and all hell with them marshalled against us, could not do us the injury that covetousness in the hearts of this people could do us, for it is idolatry.[33]

And in 1858 he added: "Whether you can see it or not, I know that this people are more or less prone to idolatry, for I see that spirit manifested every day, and hear of it from nearly every quarter."[34]

THE LAW OF CONSECRATION IS STILL REQUIRED OF A ZION PEOPLE

The fact that the early Saints did not successfully live like Zion people does not revoke the law of consecration forever. As we will discuss in the following chapter, the Saints will be required to return and build up Zion once again. And when they do, they will be required to live the law of consecration.

- **D&C 105:5–6 The law of consecration is a celestial law, and a Zion people must live it.** The Prophet Joseph Smith taught:

> Any person who is exalted to the highest mansion has to abide a celestial law, and the whole law too. But there has been a great difficulty in getting anything into the heads of this generation.... Even the Saints are slow to understand.[35]

THE UNDERLYING PRINCIPLES OF CONSECRATION

If we are slow to understand, then a little instruction in the principles of Zion and consecration might help.

- **D&C 104:13–14 The earth is the Lord's.** A person's willingness to consecrate results from the recognition that the earth and everything in it belongs to the Lord (see Psalm 24:1). Those who do not believe this will not see themselves as "stewards" over the blessings they possess, but rather as the sole owners of self-made circumstances.
- **D&C 104:15–16 The Lord's way is to exalt the poor and humble the rich.** We should not misunderstand. This is not socialism, nor taxing the rich to provide handouts for the poor. The Lord's way provides for

personal growth for both the rich and the poor as they come together in a covenant bond. The poor must work for what they receive, and every man must contribute his excess to the common good of the whole.

- **D&C 29:34–35 Consecration is a spiritual law,** not just a temporal or economic program. It helps participants prepare for eternal life in a celestial kingdom, whose inhabitants live the law of consecration.
- **D&C 19:26 We must not "covet" our possessions.** This is an interesting use of the word *covet,* since we normally think of it as unrighteous wishing that we possessed the means or circumstances of another. But we must also not covet our own possessions.
- **D&C 64:34 Consecration must be done willingly, not grudgingly or by force.** Consistent with all spiritual laws, participation in consecration is voluntary, not forced. God insists that every man "should be an agent unto himself" (D&C 29:35). In the matter of consecration, "the Lord requireth the heart and a willing mind," and only the "willing" and the "obedient" may participate in this celestial program among a Zion people.

Consecration Is Neither Socialism Nor Communism

Some have suggested that the law of consecration and the system of the united order are a religious kind of socialism or communism. These assumptions are false.

Consecration was not a call to socialism. The Church would not hold title to everyone's property. Rather, a system of stewardships would make it possible for "every man [to] improve upon his talent, that every man may gain other talents, yea, even an hundred fold," with all excess property "to be cast into the Lord's storehouse, to become the common property of the whole church" (D&C 82:18), for the purpose of taking care of widows, orphans, and the poor (see D&C 83:6).

President J. Reuben Clark Jr. stated:

> The united order has not been generally understood. . . . The united order was not a communal system. . . . The united order and [communism/socialism] are not synonymous. Communism is Satan's counterfeit for the united order. There is no mistake

about this and those who go about telling us otherwise either do not know or have failed to understand or are willfully misrepresenting.[36]

Vladimir Lenin

The Prophet Joseph Smith attended a presentation on socialism in September 1843 at Nauvoo. His response was to declare that he *"did not believe the doctrine."*[37] Later that month he reported: "I preached on the stand about one hour on the 2nd chapter of Acts, designing to show the folly of common stock [holding property in common]. In Nauvoo every one is steward over his own [property]."[38]

THE PROCESS OF CONSECRATION

To fully appreciate the difference between a welfare state and the law of consecration, we need to examine the process by which consecration is accomplished under the Lord's plan. It can be thought of as a four-step process:

- **Step #1: Consecrating Possessions**

1. Church members voluntarily consecrate their possessions to the Church by legal deed (see D&C 42:30–32). This is the first step and perhaps the one that requires the most faith. To be effective, and to allow the issuance of stewardships, this had to be done voluntarily (v. 31; see also D&C 64:34) and with a legal deed of ownership—secure enough that ownership of the properties was sure and "cannot be taken from the church" (v. 32). Not everything

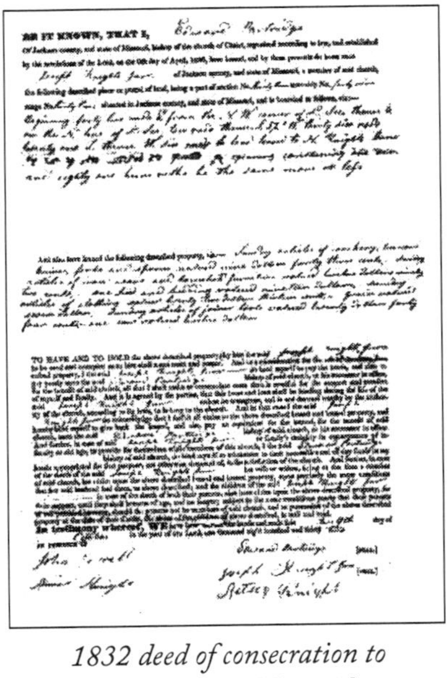

BE IT KNOWN, THAT I,

1832 deed of consecration to Bishop Edward Partridge

was thus consecrated—only those things that had real value (e.g., property) or could be used to make a living (e.g., farm animals, tools), plus money and goods that could be used to help the poor.

2. These consecrated properties are "laid before the bishop" (D&C 42:31). The bishop was thus the agent through whom consecration was made. A bishop had to be a man of uncommon character, a man whose "heart is pure before me . . . [and] in whom there is no guile" (D&C 41:11).

- **Step #2: Receiving a Stewardship**

1. In return, the bishop deeds back the man's property, with a covenant of stewardship (see D&C 42:32). The Lord said, "Every man shall be made accountable unto me, *a steward over his own property*" (v. 32; emphasis added). Why was property deeded to the bishop and then deeded right back? The answer is covenant stewardship. When I receive it back, I do so with a covenant and promise to take care of it and use it for the blessing and benefit of all.
2. The stewardship property is owned by the recipients (see D&C 51:4). This is private property, not communal property. It is given to them with a deed of ownership so each member will be fully responsible and accountable for managing it.
3. Stewardships come with a covenant of accountability for their use and management (see D&C 104:11–13).
4. The size of the stewardship depends on the circumstances, wants, and needs of the family (see D&C 42:32). In every case, he was to receive "sufficient for himself and family" (v. 32). This would mean that the size and nature of stewardships would vary according to the size and needs of each individual family. The bishop was commanded to "appoint unto this people their portions, every man *equal according to his family*, according to his circumstances and his wants and needs" (D&C 51:3; emphasis added). Notice that the bishop was to take into account the family's righteous "wants" so long as they were "just" and not selfish (see D&C 82:17).

5. The bishop and the member decide by mutual consent how much is enough. The Prophet Joseph Smith taught: "The matter of consecration must be done by the mutual consent of both parties; for to give the bishop power to say how much every man shall have, and he be obliged to comply with the bishop's judgment, is giving to the bishop more power than a king has; and upon the other hand, to let every man say how much he needs, and the bishop be obliged to comply with his judgment, is to throw Zion into confusion, and make a slave of the bishop. The fact is, there must be a balance or equilibrium of power, between the bishop and the people, and thus harmony and good will may be preserved among you."[39]
6. The stewardship also depends on the particular training, skills, knowledge, talents, and interests of the recipient, recognizing the uniqueness of each individual. A blacksmith received what was needed to operate a blacksmith shop. A printer received a print shop. A baker received a bakery. For example, individual stewardships were granted to Church leaders at Kirtland, based on their personal skills and desires (see D&C 104:19–46).
7. Participants must be righteous in order to participate (see D&C 51:4). If a steward "transgresses and is not accounted worthy," he is no longer eligible to participate. In such cases, the participant is given back the money and property he consecrated and is required to leave the system (see D&C 51:5; 56:10).

- **Step #3: Managing Stewardships and Contributing Surpluses**

1. Stewards must regularly report to the bishop on their stewardships (see D&C 72:3–4). This "return and report" process can be seen throughout the plan of salvation. By this process the Lord can determine "who is faithful and wise" both in this world and when we "inherit the mansions prepared for [us] of my Father" (v. 4).

Bishop Newel K. Whitney

2. Stewards consecrate any surplus they have generated to the bishop (see D&C 42:33).
3. The bishop places all surplus property and goods into a bishop's storehouse (see D&C 51:13).
4. The lazy and indolent do not receive a stewardship (see D&C 42:42, 53). The system rewards those willing to work with the means to make their living. It does not provide handouts to the lazy and indolent.
5. Participants pay for whatever they obtain from each other (see D&C 42:54). People were not to borrow from their neighbors but to pay for whatever they received from anyone else. In this way, every person's stewardship is productive, with nobody taking advantage of any other person's labor. Each has a profitable enterprise from which they can generate the means to purchase whatever they need from others.
6. New stewards participate like all other stewards (see D&C 42:53, 55).

- **Step #4: Managing Surpluses**

  1. The surplus is used to provide new stewardships to others (see D&C 42:33).
  2. The bishop also uses the surplus to care for the poor, to build houses of worship, and for other worthy purposes (see D&C 42:34–35).

AN EXAMPLE OF HOW CONSECRATION WORKS

A new dentist in his practice

To illustrate this celestial principle and how it might work among a righteous people, let us take an imaginary example of a young man who has recently come of age to receive his own stewardship. He wants to be a dentist, and he has prepared himself for this stewardship by attending dental school, graduating, and obtaining a license to practice. How does he now proceed?

- **Step #1: Consecrating Possessions.**

  The bishop's storehouse already contains sufficient money and equipment to set this young man up in his dental practice. Perhaps a member whose stewardship is manufacturing has already donated the necessary equipment. Or, if not, then the funds of the storehouse can be used to purchase the equipment from a vendor. Also, because of the consecrations that have been made, land and building materials are available to construct him an office. The young man needs only to go to his bishop and consecrate to the system whatever he possesses of value and express a desire to receive a stewardship.

- **Step #2: Receiving a Stewardship.**

  Seeing that he is fully qualified, worthy, and willing to enter into his stewardship with a covenant, the bishop arranges for him to receive his stewardship—everything necessary for him to practice dentistry. He makes a covenant with the bishop to manage and maintain his stewardship to the best of his ability, and to consecrate to the storehouse any surplus he may generate from his practice. He and the bishop agree together as to what his family's needs and wants are, and anything above that will be considered to be "surplus." He receives his property and equipment with a deed, makes his solemn covenant of stewardship, and begins his practice.

- **Step #3: Managing Stewardships and Contributing Surpluses.**

  To understand the genius of this system, we should ask ourselves three questions at this point:

  — **First, how much debt does the young man have?** He has none. The land and building and equipment are all paid for. So, too, is his house and his car. All were received as part of his stewardship. So he begins his stewardship debt-free and able to concentrate on managing his practice and spending plenty of time with his family. He is truly free.

- **Second, how expensive will his fees need to be in order for him to practice?** Not very expensive. People can obtain dental services from him for a reasonable cost that does not have to cover the cost of his equipment or facilities. Nor does he have to generate unreasonable sums of money to satisfy his desired lifestyle. That has already been negotiated and agreed to with his bishop, and his home and cars, etc., are all paid for. The entire community benefits from dental services at a very reasonable price.
- **Third, how much excess will he generate from his practice?** Quite a bit, since he has no payments to make. After keeping what he and the bishop have agreed he should keep to satisfy his family's needs and wants, he then gives back to the storehouse all of the excess he generates each year. It might be safe to say that at least half of what he generates will be excess, if not more. A large amount of money flows back into the storehouse from this young man every year of his life, providing the means to set others up in their own stewardships.

- **Step #4: Managing Surpluses.**

  It should not be difficult to imagine how an entire community would benefit from such a system. Nobody is in debt. Everybody has what they need and want. And this young man's story is multiplied by thousands of people, from all walks of life, who are consecrated stewards. It is not surprising, therefore, that societies that have lived this law have become extremely blessed as a people. They all get rich—together. And they all stay focused on the more important things of life—family, church, and the welfare of their neighbors. They become, indeed, a celestial people.

THE PURPOSES OF CONSECRATION

The goal of the system is not just "to get rich," but to shape a people into a Zion society where they have "all things common" (Acts 4:32) and there are "no poor among them" (Moses 7:18). Both temporally and spiritually, they are united and unfettered and blessed. Thus, consecration achieves a number of important things for those who live it.

Temporal Reasons for Consecration

- **To care for the poor and needy** (see D&C 42:31).
- **To teach us to be industrious and to avoid idleness** (see D&C 42:42). In our modern society we see thousands of "idle poor" who feel entitled to the care of others without regard for their own productivity. That is not the Lord's way. The poor must labor for what they receive, both as their way of contributing to the blessings of others, and also for the sake of their own self-dignity.
- **To make us "equal" in earthly opportunities** (see D&C 51:3, 9). Bishop Edward Partridge was charged to "appoint unto this people their portions, every man equal according to his family, according to his circumstances and his wants and needs" (v. 3). This did not mean everyone would receive identical portions, but rather that every steward would have all that he needs and desires in righteousness.
- **To provide a common pool of resources from which to help people** (see D&C 82:18). Notice that it is what goes into the *storehouse* that becomes common property, and not the *private property* of the people. Each stewardship is considered private property. This is not communism but joint-capitalism.
- **To make it possible to focus on spiritual things** (see D&C 78:5–6). People who are unequally yoked with the cares of the world will be unequally able to give their attention to spiritual things.
- **To improve our talents for the benefit of all** (see D&C 82:18). While taking a stewardship upon himself and learning to manage it "for the benefit of the church of the living God," "every man may improve upon his talent, [and] . . . gain other talents, yea, even an hundred fold."
- **To purchase lands and build buildings** (see D&C 42:35). The Church needs places of worship and temples and administrative buildings around the world. Thus, the money and goods that are consecrated to the Lord may be used for these purposes.
- **To support full-time Church officers and workers** (see D&C 42:70–73). Those who labor full-time in the management of the affairs of the Church are entitled to either be paid for their service or to receive goods from the bishop's storehouse.

- **To help the Church "stand independent above all other creatures"** (D&C 78:14). The traumatic events of these last days would be much worse if the Church and its people were financially insolvent.

Spiritual Reasons for Consecration

- **To help us overcome pride** (see D&C 42:40).
- **To teach us to be honest** (see D&C 51:9). This is a system which requires households to declare their needs and wants to the bishop. There are all kinds of opportunities for greed and selfishness under such a system. The Lord said as He implemented this plan, "And let every man deal honestly."
- **To teach us to be accountable, faithful, and wise** (see D&C 51:19). Managing a stewardship which requires us to report its results teaches us to be accountable. Being properly and consistently accountable makes us faithful. And learning to make the proper decisions along the way makes us wise. These are all godlike characteristics which we must obtain if we wish to be exalted.
- **To teach us to be unselfish** (see D&C 70:14). Consecrating against our will or with a bad attitude will not bless us. We might as well not give the gift because there will be no reward for giving grudgingly.
- **To teach us to be just and fair** (see D&C 82:17). While living this law, "you are to have equal claims on the properties, for the benefit of managing . . . your stewardships, every man according to his wants and his needs, inasmuch as his wants are just." In other words, we need to learn to be fair and equitable in our requests from the system, not greedy and self-serving.
- **To provide for the salvation of the Saints** (see D&C 78:3–4). The Lord intended this practice to be "permanent and everlasting" and to "advance the cause" of Zion (v. 4). Its purpose was to provide for "the salvation of man" and for "the glory of your Father who is in heaven" (v. 4). How does consecration do this? By teaching us how to hold and manage wealth without it destroying us spiritually.
- **To learn to live a celestial principle while still on earth** (see D&C 78:7). Consecration is a celestial law—the inhabitants of the celestial

world live by this law. Therefore, "if you will that I give unto you a place in the celestial world, you must prepare yourselves by doing the things which I have commanded you and required of you" (that is, to consecrate).

- **To keep our "eye single to the glory of God"** (D&C 82:19). Instead of self-interest and self-aggrandizement, consecration encourages "every man seeking the interest of his neighbor, and doing all things with an eye single to the glory of God." It is charity in action.

HOW WE CAN CONSECRATE TODAY

Though we do not live the law of consecration as a people, we are nonetheless asked to consecrate as individuals. We have made covenants to do so. But how can we live the law of consecration in a time when there is no organized process for us to do it as a people?

1. **Make the sacrifices the Lord requires now**—our time, talents, and possessions—for the building up of the kingdom of God upon the earth, and for the establishment of Zion.
2. **Pay tithing and fast offerings, and give generously in other ways to those in need.** By doing this, we can help care for the poor and carry on the important activities of the Church. Thus, each of us could, individually, calculate what is surplus in our means and give it willingly to the Church in support of any of its vital programs.
3. **Serve willingly in the Church.** The Lord has admonished each person to "learn his duty, and to act in the office in which he is appointed, in all diligence" (D&C 107:99).
4. **Serve as a full-time missionary**. Elder Robert D. Hales observed, "Going on a mission teaches you to live the law of consecration. It may be the only time in your life when you can give to the Lord all your time, talents, and resources. In return, the Lord will bless you with His Spirit to be with you. He will be close to you and strengthen you."[40]
5. **Develop Christlike love for others.** "Every man seeking the interest of his neighbor" (D&C 82:19) is the foundation of the law of consecration.

6. **Strive to consecrate willingly.** We must willingly consecrate, not do so grudgingly. The revelations tell us that "the Lord requireth the heart and a willing mind; and the willing and obedient shall eat the good of the land of Zion in these last days" (D&C 64:34). Willingness is manifested by our attitude as well as our actions.

THE CONNECTION BETWEEN CONSECRATION AND ZION

- **D&C 82:19–21 Zion is "every man seeking the interest of his neighbor."** I know of no more precise definition of Zion than this one—that every man should seek "the interest of his neighbor, and [do] all things with an eye single to the glory of God" (v. 19). This is the order of things that the Lord has "appointed to be an everlasting order unto you, and unto your successors" (v. 20).

  Christ will not come until a Zion people are prepared to receive Him. And we will never become a Zion people until we lose the tendency to care only for ourselves without regard for the welfare of our neighbors, both member and nonmember. Selfishness and isolation can have no place in Zion. And he who "hardeneth his heart against [this law], . . . shall be delivered over to the buffetings of Satan until the day of redemption" (v. 21).

- **D&C 97:18–20 Zion will become "very glorious" and "very great."** The promise of the Lord concerning Zion is sure: "Behold, if Zion do these things she shall prosper, and spread herself and become very glorious, very great, and very terrible. And the nations of the earth shall honor her, and shall say: Surely Zion is the city of our God, and surely Zion cannot fall, neither be moved out of her place, for God is there, and the hand of the Lord is there; and he hath sworn by the power of his might to be her salvation and her high tower."

- **D&C 97:21 Zion is "the pure in heart."** "Zion is not only a location but a condition as well. The Lord declares that a person worthy of

Zion is one who is 'pure in heart.'"[41] Hyrum Smith characterized Zion as "the honest and pure in heart that will h[e]arken to the everlasting covenant."[42]

Notes

1. See Moses 7:17–21, 67–69.
2. See Joseph Smith Translation, Genesis 14:25–40 (in the Bible appendix).
3. See Doctrine and Covenants 84:23–25.
4. See 4 Nephi 1:2–3, 15–16, 22–26.
5. Joseph Smith, in "Lucy Mack Smith, History, 1844–1845, Pages [6–7], bk. 14," pp. [6–7], bk. 14, The Joseph Smith Papers, accessed August 9, 2017, http://www.josephsmithpapers.org/paper-summary/lucy-mack-smith-history-1844-1845/172
6. Joseph Smith, in *History of the Church,* 2:487, 488.
7. Heber C. Kimball, in Orson F. Whitney, *Life of Heber C. Kimball* (1945), 99.
8. Hugh W. Nibley, *Approaching Zion,* ed. Don E. Norton (1989), 347.
9. Heber C. Kimball, in Orson F. Whitney, *Life of Heber C. Kimball,* 101.
10. Heber C. Kimball, in Orson F. Whitney, *Life of Heber C. Kimball,* 101.
11. Orson F. Whitney, in *Life of Heber C. Kimball,* 181.
12. Joseph Smith, in Edward Stevenson, *The Life and History of Elder Edward Stevenson* (n.d.), 40–41.
13. Brigham Young, "Discourse," *Deseret News,* June 20, 1855, 117.
14. Hugh W. Nibley, *Approaching Zion,* 349–50.
15. *Teachings of Presidents of the Church: Joseph Smith* (2007), 427.
16. Joseph Smith, in *History of the Church,* 3:301.
17. Joseph Smith, in *History of the Church,* 3:391.
18. *Teachings of Presidents of the Church: Joseph Smith,* 213.
19. *Teachings of Presidents of the Church: Joseph Smith,* 278.
20. *Teachings of Presidents of the Church: Joseph Smith,* 144.
21. Hugh W. Nibley, *Approaching Zion,* 353.

22. Wilford Woodruff, in *Wilford Woodruff: History of His Life and Labors as Recorded in His Daily Journals,* ed. Matthias F. Cowley (1909), 166.

23. Wilford Woodruff, in *Wilford Woodruff: History of His Life and Labors as Recorded in His Daily Journals,* 169.

24. Brigham Young, in *Wilford Woodruff: History of His Life and Labors as Recorded in His Daily Journals,* 320.

25. *Teachings of Presidents of the Church: Brigham Young* (1997), 114.

26. Heber C. Kimball, in Orson F. Whitney, *Life of Heber C. Kimball,* 389.

27. Matthias F. Cowley, in *Wilford Woodruff: History of His Life and Labors as Recorded in His Daily Journals,* 328–29.

28. Matthias F. Cowley, in *Wilford Woodruff: History of His Life and Labors as Recorded in His Daily Journals,* 317.

29. Heber C. Kimball, in *Wilford Woodruff: History of His Life and Labors as Recorded in His Daily Journals,* 356.

30. Hugh W. Nibley, *Approaching Zion,* 356.

31. From the *Manuscript History of Brigham Young* (Church Historical Archives).

32. Brigham Young, "To the Saints in Utah," *Deseret News,* Sept. 14, 1854, 96. Also in *Millennial Star,* Feb. 24, 1855, 120.

33. Brigham Young, "Remarks," *Deseret News,* Nov. 18, 1857, 291.

34. Brigham Young, "Discourse," *Deseret News,* Feb. 17, 1858, 396.

35. Joseph Smith, in *History of the Church,* 6:184.

36. J. Reuben Clark Jr., in Conference Report, Oct. 1943, 11.

37. Joseph Smith, in *History of the Church,* 6:33.

38. Joseph Smith, in *History of the Church,* 6:37–38.

39. Joseph Smith, in *History of the Church,* 1:364.

40. Robert D. Hales, "If Thou Wilt Enter into Life, Keep the Commandments," *Ensign,* May 1996, 36.

41. "Section 97: 'This Is Zion—the Pure in Heart,'" *Doctrine and Covenants Student Manual,* 2nd ed. (Church Educational System manual, 2001), 230.

42. Hyrum Smith, in *History of the Church,* 6:320.

CHAPTER 10

The Loss and Redemption of Zion

(D&C 3; 10; 57–58; 82; 85; 97–98; 101; 103; 105; 136)

A FAILURE TO ESTABLISH ZION

As soon as the Saints knew that the latter-day Zion would be established in Missouri, many of them began to gather there. They were told not to gather in haste (see D&C 58:56; 63:24; 101:68), but many did so anyway. Then, to make matters worse, as hundreds of them arrived in Missouri, they told the settlers there that they would soon own the entire countryside because this was going to be the Lord's Zion.

We can imagine what it might have been like to be Missourians, having a large number of exuberant religious people moving in among you and listening to them say they would soon own everything. Little wonder that the Saints were not warmly welcomed. Their disobedience in "gathering in haste" and lack of charity toward all men were setting the stage for violence.

The Prophet Joseph Smith sent a letter to Church leaders in Missouri on August 6, 1833, in response to questions concerning the School of Zion. The letter contained Doctrine and Covenants 97 (given August 2, 1833) and Doctrine and Covenants 98 (given August 6, 1833). In Doctrine and Covenants 97, the Lord warned the inhabitants of Zion to observe His commandments or they would be visited "with sore affliction, with pestilence, with plague, with sword, with vengeance, with devouring fire" (v. 26). As it turned out, the Saints did not fully repent, and the promised devastation followed in late October and early November of 1833.[1]

"Increased settlement of Church members in Missouri troubled some other settlers, who felt threatened by the Saints' numbers, political and economic influence, and cultural and religious differences."[2] Worse still, the Saints were largely Notherners while the Missourians were largely Southerners, making the issue of slaveholding a point of further contention.

SAINTS DRIVEN FROM JACKSON COUNTY,

It did not take long until the citizens of Jackson County took up arms in order to drive the Saints off their lands. The mobs were merciless, driving the Saints north across the Missouri River (out of Jackson County into Clay County) in winter conditions that caused great suffering.

- **D&C 97:1–2, 25–26 The Lord blessed many of the Saints in Zion (Jackson County) for their faithfulness.** In this revelation, the Lord said He desired to make known His will concerning the Saints in Zion. Many of them had truly humbled themselves and were seeking wisdom (v. 1). Because of their repentance they could be blessed, but those who would not humble themselves would be brought "unto judgment" (v. 2). The Lord also said that if Zion would do His will she would escape punishment (v. 25), but if not, she would be visited "with sore affliction, with pestilence, with plague, with sword, with vengeance, with devouring fire" (v. 26).

  When the Prophet Joseph Smith received Doctrine and Covenants sections 97 and 98, the trouble between the Saints and the Missourians had violently escalated, and some of the Saints had been savagely driven from their homes.[3] "Although some news of the problems in Missouri had no doubt reached the Prophet in Kirtland (nine hundred miles away), the seriousness of the situation could have been known to him at this date [August 6, 1833] only by revelation."[4]

- **D&C 97:6–9 The Lord accepted those who observed their covenants.** But for those who did not keep their covenants, the "ax [was] laid" for their destruction (v. 7). Some of the brethren in Zion needed to be "chastened" and "their works . . . made known" (v. 6). Those among them whose "hearts [were] honest, and . . . broken, and their spirits contrite, and [were] willing to observe their covenants by sacrifice—yea, every sacrifice which I, the Lord, shall command—they are accepted of me" (v. 8). The Lord will "cause them to bring forth as a very fruitful tree which is planted in a goodly land, by a pure stream, that yieldeth much precious fruit" (v. 9).

- **D&C 97:22–28 Zion shall escape the Lord's scourge if she is faithful.** We are in the last days, and "vengeance cometh speedily upon the ungodly as the whirlwind; and who shall escape it? The Lord's scourge shall pass over by night and by day, and the report thereof shall vex all people; yea, it shall not be stayed until the Lord come; for the indignation of the Lord is kindled against their abominations and all their wicked works" (vv. 22–24).

  Nevertheless, in the midst of all these judgments upon the world, "Zion shall escape if she observe to do all things whatsoever I have commanded her" (v. 25). "But if she observe not to do whatsoever I have commanded her, I will visit her according to all her works, with sore affliction, with pestilence, with plague, with sword, with vengeance, with devouring fire" (v. 26)—punishments similar to those reserved for the wicked.

  The Saints in Missouri were guilty of serious transgressions. They were now, for a while, in a repentant state of mind, and the Lord "accepted of her [Zion's] offering; and if she sin no more none of these things shall come upon her; and I will bless her with blessings, and multiply a multiplicity of blessings upon her, and upon her generations forever and ever" (vv. 27–28).

  The Prophet Joseph Smith warned:

  > Repent, repent, is the voice of God to Zion; and strange as it may appear, yet it is true, mankind will persist in self- justification until all their iniquity is exposed, and their character past being redeemed. . . . Hear the warning voice of God, lest Zion fall, and the Lord swear in His wrath the inhabitants of Zion shall not enter into His rest.[5]

That which followed was an echo of the failures of Zion among the children of Israel and also among the early Christian Church.

Wickedness and Covetousness

In Kirtland, the Prophet Joseph Smith said that "he had been trampled under foot by aspiring Elders, for all were infected with that spirit."[6] What was that spirit?—searching for riches.

- **D&C 104:52 In both Kirtland and Missouri, "the covenants [were] being broken through transgression, by covetousness and feigned words."** Greed, hypocrisy, and pious self-justification were everywhere,[7] even among some of the Apostles and other leaders.
- **D&C 105:3 The Saints failed to fully repent, and were "full of all manner of evil."** The Prophet Joseph Smith observed that "intemperance, immorality, extravagance, pride, blindness of heart, idolatry, the loss of natural affection, the love of this world, and indifference toward the things of eternity [are] increasing among those [Latter-day Saints] who profess a belief in the religion of heaven."[8]
- **D&C 105:1 Zion might have been established already** "were it not for the transgressions of my people."
- **D&C 105:5–6 The Saints would need to be chastened until they learned obedience** "if it needs be, by the things which they suffer."

A Failure to Live the Law of Consecration

- **D&C 105:3–4 The Saints failed to live the law of consecration.** They did not "impart of their substance, as becometh saints, to the poor and afflicted among them," as well as disunity.
- **D&C 105:9, 34 As a result of all this, the law of consecration was revoked,** and by 1834 the plan for an early Zion was abandoned (D&C 104:47).

The Saints were driven out of Jackson County and eventually out of the state of Missouri. The establishment of Zion would have to wait.

WHEN WILL ZION BE REDEEMED?

Was this to be a repeat of the total failure of the children of Israel under Moses to establish Zion? Certainly, disobedience and a lack of holiness (including consecration) had made the early Latter-day Saints unworthy of Zion. But this is the final dispensation, and the Lord will yet establish a Zion people in Jackson County Missouri, prior to His Second Coming.

- **D&C 101:43–62 A parable concerning the redemption of Zion.** With the parable contained in these verses, the Lord reminded the Saints that disobedience had weakened them and allowed their enemies to overpower them. Thus, the redemption of Zion could not take place at that time.

JOHN MARTIN, 1841

However, the Lord assured them that Zion would eventually be redeemed. In the meantime, the servant (who represents the Prophet Joseph Smith) was commanded to "go ye straightway, and do all things whatsoever I have commanded you" (v. 60; see also v. 55; D&C 103:21).

— **D&C 101:60 The redemption of Zion will occur "when I will."** We must focus on doing "all things whatsoever I have commanded you" and become a Zion people who are worthy of inheriting that blessed land.

— **D&C 101:62 The promise concerning Zion will be fulfilled "after many days,"** which indicates that a long period of time will pass before Zion will be redeemed.[9]

— **D&C 136:18 "Zion shall be redeemed in mine own due time."** The Lord told President Brigham Young that the Saints should not worry about the land of Zion until the Lord is ready to redeem it. The redemption of Zion still had not taken place even after the Saints had been expelled from Missouri and from Nauvoo. The redemption of Zion (meaning the city of New Jerusalem in Missouri) is still future, although of course it is much closer now than it was when the Saints first sought to regain their inheritance in the land of Zion.[10]

— **D&C 58:44 The time for Zion's redemption "has not yet come."** And it will not come "for many years." The Saints will "receive their inheritance in this land" only when they "desire it through the prayer of faith, only as it shall be appointed unto them of the Lord."

— **D&C 105:15, 37 The Lord will destroy His enemies "not many years hence."** The Lord has sent forth His angels "to destroy and lay waste mine enemies," and none will be "left to pollute mine heritage, and to blaspheme my name upon the lands which I have consecrated for the gathering together of my saints" (v. 15). And then the Saints will be given "power after many days to accomplish all things pertaining to Zion" (v. 37).

WHAT SHOULD WE DO UNTIL THEN?

- **D&C 101:63–75 Continue the work of the gathering.** Even though the center place of Zion had fallen to the enemy, the Lord made it clear that the Saints were to continue to gather together in whatsoever places He had appointed for the gathering of His people (v. 67).[11]

  — **The "wheat" will be gathered together and "secured in the garners** [stakes and temples] to possess eternal life, and be crowned with celestial glory, when I shall come in the kingdom of my Father to reward every man according as his work shall be" (v. 65).

  — **The "tares" will be bound together "in bundles,"** so that "their bands [can be] made strong, that they may be burned with unquenchable fire" (v. 66).

  — **The Saints are commanded to "continue to gather together unto the places which I have appointed"** (v. 67). In our day, these places are the stakes of Zion throughout the world, which are "holy places" (see D&C 101:21–22).

  — **The gathering is to be orderly, not chaotic.** "Let not your gathering be in haste, nor by flight; but let all things be prepared before you" (v. 68; see also D&C 58:56; 63:24).

- **"Purchase all the lands [of gathering] with money."** There can be no question about the title to those lands, including the properties in the land of Zion (v. 70). The Saints were to buy "all the land which can be purchased in Jackson county, and the counties round about, and leave the residue in mine hand" (v. 71; see also D&C 42:35; 48:4; 57:4–5, 8).
- **"Let these things be done in their time, but not in haste;** and observe to have all things prepared before you" (v. 72).
- **"Honorable men" and "wise men" should be appointed to purchase and manage these lands** so that the Saints can "gather together upon them" and in this way "establish Zion" (vv. 73–74).

- **D&C 101:96–101 Hold claim on all property in Jackson County.** Even though Zion had been temporarily abandoned, the Lord had not set it aside: it shall yet become the center place of Zion. Although the Saints' properties had been taken from them, they were not to consent to it legally by selling their property in Zion (vv. 96–97). "Therefore, it is my will that my people should claim, and hold claim upon that which I have appointed unto them, though they should not be permitted to dwell thereon" (v. 99). The day will come when the Saints "shall dwell thereon" (v. 100). "They shall build, and another shall not inherit it; they shall plant vineyards, and they shall eat the fruit thereof" (v. 101; see also Isaiah 65:21; D&C 64:34).

- **D&C 103:20 "In time ye shall possess the goodly land."** These words, pronounced by the Lord in 1834, do not suggest an immediate redemption of Zion. Rather, they imply a period somewhat distant in time from that moment.

  President Joseph Fielding Smith provided this insight:

  > It appears from this declaration ["in time"] that the redemption of Zion was not to come immediately, but was to be postponed to some future day. Moreover, that day would not come until the members of the Church were willing to keep their covenants and walk unitedly, for until the members of the Church learn to walk in full accord and in obedience with all of the commandments, this day cannot come. It may be necessary in order to bring this to pass for the Lord to use drastic measures and cleanse the Church

from everything that offends. This He has promised to do when He is ready to redeem Zion [see Matthew 13:41].[12]

- **D&C 82:14 "Zion must increase in beauty."** Before Zion can be acceptable to the Lord, she must increase "in beauty, in holiness; her borders must be enlarged; her stakes must be strengthened" and "Zion must arise and put on her beautiful garments" (suggesting temple ordinances and covenants). This is what the Church is doing today, preparing and improving herself until the time when she will be fully acceptable unto the Lord.

  President Harold B. Lee expounded:

  > To be worthy of such a sacred designation as Zion, the Church must think of itself as a bride adorned for her husband, as John the Revelator recorded when he saw in vision the Holy City where the righteous dwelled, adorned as a bride for the Lamb of God as her husband. Here is portrayed the relationship the Lord desires in His people in order to be acceptable to our Lord and Master even as a wife would adorn herself in beautiful garments for her husband.
  >
  > The rule by which the people of God must live in order to be worthy of acceptance in the sight of God is indicated [in D&C 82:14]. This people must increase in beauty before the world; have an inward loveliness which may be observed by mankind as a reflection in holiness and in those inherent qualities of sanctity. The borders of Zion, where the righteous and pure in heart may dwell, must now begin to be enlarged. The stakes of Zion must be strengthened. All this so that Zion may arise and shine by becoming increasingly diligent in carrying out the plan of salvation throughout the world.[13]

HOW WILL ZION BE REDEEMED?

- **D&C 103 On February 24, 1834, the Lord commanded that Zion's Camp be organized.** The brethren in Kirtland, including the Prophet Joseph Smith, felt the need to organize an army to go to Missouri and restore the Saints to their lands in Jackson County. "Zion's Camp was formally organized in New Portage, Ohio," on May 6, 1834.

"[Zion's Camp] eventually included 207 men, 11 women, and 11 children."[14] Joseph led one company west from Ohio, and Hyrum Smith led another one from areas northward and westward, including Ohio, Michigan, and Illinois. Both companies united at the Salt River in eastern Missouri on June 8 before heading west across the state toward Liberty. By June 18, "Zion's Camp arrived within a mile of Richmond, the county seat of Ray County."[15] "Instead of reaching their intended destination of Liberty, they camped just inside Clay County on a hill between two branches of the Fishing River."[16] There the Lord provided a miraculous, fierce storm that prevented angry Missouri mobbers from attempting to kill the members of Zion's Camp.

- **D&C 103:13–16 Zion will be redeemed "by power."** The Lord promised the redemption of Zion and its people, "even their restoration to the land of Zion, to be established, no more to be thrown down" (v. 13). But if they polluted their inheritances "they shall be thrown down" (v. 14). "The redemption of Zion must needs come by power" and the Lord will "raise up unto my people a man, who shall lead them like as Moses led the children of Israel" (vv. 15–16).

No doubt the Saints thought Zion's Camp would be the means whereby Zion would be redeemed "by power." However, by the time Zion's Camp arrived in Missouri, Governor Daniel Dunklin had changed his mind about helping them, and any ensuing bloodshed would have accomplished nothing positive. Some of the men in the camp were angry and rebellious when they learned that the Lord did not want them to fight, and, as a result, He sent a plague of cholera upon them. Fourteen members of Zion's Camp died from this plague.

The true purpose of the march of Zion's Camp was to identify those men who would remain faithful under all circumstances. It was also to give them a chance to be with the Prophet Joseph Smith for an extended period of time, where they could observe the miracles he performed and the righteousness with which he led. Also, members of Zion's Camp learned how to move the Saints through the wilderness as an organized body. This would become important to Brigham Young and others later on when the Saints were driven from Missouri and subsequently driven out of Nauvoo.

"In February 1835, [several] months after [Zion's Camp] was disbanded, the Quorum of the Twelve Apostles and the First Quorum of the Seventy were organized. Nine of the Twelve Apostles and all 70 members of the Quorum of the Seventy had served in Zion's Camp."[17]

The Saints Will Return to Build Up Zion

- **D&C 103:11–12 The redemption of Zion will come later, "after much tribulation."** (v. 12; see also D&C 58:4). A careful reading of Doctrine and Covenants 103 shows that the Lord did not intend to redeem Zion immediately. There were yet many years of tribulation, growth, and repentance that would be necessary to prepare a Zion people.
- **D&C 58:2–4 Great blessings come only "after much tribulation."** The Lord told the Saints about two and a half years earlier, in August 1831, that those who "keepeth my commandments, whether in life or in death; and [are] faithful in tribulation" will receive a reward that is "greater in the kingdom of heaven" (v. 2).

  "Ye cannot behold with your natural eyes, for the present time, the design of your God concerning those things which shall come hereafter, and the glory which shall follow after much tribulation" (v. 3).

  "For after much tribulation come the blessings. Wherefore the day cometh that ye shall be crowned with much glory; the hour is not yet, but is nigh at hand" (v. 4).
- **D&C 85:7 "One mighty and strong" will lead the Saints to Zion.** This prophecy is not crystal clear even to us today. Some apostates claim that the Church has gone astray and that this "one mighty and strong" will return it to its purity. And, as Elder Mark E. Petersen noted, "Without any evidence of modesty whatsoever on their parts, they themselves volunteer for the position."[18] Suffice it to say, the Saints will be returned to Zion "by power" (see D&C 103:15–16).

Building Up the "Waste Places of Zion"

- **D&C 101:18 The "pure in heart" will "build up the waste places of Zion."** The meaning of the term *waste* is "wild and uninhabited."[19]

This seems to suggest that Zion, at the time of its redemption, will be "empty." But we need to be careful in our interpretations of these prophecies. Like Zion's Camp, we may be "looking beyond the mark" (see Jacob 4:14) and reasoning literally rather than symbolically.

Elder Orson Hyde stated:

> The scripture [D&C 101:18; see also D&C 103:11] says that in the last days His people will go forth and build up the waste places of Zion. But they must first be made desolate, before they can be called "the waste places of Zion." Then the hands of the Saints will be required to build them up.[20]

Palmyra New York Temple (near the Sacred Grove)

However, this does not say that Zion will be "empty" or "desolate" in the physical sense.

Nauvoo Illinois Temple (built on the original site)

Consider, for example, how all the former places of Zion in these last days were abandoned by the Saints and then, after many years, built back up. Virtually all the historical sites in Vermont, New York, Ohio, Missouri, and Illinois have been "redeemed" and "built up" as locations for Zion's people. Many of these sites are now numbered among the stakes of Zion and some even have temples located on or near them. Is not this the building up of "waste places" in terms of Zion's purpose?

Winter Quarters Nebraska Temple (near the cemetery)

Some might insist on a literal interpretation of an "empty Zion" because of statements like the "yellow dog" prophecy, which says there will not be left so much as a yellow dog to wag its tail in welcome when we return to Zion in Missouri. Careful examination of this so-called prophecy shows that it is an unsubstantiated myth.[21]

President Joseph F. Smith made a more substantiated statement in 1882:

> When God leads the people back to Jackson County, how will He do it? Let me picture to you how some of us may be gathered and led to Jackson County. I think I see two or three hundred thousand people wending their way across the great plain, enduring the nameless hardships of the journey, herding and guarding their cattle by day and by night, and defending themselves and little ones from foes on the right hand and on the left, as when they came here. They will find the journey back to Jackson County will be as real as when they came out here. Now, mark it. . . . This is one way to look at it. It is certainly a practical view. Some might ask, what will become of the railroads? I fear that the sifting process would be insufficient were we to travel by railroads.[22]

Elder Graham W. Doxey commented on President Joseph F. Smith's foregoing statement:

> This is a vivid mental picture, but people frequently remember the picture and forget he said "*some* of us" and "*may* be gathered." We should also keep in mind that he said this is "one way to look at it," remembering also the perspective of 1882. From our perspective [as of] 1979, it seems even less likely that we would sell our automobiles and herd cattle along our freeway systems. But we simply have no scriptural information about who—if any general Church members—will be called to go back and the means that they might use. The prophets of our day have not found it timely or necessary to speak on the matter.[23]

Kansas City Missouri Temple (near Independence, Missouri)

"Elder Orson Pratt taught that the Saints would go back to Missouri and possess the properties they had once inhabited in the early days of the Church, after God's judgments have made the cities desolate."[24] We should remember that Missouri was made more desolate during the Civil War than any other state in the Union.[25] And it has only been in recent years that Missouri's spiritual desolation has begun to be mitigated. Now we actually have two temples there: one in St. Louis and another in Kansas City.

Where Will the Saints Gather?

Some have imagined that the entire membership of the Church from around the world will gather to the New Jerusalem. This is not the case. Zion has now become worldwide, with stakes on every continent, and most of those stakes have a temple nearby.[26]

Elder Bruce R. McConkie explained:

> The place of gathering for the Mexican Saints is in Mexico; the place of gathering for the Guatemalan Saints is in Guatemala; the place of gathering for the Brazilian Saints is in Brazil; and so it goes throughout the length and breadth of the whole earth. Japan is for the Japanese; Korea is for the Koreans; Australia is for the Australians; every nation is the gathering place for its own people.[27]

And Elder Doxey observed:

> During the time of Joseph Smith and Brigham Young, it was essential for members of the Church to "gather to Zion" for their own spiritual and physical safety. But now that temples, welfare projects, educational facilities, genealogical research libraries, and the blessings of a full church organization in stakes are available, this gathering is no longer required or wise. And although the Church purchased some [Clay County, Missouri] land last December [in 1978], it was solely for investment purposes—not for other Church use.[28]

Some Will Return to Jackson County

Still, some will in fact be called upon to build the New Jerusalem in Jackson County, Missouri. President Brigham Young revealed, "A portion of the Priesthood will go and redeem and build up the cent[er] Stake of Zion."[29] He later added, "Are we going back to Jackson County? Yes. When? As soon as the way opens up. Are we all going? O no! of course not. The country is not large enough to hold our present numbers."[30]

President Joseph Fielding Smith remarked: "The *center place* where the City New Jerusalem is to be built, is in Jackson County, Missouri. It was never the intention to substitute Utah or any other place for Jackson County."[31]

And Elder Orson F. Whitney asked:

> Will our mission end here [in Utah]? Is the State of Utah the proper monument of the "Mormon" People? No. . . . The monument to "Mormonism" will stand in Jackson County, Missouri. There the great City will be built: there Zion will arise and shine, "the joy of the whole earth," and there the Lord will come to His Temple in His own time, when His people shall have made the required preparation.[32]

In 1853, President Heber C. Kimball promised the Saints in Utah:

> I know you will prosper and live in peace in the mountains of the Great Salt Lake, and be perfectly independent. You will have food and raiment, houses and lands, flocks and herds, and everything your hearts can desire, that there is in heaven and on earth, *if you will do as you are told*. . . . You will live in peace and God will be your defen[s]e . . . I have said often, you may go and write blessings for yourselves, and insert every good thing you can think of, . . . and it will all come to pass on your heads, *if you do right*.[33]

Four years later, President Kimball predicted:

> We never shall leave these valleys—till we get ready; no, never; no, never[!] We will live here till we go back to Jackson County, Missouri. I prophesy that, in the name of Israel's God.[34]

Only a Zion People Can Build the New Jerusalem

While Zion is now all over the world, there is no doubt that the central location of Zion in Jackson County, Missouri, will be a special place. That is where the New Jerusalem will be built, and only a Zion people will be permitted to do that. This means a people who will obey all the laws of the celestial kingdom, including consecration (see D&C 105:5). Can we expect to build "the city of our God" (D&C 97:19) on any other basis?

President Joseph F. Smith inquired:

> But when shall I be prepared to go there? Not while I have in my heart the love of this world more than the love of God. Not while I am possessed of that selfishness and greed that would induce me to cling to the world or my possessions in it, at the sacrifice of principle or truth. But when I am ready to say, "Father, all that I have, myself included, is Thine; my time, my substance, everything that I possess is on the altar, to be used freely, agreeable to Thy holy will, and not my will, but Thine, be done," then perhaps I will be prepared to go and help to redeem Zion.[35]

THE ULTIMATE TRIUMPH OF GOD'S WORK

- **D&C 3:3; 10:43 God's work will not be frustrated.** The enemies of the Church, including its apostates, vainly imagine that they can change the course of the Lord's kingdom in these latter days. However, "it is not the work of God that is frustrated, but the work of men" (D&C 3:3). The Lord promised that He "will not suffer that they shall destroy my work; yea, I will show unto them that my wisdom is greater than the cunning of the devil" (D&C 10:43).
- **D&C 58:3–4, 6–7 Great blessings are in store for the Lord's righteous Saints.** "Ye cannot behold with your natural eyes, for the

present time, the design of your God concerning those things which shall come hereafter, and the glory which shall follow after much tribulation. For after much tribulation come the blessings. Wherefore the day cometh that ye shall be crowned with much glory; the hour is not yet, but is nigh at hand" (vv. 3–4).

The Lord said further, "Behold, verily I say unto you, for this cause I have sent you—that you might be obedient, and that your hearts might be prepared to bear testimony of the things which are to come; and also that you might be honored in laying the foundation, and in bearing record of the land upon which the Zion of God shall stand" (vv. 6–7). Can we imagine any greater honor than that?

No Unhallowed Hand Can Stop God's Work

In his letter to John Wentworth, the Prophet Joseph Smith proclaimed that nothing can stop the progress of this latter-day work:

> No unhallowed hand can stop the work from progressing; persecutions may rage, mobs may combine, armies may assemble, calumny may defame, but the truth of God will go forth boldly, nobly, and independent, till it has penetrated every continent, visited every clime, swept every country, and sounded in every ear, till the purposes of God shall be accomplished, and the Great Jehovah shall say the work is done.[36]

Joseph Smith

When Will These Things Occur?

The Prophet Joseph Smith wrote:

> I know that Zion, in the due time of the Lord, will be redeemed; but how many will be the days of her purification, tribulation, and affliction, the Lord has kept hid from my eyes; and when I inquire concerning this subject, the voice of the Lord is: Be still, and know that I am God! All those who suffer for my name shall

> reign with me, and he that layeth down his life for my sake shall find it again.[37]

President Wilford Woodruff testified:

> I will say to the Latter-day Saints, as an Elder in Israel and as an Apostle of the Lord Jesus Christ, we are approaching some of the most tremendous judgments God ever poured out upon the world. You watch the signs of the times, the sign of the coming of the Son of Man. . . . Christ will not come until these things come to pass. Jerusalem has got to be rebuilt. The temple has got to be built. Judah has got to be gathered and the house of Israel. And the Gentiles will go forth to battle against Judah and Jerusalem. . . . These things have been revealed by the prophets; they will have their fulfillment. . . . All that the Latter-day Saints have to do is to be quiet, careful, and wise before the Lord, watch the signs of the times, and be true and faithful; and when you get through you will understand many things that you do not today.[38]

And Elder Bruce R. McConkie affirmed:

> We shall go forward according to the divine timetable, a timetable under which the Lord will prepare the way for us to teach the gospel in one nation after another as rapidly as our strength and means are sufficient for us to do the work.
>
> Nephi foresaw that we shall establish congregations of the Saints in all nations and among all peoples and kindreds before the promised unity of the faith. Speaking of this dispensation, he said: [1 Nephi 14:12]. . . .
>
> . . . Before the millennial era, before the time when Christ shall reign personally upon the earth, the elect of God among every kindred, the Saints who speak every tongue, the converts among all peoples and nations, having first believed the restored gospel, will go to the temples of God and receive the ordinances of exaltation whereby they qualify to become kings and priests.[39]

Notes

1. Adapted from "Section 97: 'This Is Zion—the Pure in Heart,'" *Doctrine and Covenants Student Manual,* 2nd ed. (Church Educational System manual, 2001), 228. See also *History of the Church,* 1:390–93, 400.
2. Doctrine and Covenants 98, section introduction.
3. See Joseph Fielding Smith, *Church History and Modern Revelation,* 2 vols. (1953), 1:430, 459.
4. Doctrine and Covenants 98, section introduction.
5. *Teachings of Presidents of the Church: Joseph Smith* (2007), 187.
6. Joseph Smith, in *History of the Church,* 4:604.
7. See Hugh W. Nibley, *Approaching Zion,* ed. Don E. Norton (1989), 345.
8. *Teachings of Presidents of the Church: Joseph Smith,* 151.
9. Adapted from "Section 101: 'The Saints Are "Cast Out from the Land of Their Inheritance,"'" *Doctrine and Covenants Student Manual,* 243.
10. Adapted from "Section 101: 'The Saints Are "Cast Out from the Land of Their Inheritance,"'" 243.
11. Adapted from "Lesson 27: 'They Must Needs Be Chastened and Tried, Even as Abraham,'" *Doctrine and Covenants and Church History Gospel Doctrine Teacher's Manual,* 156.
12. Joseph Fielding Smith, *Church History and Modern Revelation,* 1:484.
13. Harold B. Lee, "Strengthen the Stakes of Zion," *Ensign,* July 1973, 3.
14. "Chapter Three: Building the Kingdom in Kirtland, Ohio," *Our Heritage: A Brief History of The Church of Jesus Christ of Latter-day Saints* (1996), 27.
15. "Chapter Twelve: Zion's Camp," *Church History in the Fulness of Times Student Manual,* 2nd ed. (Church Educational System manual, 2003), 148.
16. "Chapter Twelve: Zion's Camp," 148.
17. "Lesson 27: 'They Must Needs Be Chastened and Tried, Even as Abraham,'" 153.
18. Mark E. Petersen, "Salvation Comes through the Church," *Ensign,* July 1973, 110.
19. *Webster's New Collegiate Dictionary,* "Waste."
20. Orson Hyde, "Remarks," *Deseret News,* Jan. 25, 1865, 130.
21. See Graham W. Doxey, "Missouri Myths," *Ensign,* Apr. 1979, 65.
22. Joseph F. Smith, "Discourse," *Deseret News,* July 18, 1883, 403. This discourse was originally delivered in the Provo Tabernacle, Sunday, Dec. 3, 1882.
23. Graham W. Doxey, "Missouri Myths," 64–65.

24. "Section 101: 'The Saints Are "Cast Out from the Land of Their Inheritance,"'" 240. See also Orson Pratt, in *Deseret Evening News,* Oct. 2, 1875, 265.

25. See Paul DeBry, *The Destruction of Jackson County, Missouri, in the Civil War,* rev. ed. (2010), xiv–xv, 47–59, 80–81. See also B. H. Roberts, *A Comprehensive History of the Church,* 1:533–59. See also Oliver B. Huntington, in Hyrum L. Andrus and Helen Mae Andrus, comps., *They Knew the Prophet: Personal Accounts from over 100 People Who Knew Joseph Smith* (2004), 62–63.

26. See Thomas S. Monson, "The Holy Temple—a Beacon to the World," *Ensign* or *Liahona,* May 2011, 92.

27. Bruce R. McConkie, in Conference Report, Mexico and Central America Area Conference 1972, 45.

28. Graham W. Doxey, "Missouri Myths," 65.

29. Brigham Young, "Remarks," *Deseret News,* Dec. 28, 1864, 98.

30. Brigham Young, "Discourse," *Deseret News,* May 23, 1877, 247.

31. Joseph Fielding Smith, *Doctrines of Salvation,* comp. Bruce R. McConkie, 3 vols. (1954–56), 3:72.

32. Orson F. Whitney, in Conference Report, Apr. 1916, 68.

33. Heber C. Kimball, "Discourse," *Deseret News,* Mar. 30, 1854, 38; emphasis added. This discourse was originally delivered at a special conference in Salt Lake City, Saturday, Aug. 13, 1853. See also Heber C. Kimball, in Orson F. Whitney, *Life of Heber C. Kimball* (1945), 398.

34. Heber C. Kimball, "Discourse," *Deseret News,* Sept. 9, 1857, 211. See also Heber C. Kimball, in Orson F. Whitney, *Life of Heber C. Kimball* (1945), 398.

35. Joseph F. Smith, in *Millennial Star,* June 18, 1894, 385–86.

36. *Teachings of Presidents of the Church: Joseph Smith,* 142.

37. *Teachings of Presidents of the Church: Joseph Smith,* 186.

38. Wilford Woodruff, in *Millennial Star,* Nov. 24, 1890, 740. Also in *The Discourses of Wilford Woodruff,* sel. G. Homer Durham (1946), 211.

39. Bruce R. McConkie, in Conference Report, Apr. 1969, 144.

CHAPTER 11

Return of the Lost Ten Tribes[1]

(DEUT. 30; ISAIAH 11; JER. 23; REVELATION 7; 1 NEPHI 22; 2 NEPHI 21; 3 NEPHI 21; D&C 77; 110; 133)

THE LOST TEN TRIBES

How Were They Lost?

J.S.V. CAROLSFELD, CA. 1852–60

When Assyria conquered the Northern Kingdom of Israel (ca. 722–21 B.C.), they took at least 27,290 captives from Samaria (the Northern Kingdom's capital city). It may be that the total number taken captive by the Assyrians was in the hundreds of thousands. These captives were resettled in the area of northwestern Mesopotamia, toward the upper reaches of the Tigris and Euphrates rivers. This region to which they were exiled corresponds to modern-day eastern Syria, northern Iraq, northwestern Iran, and the Armenian region of eastern Turkey.

When Assyria later fell to the Medes led by Cyaxares (ca. 614–10 B.C.), the lands occupied by many of these captive Israelites (including Halah and Habor) also came under the control of the Medes. Subsequently, sometime during the early part of the sixth century B.C., some of the Israelites held captive by Assyria migrated northward.

- **1 Nephi 22:4 Nephi may have been speaking of these migrants when he wrote:** "Behold, there are many who are already lost from the knowledge of those who are at Jerusalem. Yea, the more part of all the tribes have been led away."

- **2 Esdras (4 Ezra) 13:40–47 The best account of this departure** is found in the apocryphal book of 2 Esdras (also called 4 Ezra), written by Jewish record keepers:

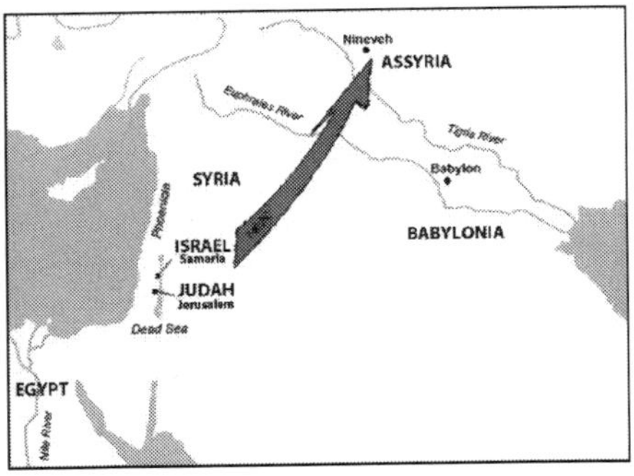

  "These are the ten tribes which were led away captive out of their own land in the days of Josiah [Hoshea] the king, which (tribes) [Shalmaneser] the king of the Assyrians led away captive; he carried them across the River, and (thus) they were transported into another land. But they took this counsel among themselves, that they would leave the multitude of the heathen, and go forth into a land further distant, where the human race had never dwelt, there at least to keep their statutes which they had not kept in their own land. And they entered by the narrow passages of the river Euphrates. For the Most High then wrought wonders for them, and stayed the springs of the River until they were passed over. And through that country there was a great way to go, (a journey) of a year and a half; and that region was called Arzareth. There they have dwelt until the last times."[2]

- **2 Kings 17:6, 18:11; 1 Chronicles 5:26 The ten tribes were taken across the Euphrates River on the way to their places of captivity.** Dr. Vern G. Swanson pointed out that "an escape 'by the narrow passages of the river Euphrates' (that is, in its upper reaches—see map) into 'a land further distant, where the human race had never dwelt' points to a northward direction for the subsequent migration of the tribes (the lands east, west, and south of Assyria were already inhabited at that time). This, too, agrees with a number of scriptural prophecies relative to the eventual return of those Other Tribes from the 'land of the north,' or 'north countries.'"[3]

- **Jeremiah 23:7–8 Jeremiah said this migration was a great miracle.** "Behold, the days come, saith the Lord, that they shall no more say, The Lord liveth, which brought up the children of Israel out of the land of Egypt; but, The Lord liveth, which brought up and which led the seed of the house of Israel out of the north country, and from all countries whither I had driven them; and they shall dwell in their own land."

Where Did They Go?

The Lord scattered the tribes of Israel all over the world. Precisely where we do not know for most of these tribes. We do know about the Mulekites and Lehites, who departed from Jerusalem and migrated to the New World. The word *Arzareth* itself, used in the accounts of the lost tribes, simply means "another land." Ultimately, they were scattered among many nations, leaving small remnants behind in the Northern Kingdom, in Assyria, and in the "land of the north."

- **Isaiah 11:11; 2 Nephi 21:11 Isaiah wrote about all these remnants in this well-known prophecy:** "And it shall come to pass in that day, that the Lord shall set his hand again the second time to recover the remnant of his people, which shall be left, from Assyria, and from Egypt, and from Pathros, and from Cush, and from Elam, and from Shinar, and from Hamath, and from the islands of the sea." Assyria, Elam, Shinar, and Hamath were all lands involved in the Assyrian captivity. The same principle applies to Judah: many Jews did not return to Jerusalem after establishing themselves in Babylon and in places where they fled, including the Mulekites and Lehites in the New World.

- **The lost ten tribes went forth "into a land further distant,"** and some of them undoubtedly chose to settle in the lands through which they traveled. Where were these lands? "A variety of Christian authors [have claimed that these tribes can be] identified with the Japanese, Chinese, Turks, Ethiopians, Persians, Yemenites, Nestorians, Afghans, Arabians, Britons, Kassites of Russia, Hindus and Buddhists of India, Scythians, Cimmerians, Celts, Kareens of Burma, North and South American Indians, Australians, and Eskimos. Indeed it is possible that remnants of the Other Tribes may have spread out and became part of all these peoples in fulfillment of the prophecies that Israel would spread itself throughout many countries."[4]

It was in this vacuum of reliable reformation regarding the ten tribes that in November 1831 Joseph Smith received the following revelation from the Lord:

The Ten Tribes Will Return

- **D&C 133:26–27, 30–33 "They who are in the north countries shall come in remembrance before the Lord;** and their prophets shall hear his voice, and shall no longer stay themselves; and they shall smite the rocks, and the ice shall flow down at their presence.

  "And an highway shall be cast up in the midst of the great deep. . . . And they shall bring forth their rich treasures unto the children of Ephraim, my servants. And the boundaries of the everlasting hills shall tremble at their presence.

  "And there shall they fall down and be crowned with glory, even in Zion, by the hands of the servants of the Lord, even the children of Ephraim. And they shall be filled with songs of everlasting joy."

- **D&C 110:11 Moses committed to the Prophet Joseph Smith the "keys of the gathering of Israel from the four parts of the earth, and the leading of the ten tribes from the land of the north"** on April 3, 1836, in the Kirtland Temple. Thus, we can conclude that the lost ten tribes will come to Zion, "upon the American continent" (Articles of Faith 1:10), and receive their blessings from Ephraim.

  Since Ephraim itself was one of the lost ten tribes, we can see that the promised gathering of the tribes of Israel had already begun in 1836. And since then, many individuals have been identified with other tribes, including Manasseh, in their patriarchal blessings.

- **D&C 133:18 The 144,000 who will assist in this work will stand on Mount Zion with the Lord** when He comes again, "having his Father's name written on their foreheads." According to the Prophet Joseph Smith, this "signifies sealing the blessing upon their heads, meaning the everlasting covenant, thereby making their calling and election sure."[5]

  — **D&C 77:11 Who are these 144,000?** The Prophet Joseph Smith asked and answered this question in Doctrine and Covenants 77 in the following manner:

  > Q[uestion:] What are we to understand by sealing the one hundred and forty-four thousand, out of all the tribes of Israel—twelve thousand out of every tribe?
  >
  > A[nswer:] We are to understand that those who are sealed are high priests, ordained unto the holy order of God, to administer the everlasting gospel; for they are they who are ordained out of every nation, kindred, tongue, and people, by the angels to whom is given power over the nations of the earth, to bring as many as will come to the church of the Firstborn.

- **Revelation 7:2–8 All of the tribes will be represented in the calling of the "hundred and forty and four thousand"** mentioned in John's revelation—twelve thousand high priests out of each of the twelve tribes of Israel.

- **Deuteronomy 30:1–5 Eventually, all of the tribes of Israel will return to the Old Jerusalem,** to receive with Judah the lands of their first inheritance.

  But first, "they who are in the north countries" (D&C 133:26) will come to "the boundaries of the everlasting hills" (D&C 133:31) to receive their priesthood and temple blessings.

- **D&C 133:26–33 The lost ten tribes will first gather to the New Jerusalem.**

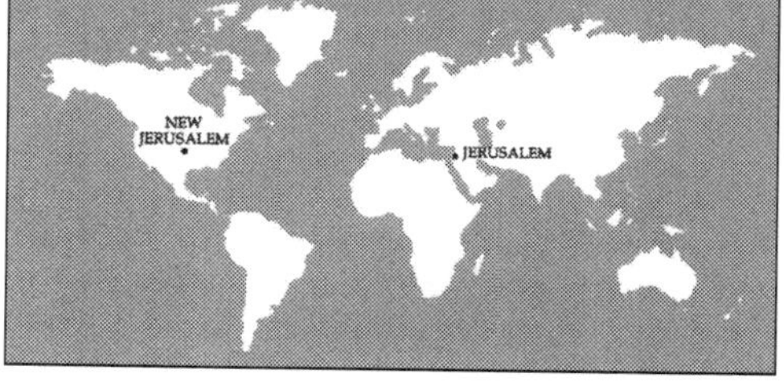

  "And they who are in the north countries shall come in remembrance before the Lord; and their prophets shall hear his voice, and shall no longer stay themselves; and they shall smite the rocks, and the ice shall flow down at their presence. And an highway shall be cast up in the midst of the great deep" (vv. 26–27).

"Their enemies shall become a prey unto them" (v. 28). "And in the barren deserts there shall come forth pools of living water; and the parched ground shall no longer be a thirsty land" (v. 29).

These tribes shall bring with them "rich treasures" to give "unto the children of Ephraim, my servants" (the priesthood leaders of the Church) (v. 30). "And the boundaries [mountains] of the everlasting hills shall tremble at their presence" (v. 31). "And there shall they fall down and be crowned with glory, even in Zion, by the hands of the servants of the Lord, even the children of Ephraim" (v. 32). This means that they will receive their temple blessings from the priesthood leaders of "Ephraim" (this Church). "And they shall be filled with songs of everlasting joy" (v. 33).

Elder Orson Pratt asked:

> How long will they who come from the north countries tarry in the heights of Zion? . . . They will dwell in Zion a good while, and during that time, there will be twelve thousand chosen out of each of these ten tribes, besides twelve thousand that will be chosen from Judah, Joseph, and the remaining tribes, one hundred and forty-four thousand in all. . . . For what purpose? . . . These parties . . . will go forth among all people, nations, and tongues, and gather up and hunt out the house of Israel, wherever they are scattered, and bring as many as they possibly can into the Church . . . , preparatory to the great day of the coming of the Lord. One hundred and forty-four thousand missionaries! Quite a host. All this has got to take place.[6]

Are the Lost Ten Tribes All in One Place?

There seems to be some controversy concerning the answer to this question. Given the information quoted above, it would appear they are in an unknown location as a "distinct remnant"[7] and will be discovered when the continents reunite (see D&C 133:23–35). Here is another point of view:

Elder Bruce R. McConkie wrote:

> *But,* says one, *are they [the lost tribes of Israel] not in a body somewhere in the land of the north?* Answer: They are not; they are scattered in all nations. The north countries of their habitation are all the countries north of their Palestinian home, north of Assyria from whence they escaped. . . .
>
> Query: *What happened to the ten tribes after the visit of the Savior to them . . . ?* Answer: The same thing that happened to the Nephites. There was righteousness for a season, and then there was apostasy and wickedness. . . .
>
> . . . In this day when the head of the Church can communicate with all men on earth, there is no longer any need for one kingdom in Jerusalem and another in
>
> Bountiful and others in whatever place or places the ten tribes were when Jesus visited them. This is the promised day when there shall be one God, one Shepherd, one prophet, one gospel, one church, and one kingdom for all the earth. This is the day when one man shall direct all of the Lord's work in all the earth; the day when he shall bring all Israel into one fold.[8]

It seems likely that both viewpoints are true. There may indeed be a group of people who will come, as a distinct body, from some location unknown to us at this time. But it is also true that these tribes are scattered all over the earth, as witnessed by the fact that patriarchal blessings of our time are revealing and naming descendants of nearly all the tribes. God knows where His children are, and wherever they are He will guide them back to His kingdom and to Zion.

Missionary Work to the Lost Ten Tribes

Missionary work was underway among the lost ten tribes during Jesus's post-Resurrection ministry to them (see 3 Nephi 16:1–4; 17:4) and also when John the Beloved was sent to them (see Revelation 10:1–2, 8–11; D&C 7:1–6).

- **D&C 77:14 The Prophet Joseph Smith gave this explanation concerning John the Beloved's mission to the lost tribes:**

  "Q. What are we to understand by the little book which was eaten by John, as mentioned in the 10th chapter of Revelation?

  "A. We are to understand that it was a mission, and an ordinance, for him to gather the tribes of Israel . . ."

- **3 Nephi 21:26–29 The gospel will be preached unto the lost ten tribes again in the latter days.** The Lord said, "The work of the Father [shall] commence at that day . . . when this gospel shall be preached among the remnant of this people . . . [and] among all the dispersed of my people, yea, even the tribes which have been lost, which the Father hath led away out of Jerusalem" (v. 26)—a reference to the lost ten tribes.

  The gospel will be preached "among all the dispersed of my people . . . to prepare the way whereby they may come unto me, that they may call on the Father in my name" (v. 27). This work will be done "among all nations in preparing the way whereby his people may be gathered home to the land of their inheritance" (v. 28). These converts will "go out from all nations; and they shall not go out in haste, nor go by flight, for I will go before them, saith the Father" (v. 29).

- **D&C 133:16–17 The gospel message will be taken to all the earth.** "Hearken and hear, O ye inhabitants of the earth. Listen, ye elders of my church together, and hear the voice of the Lord; for he calleth upon all men, and he commandeth all men everywhere to repent" (v. 16). He has sent angels from the midst of heaven with the message, "Prepare ye the way of the Lord, and make his paths straight, for the hour of his coming is nigh" (v. 17). These are the messages we are to take to all the world.

The Earth Has Been Blessed by These Tribes

President Joseph Fielding Smith explained:

> Through this scattering the Lord has caused Israel to mix with the nations and bring the Gentiles within the blessings of the seed of Abraham. We are preaching the gospel now in all parts of

> the world, and for what purpose? To gather out from the Gentile nations the lost sheep of the house of Israel. It is by this scattering that the Gentile nations have been blessed, and if they will truly repent they are entitled to all the blessings promised to Israel.[9]

And President Wilford Woodruff taught:

> Again, here are the ten tribes of Israel; we know nothing about them only what the Lord has said by His prophets. There are prophets among them, and by and by they will come along, and they will smite the rocks, and the mountains of ice will flow down at their presence, and a highway will be cast up before them, and they will come to Zion, receive their [temple] endowments, and be crowned under the hands of the children of Ephraim.[10]

In the meantime, all nations of the world have been blessed by the presence of the believing blood within their boundaries. These descendants of the tribes of Israel have been a leavening influence of righteousness in the world and are the focus of all missionary work in these last days— finding the children of Israel wherever they are and restoring to them the true knowledge of their God and King, Jesus Christ.

Notes

1. Much of the information in this chapter is adapted from Vern G. Swanson, "Israel's 'Other Tribes,'" *Ensign,* Jan. 1982, 26–31.
2. R. H. Charles, *The Apocrypha and Pseudepigrapha of the Old Testament,* 2 vols. (1964), 2:619.
3. Vern G. Swanson, "Israel's 'Other Tribes,'" 29. See also Topical Guide in the Latter-day Saint edition of the King James Version of the Bible, "Israel, Ten Lost Tribes of."
4. Vern G. Swanson, "Israel's 'Other Tribes,'" 29–30.
5. Joseph Smith, in *History of the Church,* 5:530.
6. Orson Pratt, "Discourse," *Deseret News,* June 30, 1875, 341.
7. Vern G. Swanson, "Israel's 'Other Tribes,'" 29, 30–31.

8. Bruce R. McConkie, *The Millennial Messiah: The Second Coming of the Son of Man* (1982), 216–17.

9. Joseph Fielding Smith, *Answers to Gospel Questions,* comp. Joseph Fielding Smith Jr., 5 vols. (1957–66), 2:57.

10. Wilford Woodruff, "Discourse," *Deseret News,* Mar. 4, 1857, 411. Also in *The Discourses of Wilford Woodruff,* sel. G. Homer Durham (1946), 119.

CHAPTER 12

A Temple in Old Jerusalem

(EZEKIEL 20; 28; 36–37; 40; ZEPHANIAH 3; ZECHARIAH 1–2; 8–9; 14; MALACHI 3)

We discussed in chapters 10 and 11 the redemption of the new Zion and the New Jerusalem, and the return of the ten tribes. But what about the Old Jerusalem? And what about the tribe of Judah? The Jews will also be restored and redeemed.

JUDAH AND JERUSALEM RESTORED[1]

After the fall of Jerusalem (ca. 587–86 B.C.), Ezekiel ceased prophesying about God's judgments on the people of his time. He then turned his attention to the gathering and redemption of Israel in the latter days.

This makes Ezekiel, like Isaiah and Jeremiah, a prophet of the Restoration. It also makes his writings and prophecies of particular interest to us today.

Ezekiel recorded twelve visions, and seven of them deal specifically with the last days:

— The building of the kingdom of Judah under a leader named David.

— The gathering of scattered Israel.

— The unification of all the tribes of Israel.

— The joining of the Bible and the Book of Mormon.

— The battle of Armageddon.

— The building of a modern temple in Old Jerusalem.

Israel Will Be Gathered to Her Own Lands

- **Ezekiel 20:33–34 The gathering will be accomplished with great power.** "As I live," the Lord promised, "surely with a mighty hand, and with a stretched out arm, and with fury poured out, will I rule over you" (v. 33). The evil designs of the wicked will not prevent His kingdom from being established. By His mighty power, He assured, "I will bring you out from the people, and will gather you out of the countries wherein ye are scattered" (v. 34).

- **Ezekiel 20:35–36 The gathering will be accomplished through revelation.** "And I will bring you into the wilderness of the people, and there will I plead [speak] with you face to face" (v. 35). "Like as I pleaded with your fathers in the wilderness of the land of Egypt, so will I plead with you, saith the Lord God" (v. 36).

- **Ezekiel 20:37 The people will be made "the Lord's" by covenant.** The Lord says, "I will cause you to pass under the rod [to be numbered as the flock[2]], and I will bring you into the bond of the covenant." "Passing under the rod" is a figure of speech that "alludes to the custom of *tithing* the *sheep*. . . . The sheep were all penned; and . . . only one sheep could come out *at once*. . . . [The shepherd] counted . . . and as the *tenth* came out, he marked it with the rod [dipped in vermilion], and said, 'This is . . . set apart for the Lord.'"[3] Thus, the converted Israelites will all be "marked" in the Lord's eyes as being His, and will become so through "the bond of the covenant."

- **Ezekiel 20:38 The unrighteous will be purged from among the people.** The Lord will purge out from among His people "the rebels, and them that transgress against me." These, He says, "shall not enter into the land of Israel."

- **Ezekiel 20:40–41 The gathering will be to the Lord's temple.** "For in mine holy mountain [the temple], in the mountain of the height of Israel, saith the Lord God, there shall all the house of Israel, all of them in the land, serve me: there will I accept them." In His temple He will expect His people to make covenants of sacrifice ("your offerings"), to give thanks ("the firstfruits of your oblations"), and to do all other "holy things" that are required there (v. 40). "I will accept you with your sweet savour [sacrifices], when I bring you out from the people, and gather you out of the countries wherein ye have been scattered; and I will be sanctified in you before the heathen" (v. 41).
- **Ezekiel 20:42 The gathering will be to the promised lands in the Old World and the New World.** "And ye shall know that I am the Lord, when I shall bring you into the land of Israel, into the country for the which I lifted up mine hand [covenanted[4]] to give it to your fathers." This includes, of course, the land of Israel, which was promised unto Abraham and his posterity. But it also includes the American continent, which was given to Joseph and his posterity as their own land of inheritance.
- **Ezekiel 20:43–44 When the Israelites recognize that they have rebelled against the Lord and failed to keep His commandments from the time of their deliverance from Egypt, they will "lothe" themselves in their "own sight."** "And there shall ye remember your ways, and all your doings, wherein ye have been defiled; and ye shall lothe yourselves in your own sight for all your evils that ye have committed" (v. 43). "And ye shall know that I am the Lord, when I have wrought [worked] with you for my name's sake [to keep my covenant concerning Abraham's posterity]" despite Israel's "wicked ways" and "corrupt doings" over the centuries (v. 44).
  - **D&C 45:48–53 The Savior described what the Jews' response will be when He descends onto the Mount of Olives** to save them from utter destruction at the height of the battle of Armageddon, and they see the wounds in His hands and feet: "And then shall the Lord set his foot upon this mount, and it shall cleave in twain, and the earth shall tremble, and reel to and fro, and the heavens also shall shake. And the Lord shall utter his voice, and all the ends of the earth shall hear it; and the nations of the earth shall mourn,

> and they that have laughed shall see their folly. And calamity shall cover the mocker, and the scorner shall be consumed; and they that have watched for iniquity shall be hewn down and cast into the fire. And then shall the Jews look upon me and say: What are these wounds in thine hands and in thy feet? Then shall they know that I am the Lord; for I will say unto them: These wounds are the wounds with which I was wounded in the house of my friends. I am he who was lifted up. I am Jesus that was crucified. I am the Son of God. And then shall they weep because of their iniquities; then shall they lament because they persecuted their king." (See Zechariah 12:9–14; 13:6.)

President Joseph Fielding Smith told what will happen next:

> Then they will accept Him as their Redeemer, which they have never been willing to do. Then is the time as spoken of in this passage from Zechariah when every family will go and mourn apart; the house of David, the house of Nathan, the Jews [see Zechariah 12:10–14]. They will fall down. They will rend their garments, and they will mourn and they will weep because they were not willing to accept the Son of God but accepted the teachings of their fathers and rejected their Redeemer and Messiah. Then they will fall down at His feet and worship Him. After these days will come their redemption and the building of Jerusalem. They will be given their own land again, and every man will live under his own vine and his own fig tree and they will learn to love the Lord and keep His commandments and walk in the light, and He will be their God and they will be His people.[5]

Elder Orson Pratt spoke of how the gathering of scattered Israel will be brought to pass:

> You young men who sit here on these seats will live to see the times of the Gentiles fulfilled; . . . the mission which you will receive, young men, will be to go to the scattered remnants of the house of Israel among all the nations and kingdoms of the Gentiles. To search them out and proclaim to them the message restored by the angel, that it may be preached to Israel as well as to the Gentiles. That is your destiny; that, young men, is what the Lord will require at your hands. [See 1 Nephi 13:42.] . . .

> ... And you will have the pleasure of gathering them up by thousands, tens of thousands, and hundreds of thousands, from the islands of the sea and from all quarters of the earth; for that will be a day of power far more than it is while the Gospel continues among the Gentiles.
>
> ... When the day of His power comes they [Israel] will be willing to hearken, they will gather up to their promised land, for it will be the day of the Lord's power. In what respect will there be power manifested then? As power was manifested when the Lord brought Israel from the Egyptian nation into the wilderness of Sinai and spoke to them by His own voice, so will the power of Almighty God be made manifest among all the nations of the earth when He brings about the redemption and restoration of His people Israel; or, in other words, the former display of power will be eclipsed, for that which was done in one land, among the Israelites and Egyptians in the wilderness, will be performed among all nations....
>
> ... So will He plead with Israel in the latter days, and show forth His mighty hand and power, when He gathers them from the nations; and He will give revelation as He did to their fathers in the wilderness of the land of Egypt.[6]

- **Ezekiel 28:24–26 The Lord's gathered people will dwell in peace and safety.** There will be no more "pricking brier[s]" or "grieving thorn[s]"—nations that torment and despise Israel (v. 24). For "thus saith the Lord God; When I shall have gathered the house of Israel from the people among whom they are scattered, and shall be sanctified in them in the sight of the heathen [nations or Gentiles[7]], then shall they dwell in their land that I have given to my servant Jacob. And they shall dwell safely therein, and shall build houses, and plant vineyards; yea, they shall dwell with confidence [in safety[8]], when I have executed judgments upon all those that despise them round about them; and they shall know that I am the Lord their God" (vv. 25–26).
- **Ezekiel 36:2–7 The heathen who have persecuted Israel will be removed from the promised land.** Israel's enemies have said for centuries, "Aha, even the ancient high places are ours in possession" (v. 2). Israel's enemies have "made [the Israelites] desolate, and swallowed

[them] up on every side, that [Israel] might be a possession unto [her enemies]" and have caused the Israelites to be "taken up in the lips of talkers" and to become "an infamy" among the heathen (v. 3). The "mountains, . . . hills, . . . rivers [ravines[9]], . . . valleys, . . . desolate wastes, and . . . cities" of Israel have been "forsaken" and have become "a prey" (reward of a conqueror) and a "derision to the residue of the heathen" (nations that surround and hate Israel) (v. 4). The Lord is angry with these nations, which have "appointed my land into their possession with the joy of all their heart, with despiteful minds" (v. 5). But in the last days this will end: "Thus saith the Lord God; Behold, I have spoken in my jealousy and in my fury, because ye have borne the shame of the heathen: therefore thus saith the Lord God; I have lifted up mine hand, [and now] [s]urely the heathen that are about you, they shall bear their shame" (vv. 6–7).

- **Ezekiel 36:8–12, 15 The land of Israel will blossom and prosper, and all the tribes of Israel will gather there.** Speaking to the "mountains of Israel," the Lord promised that "ye shall shoot forth your branches, and yield your fruit to my people of Israel; for they are at hand to come" (v. 8). "For, behold, I am for you, and I will turn unto you, and ye shall be tilled and sown: and I will multiply men upon you, all the house of Israel, even all of it: and the cities shall be inhabited, and the wastes shall be builded" (vv. 9–10). Notice that those who will multiply upon the land will be from *all* the tribes of Israel and not just those of the house of Judah.

THEBIBLEREVIVAL.COM, #14

The Lord will multiply both "man and beast," and increase the land's fruits, making the land of Israel "better unto you than at your beginnings" (v. 11). Once nearly bereft of inhabitants, the Lord will "cause men to walk upon you, even my people Israel; and they shall possess thee, and thou shalt be their inheritance" (v. 12). The sound of heathen inhabitants will no longer be heard in the land, and the "nations" of Israel will never fall again (v. 15).

- **Ezekiel 36:17–22, 24–30, 32–38 The Israel of the future will be obedient and spiritually worthy.** The first time the Israelites lived upon the promised land, "they defiled it by their own way and by their doings" (v. 17). The Lord poured His fury upon them because "they had shed [blood] upon the land, and for their idols wherewith they had polluted it" (v. 18). He "scattered them among the heathen, and . . . dispersed [them] through the countries" (v. 19), where they continued to "profane . . . my holy name" (v. 20). But for the sake of His "holy name," the Lord will eventually redeem them (vv. 21–22).

  The Lord will gather His people from among the heathen and from all countries and bring them back to the promised land (v. 24). This gathering will be remarkable (vv. 28–30, 33–38), and will be done for the Lord's purposes, not because Israel has earned it (v. 32). But by means of their scattering and captivity, they will be cleansed from their filthiness (v. 25), converted to the Lord, and shall receive His Spirit (vv. 26–27).

ZECHARIAH'S PROPHECIES CONCERNING JUDAH

- **Zechariah 1:14–17 The restoration of Jerusalem.** "I am jealous [zealous[10]] for Jerusalem and for Zion with a great jealousy," the Lord said (v. 14). "And I am very sore displeased with the heathen that are at ease" (v. 15).

  While the Lord "was but a little displeased" with His people, "they [the heathen] helped forward the affliction" upon His people (v. 15). But now, thus saith the Lord; I am returned to Jerusalem with mercies: my house [temple] shall be built in it" (v. 16). Judah will again prosper, cities will cover the land, and Jerusalem will be rebuilt and crowned with a temple (vv. 16–17).

- **Zechariah 1:18–19 The "four horns."[11]** Zechariah was next shown "four horns" which symbolize worldly powers that "scattered Judah,

Israel, and Jerusalem" (vv. 18–19). The horn itself is a symbol of power, and so these four horns represent four successive powerful empires. We see this more clearly in the visions of Daniel (see Daniel chapters 2 and 7), where the great image in King Nebuchadnezzar's dream and the four beasts ascending from the sea in Daniel's vision symbolize four empires which rose up in succession one after the other. But it is not clear which four empires are meant in Zechariah's prophecy of the "four horns." If Zechariah's prophecy referred to the empires of the past that engaged in the scattering, they would be Assyria, Babylonia, Persia, and Media. But if Zechariah was also looking to the future, as Daniel did, the four empires would be Assyria, Babylonia, Greece, and Rome. Persia and Media would be omitted, because they were responsible for the return of exiled Jews to Jerusalem.

- **Zechariah 2:1–5 Jerusalem will not be "measure[d]."** Zechariah observed a conversation between two heavenly visitors—one on his way to measure the size of the city of Jerusalem (vv. 1–2), and another who said it was unnecessary because "Jerusalem shall be inhabited as towns without walls for the multitude of men and cattle therein: for I, saith the Lord, will be unto her a wall of fire round about, and will be the glory in the midst of her" (vv. 3–5).

  Carl Friedrich Keil and Franz Delitzsch commented:

  > Jerusalem is in [the] future to resemble an open country covered with unwalled cities and villages; it will no longer be a city closely encircled with walls; hence it will be extraordinarily enlarged, on account of the multitude of men and cattle with which it will be blessed [compare Isaiah 49:19–20; Ezekiel 38:11]. Moreover, . . . Jerusalem will then have no protecting wall surrounding it, because it will enjoy a superior protection. Jehovah will be to it a wall of fire round about, that is to say, a defence of fire which will consume every one who ventures to attack it [compare Isaiah 4:5; Deuteronomy 4:24]. Jehovah will also be the glory in the midst of Jerusalem, that is to say, will fill the city with His glory [compare Isaiah 60:19].[12]

  It is interesting to note that only in our day has the city of Jerusalem grown beyond its walls as a sprawling metropolis. And when the Lord comes, Jerusalem will need no walls to protect it because of His glory that will be upon the city.

- **Zechariah 2:8 Jerusalem will be the "apple" of the Lord's "eye."** This figure of speech is an interesting one. The word translated as "apple" actually refers to the pupil of the eye, or the pupilla. The saying denotes someone whom one cherishes above all else. The alternative translation of the word is "little doll"—someone who is loved very much.[13] We should remember that Eve was the "apple" of Adam's eye (which apostate Christianity turned into the absurd "apple" story signifying sexual sin). In this scripture we learn that Israel will be the "apple" of the Lord's "eye" in the latter days.

- **Zechariah 8:3 Jerusalem will be a city of truth crowned with a temple.** Speaking of His future reign in the city, the Lord said through Zechariah, "I am returned unto Zion, and will dwell in the midst of Jerusalem: and Jerusalem shall be called a city of truth; and the mountain of the Lord of hosts [the temple] the holy mountain."

PUBLIC DOMAIN

- **Zechariah 8:4–9 Both young and old shall dwell in Jerusalem.** "There shall yet old men and old women dwell in the streets of Jerusalem, and every man with his staff in his hand for very age. And the streets of the city shall be full of boys and girls playing in the streets thereof " (vv. 4–5). This gathering will "be marvellous in the eyes of the remnant of this people in these [latter] days" (v. 6). "Behold, I will save [gather[14]] my people from the east country, and from the west

THEBIBLEREVIVAL.COM, #17

country; and I will bring them, and they shall dwell in the midst of Jerusalem: and they shall be my people, and I will be their God, in truth and in righteousness" (vv. 7–8). Then, speaking to "ye that hear in these [latter] days these words by the mouth of the prophets," He says, "Let your hands be strong . . . that the temple might be built" (v. 9).

- **Zechariah 8:11–15 The Lord will gather Judah and restore her to the land of Jerusalem.** "I will not be unto the residue [remainder who are restored] of this people as in the former days, saith the Lord of hosts. For [their] seed shall be prosperous; the vine shall give her fruit, and the ground shall give her increase, and the heavens shall give their dew; and I will cause the remnant of this people to possess all these things" (vv. 11–12). Though they will have been "a curse among the heathen, O house of Judah, and house of Israel; so will I save [gather[15]] you, and ye shall be a blessing" (v. 13). Though their fathers "provoked [Him] to wrath," the Lord will "in these [latter] days . . . do well unto Jerusalem and to the house of Judah" (vv. 14–15).
- **Zechariah 8:16–17 The Lord's expectations of gathered Judah.** "These are the things that ye shall do; Speak ye every man the truth to his neighbour; execute the judgment of truth and peace in your gates: and let none of you imagine evil in your hearts against his neighbour; and love no false oath: for all these are things that I hate, saith the Lord."
- **Zechariah 8:20–23 People will gather to Judah from "many cities."** "It shall yet come to pass, that there shall come people, and the inhabitants of many cities: and the inhabitants of one city shall go to another, saying, Let us go speedily to pray before the Lord, and to seek the Lord of hosts" (vv. 20–21). "Yea, many people and strong nations shall come to seek the Lord of hosts in Jerusalem, and to pray before the Lord" (v. 22). "In those days it shall come to pass, that ten men . . . out of all languages of the nations . . . shall take hold of the skirt of him that is a Jew, saying, We will go with you: for we have heard that God is with you [Hebrew: you (plural)[16]]" (v. 23).
- **Zechariah 9:1–6, 8 Wicked nations that border Israel will be destroyed.** Zechariah pronounced "the burden [curse] of the word of the Lord" against the nations surrounding Israel that have (and

will) attack and persecute her (v. 1). Tyrus, a Mediterranean merchant city north of Nazareth, though once "heaped up [with] silver as the dust, and fine gold as the mire of the streets," will be "cast . . . out, and [the Lord] will smite her power in the sea; and she shall be devoured with fire" (vv. 2–4). "Ashkelon shall see it, and fear; Gaza also shall see it, and be very sorrowful, and Ekron; for her expectation shall be ashamed; and the king shall perish from Gaza, and Ashkelon shall not be inhabited. And a bastard shall dwell in Ashdod," and the Lord will "cut off the pride of the Philistines" (vv. 5–6). "No oppressor shall pass through [Israel] any more" (v. 8).

- **Zechariah 9:13–17; 10:2, 6, 9–12 Judah and Ephraim will be gathered in from their long dispersion and united.** Using a number of metaphors and similes, the Lord promises to strengthen both Judah and Ephraim (see Zech. 9:13–15). "And the Lord their God shall save them in that day as the flock of his people: for they shall be as the stones of a crown, lifted up as an ensign upon his land. For how great is his goodness, and how great is his beauty!" (Zech. 9:16–17).

  In the days of their punishment their idols failed them and their diviners lied to them and told false dreams, "therefore they went their way as a flock, they were troubled, because there was no shepherd" (Zech. 10:2). But in the latter days, "I will strengthen the house of Judah, and I will save the house of Joseph, and I will bring them again to place them; for I have mercy upon them: and they shall be as though I had not cast them off: for I am the Lord their God, and will hear [or answer[17]] them" (Zech. 10:6). Though they will have been "sow[n] . . . among the people . . . they shall remember me in far countries; and they shall live with their children, and turn again" (Zech. 10:9). They will be gathered in such numbers that "place shall not be found for them" (Zech. 10:10). Their enemies will be destroyed, and the Lord "will strengthen them in the Lord; and they shall walk up and down in his name" (Zech. 10:11–12).

- **Zechariah 14:8 "Living waters shall go out from Jerusalem."** These are the waters of the river beheld by Ezekiel (see Ezek. 47:1–12) and the fountain that "shall come forth of the house of the Lord" seen by Joel (see Joel 3:18) and John the Revelator (see Revelation 22:1). These waters will flow year round—"in summer and in winter shall it be."

In connection with the foregoing scriptures, the Prophet Joseph Smith taught:

> Judah must return, Jerusalem must be rebuilt, and the temple, and water come out from under the temple, and the waters of the Dead Sea be healed [see Ezekiel 47:1–9]. It will take some time to rebuild the walls of the city and the temple, . . . and all this must be done before the Son of Man will make His appearance.[18]

- **Zechariah 14:10 "Jerusalem shall rise and dwell in her place"** is a better rendering of the phrase "it shall be lifted up, and inhabited in her place." The entire countryside will be "as a plain" surrounding the Holy City.

A NEW NATION AND TEMPLE

One Nation under Christ

- **Ezekiel 37:21–22 The children of Israel will be gathered together and united into one kingdom with the Savior as their King.** They will be taken from "among the heathen [nations or Gentiles[19]], whither they be gone, and . . . gather[ed] . . . on every side, and [brought] into their own land" (v. 21). There, the Lord "will make them one nation in the land upon the mountains of Israel; and one king shall be king to them all: and they shall be no more two[20] nations, neither shall they be divided into two kingdoms any more at all" (v. 22).
- **Ezekiel 37:23 They will be cleansed and purified.** They will not "defile themselves any more with their idols, nor with their detestable things, nor with any of their transgressions . . . wherein they have sinned, and [I] will cleanse them: so shall they be my people, and I will be their God."
- **Ezekiel 37:24 They will observe the Lord's statutes.** "David my servant [Christ] shall be king over them; and they all shall have one shepherd: they shall also walk in my judgments, and observe my statutes, and do them."
- **Ezekiel 37:25 They will dwell in Abraham, Isaac, and Jacob's promised land.** "They shall dwell in the land that I have given unto

Jacob my servant, wherein your fathers have dwelt; and they shall dwell therein, even they, and their children, and their children's children for ever: and my servant David [Christ] shall be their prince for ever."

A New Temple in Old Jerusalem

- **Ezekiel 40:1–7, 9–11 In the holy city of Jerusalem, a new temple will be built on the Temple Mount.** "The visions of God" came upon Ezekiel in the twenty-fifth year of Judah's captivity in Babylon, and he was carried away in the Spirit "into the land of Israel, and set . . . upon a very high mountain," from which he could see "a city on the south" (vv. 1–2) containing a prominent building with a wall around it (vv. 5–6).

PUBLIC DOMAIN

His heavenly visitor was "a man, whose appearance was like the appearance of brass, with a line of flax in his hand, and a measuring reed; and he stood in the gate" (v. 3). This was probably an angelic messenger and not the Lord Himself.[21] Ezekiel was commanded to "behold with thine eyes, and hear with thine ears, and set thine heart upon all that I shall shew thee," and then "declare all that thou seest to the house of Israel" (v. 4). Ezekiel likened this vision to his earlier visions "by the river Chebar" (see Ezekiel 1:3; 3:23; 10:15, 20).

THEBIBLEREVIVAL.COM, #15

The visitor's flax and reed were measuring instruments. The reed was "six cubits long . . . and an hand breadth," by which "he measured the breadth of the building, . . . and the height" (v. 5).

"Then came he unto the gate which looketh [or faces[22]] toward the east, and went up the stairs thereof, and measured the threshold of the gate, . . . [a]nd every little chamber . . . and the porch of the gate . . . and the posts . . . [and] the entry of the gate, . . . and the length [or height[23]] of the gate" (vv. 6–7, 9–11).

Elder James E. Talmage wrote:

> In the twenty-fifth year of the Babylonian captivity, while yet the people of Israel were in exile in a strange land, the word of the Lord came to the prophet Ezekiel; the power of God rested upon him; and he saw in vision a glorious Temple, the plan of which he minutely described [see Ezekiel, chapters 40–43]. As to whether the prophet himself considered the design so shown as one to be subsequently realized, or as but a grand yet unattainable ideal, is not declared. Certain it is that the Temple of the vision has not yet been builded.
>
> In most of its essential features Ezekiel's ideal followed closely the plan of Solomon's Temple; so close, indeed, is the resemblance, that many of the details specified by Ezekiel have been accepted as those of the splendid edifice destroyed by Nebuchadnezzar. A predominant characteristic of the Temple described by Ezekiel was the spaciousness of its premises and the symmetry of both the Holy House and its associated buildings.
>
> The area was to be a square of five hundred cubits, walled about and provided with a gateway and arches on each of three sides; on the west side the wall was to be unbroken by arch or portal. At each of the gateways were little chambers regarded as lodges, and provided with porches. In

J. GOEREE

the outer court were other chambers. The entire area was to be elevated, and a flight of steps led to each gateway. In the inner court was seen the great altar, standing before the House, and occupying the center of a square of one hundred cubits [Ezekiel 40:47]. Ample pro- vision was made for every variety of sacrifice and offering, and for the accommodation of the priests, the singers, and all engaged in the holy ritual [Ezekiel 40:44–46].

The main structure comprised a Porch, a Holy Place, and an inner sanctuary or Most Holy Place, the last named elevated above the rest and reached by steps. The plan provided for even greater exclusiveness than had characterized the sacred area of the Temple of Solomon; the double courts contributed to this end. The service of the Temple was prescribed in detail; the ordinances of the altar, the duties of the priests, the ministry of the Levites, the regulations governing oblations and feasts were all set forth [see Ezekiel, chapters 44–48].[24]

The Sons of Levi Will Make Offerings Again

- **Malachi 3:3 The sons of Levi will be purified and make offerings to the Lord.** "And he shall sit as a refiner and purifer of silver: and he shall purify the sons of Levi, and purge them as gold and silver, that they may offer unto the Lord an offering in righteousness." Offerings again? Did these not cease after Christ's infinite Atonement? No—not entirely.

The Prophet Joseph Smith explained:

> It is generally supposed that sacrifice was entirely done away when the Great Sacrifice [*i.e.*, the sacrifice of the Lord Jesus] was offered up, and that there will be no necessity for the ordinance of sacrifice in [the] future: but those who assert this are certainly

not acquainted with the duties, privileges, and authority of the priesthood, or with the Prophets.

The offering of sacrifice has ever been connected and forms a part of the duties of the Priesthood. It began with the Priesthood, and will be continued until after the coming of Christ, from generation to generation. We frequently have mention made of the offering of sacrifice by the servants of the Most High in ancient days, prior to the law of Moses; which ordinances will be continued when the Priesthood is restored with all its authority, power, and blessings. . . .

These sacrifices, as well as every ordinance belonging to the Priesthood, will, when the Temple of the Lord shall be built, and the sons of Levi be purified, be fully restored and attended to in all their powers, ramifications, and blessings. This ever did and ever will exist when the powers of the Melchizedek Priesthood are sufficiently manifest; else how can the restitution of all things spoken of by the holy Prophets be brought to pass? It is not to be understood that the law of Moses will be established again with all its rites and variety of ceremonies; this has never been spoken of by the Prophets; but those things which existed prior to [Moses's] day, namely, sacrifice, will be continued.

It may be asked by some, what necessity for sacrifice, since the Great Sacrifice was offered? In answer to which, if repentance, baptism, and faith existed prior to the days of Christ, what necessity for them since that time? The Priesthood has descended in a regular line from father to son, through their succeeding generations.[25]

- **Malachi 3:4 After all these events, Judah will be acceptable to the Lord.** "Then shall the offering of Judah and Jerusalem be pleasant unto the Lord, as in the days of old, and as in former years."

A ZION PEOPLE WILL DWELL IN JERUSALEM

- **Zephaniah 3:9 They will speak a pure language.** "For then will I turn to the people a pure language, that they may all call upon the name of the Lord, to serve him with one consent."

- **Zephaniah 3:10, 12–13 An afflicted and poor people will inherit Jerusalem.** The "daughter of my dispersed" (Judah) will come from "beyond the rivers of Ethiopia"— a figure of speech meaning from the ends of the earth (v. 10). There will be no proud among them—only "an afflicted and poor people, and they shall trust in the name of the Lord" (v. 12). "The remnant of Israel shall not do iniquity, nor speak lies; neither shall a deceitful tongue be found in their mouth: for they shall feed and lie down, and none shall make them afraid" (v. 13).

THEBIBLEREVIVAL.COM, #16

- **Zephaniah 3:14–17 The Lord will reign in their midst.** "Sing, O daughter of Zion; shout, O Israel; be glad and rejoice with all the heart, O daughter of Jerusalem. The Lord hath taken away thy judgments, he hath cast out thine enemy: the king of Israel, even the Lord, is in the midst of thee: thou shalt not see evil any more" (vv. 14–15). The city will "fear . . . not," "rest in [H]is love," and He will "joy over thee with singing" (vv. 16–17).

Notes

1. The contents of this section are adapted from "Prophecies of the Restoration (Ezekiel 25–48)," *Old Testament Student Manual: 1 Kings–Malachi*, 3rd ed. (Church Educational System manual, 2003), 279.
2. Ezekiel 20:37, footnote *a*.
3. Adam Clarke, *The Holy Bible . . . with a Commentary and Critical Notes*, 6 vols. (n.d.), 4:477.
4. Ezekiel 20:42, footnote *b*.
5. Joseph Fielding Smith, *The Signs of the Times* (1954), 171–72.

6. Orson Pratt, "Discourse," *Deseret News,* Apr. 5, 1871, 101, 102.
7. Ezekiel 28:25, footnote *c.*
8. Ezekiel 28:26, footnote *b.*
9. Ezekiel 36:4, footnote *a.*
10. Zechariah 1:14, footnote *a.*
11. The contents of this section are adapted from "Preparations for the Lord's Return in Glory (Zechariah)," *Old Testament Student Manual: 1 Kings–Malachi,* 342.
12. Carl Friedrich Keil and Franz Delitzsch, *Commentary on the Old Testament,* 10 vols. (n.d.), 10:2:245.
13. See Hugh W. Nibley, *Old Testament and Related Studies,* ed. John W. Welch, Gary P. Gillum, and Don E. Norton (1986), 87–88.
14. Joseph Smith Translation, Zechariah 8:7 (in Zechariah 8:7, footnote *a*).
15. Joseph Smith Translation, Zechariah 8:13 (in Zechariah 8:13, footnote *b*).
16. See Zechariah 8:23, footnote *a.*
17. Zechariah 10:6, footnote *a.*
18. *Teachings of Presidents of the Church: Joseph Smith* (2007), 252.
19. Ezekiel 37:21, footnote *a.*
20. "The tribes led by Judah and by Ephraim were historically adversaries (after events of 1 [Kings] 12:16–20). In the latter days this enmity will be healed" (Ezekiel 37:22, footnote *d*).
21. See "Prophecies of the Restoration (Ezekiel 25–48)," 286.
22. Ezekiel 40:6, footnote *b.*
23. Ezekiel 40:11, footnote *a.*
24. James E. Talmage, *The House of the Lord* (1912), 43–45.
25. Joseph Smith, in *History of the Church,* 4:211–12.

SECTION THREE

The Zion of Our God

The Coming Zion of Our God

We are all familiar with the Lord's example of prayer, given to His disciples in the meridian of time. The first part of this prayer says the following:

> After this manner therefore pray ye: Our Father which art in heaven, Hallowed be thy name.
>
> Thy kingdom come. Thy will be done in earth, as it is in heaven.[1]

At the very end of the book of Revelation, the Apostle John quotes the Savior as saying, "He which testifieth these things saith, Surely I come quickly." And then John concludes his record by saying in response:

> Amen. Even so, come, Lord Jesus.[2]

Each of these scriptures celebrates the coming of our Lord, Jesus Christ. We are instructed by the Savior to pray for it. And the Apostle John did pray for it as he closed his record. We also sing this sentiment in one of our beloved hymns:

"Come, O Thou King of Kings!"[3]

In the April 2015 general conference, Elder Neil L. Andersen said:[4]

> As we were singing, I was deeply moved with the thought that at this very moment hundreds of thousands, perhaps millions, of believing Saints in more than 150 countries, amazingly in 75 different languages,[5] together we were raising our voices to God, singing:
>
> *Come, O thou King of Kings! We've waited long for thee, With healing in thy wings, To set thy people free. . . .*[6]

IN HIS GLORY, © DEL PARSON, USED BY PERMISSION

> We are a very large worldwide family of believers, disciples of the Lord Jesus Christ. . . .
>
> We live, brothers and sisters, in the days preceding the Lord's Second Coming, a time long anticipated by believers through the ages. We live in days of wars and rumors of wars, days of natural disasters, days when the world is pulled by confusion and commotion.
>
> But we also live in the glorious time of the Restoration, when the gospel is being taken to all the world—a time when the Lord has promised that He "will raise up . . . a pure people"[7] and arm them "with righteousness and with the power of God."[8]

While the Lord's people have struggled in many previous dispensations to establish Zion, some with success and some without success—it falls upon us, the Latter-day Saints, to bring about a latter-day Zion that will not fail. Nor will it end with our translation into heaven as it did in the days of Enoch and of Melchizedek. It will continue on into the Millennium, where it will be joined with the heavenly Zion that will come down to earth to be joined with the New Jerusalem.

Elder Neil L. Andersen summed up the glory of that great day as follows:[9]

> Our faith grows as we anticipate the glorious day of the Savior's return to the earth. The thought of His coming stirs my soul. It will be breathtaking! The scope and grandeur, the vastness and magnificence, will exceed anything mortal eyes have ever seen or experienced.
>
> In that day He will not come "wrapped in swaddling clothes, lying in a manger,"[10] but He will appear "in the clouds of heaven, clothed with power and great glory; with all the holy angels."[11] We will hear "the voice of the archangel, and . . . the trump of God."[12] The sun and the moon will be transformed, and "stars [will] be hurled from their places."[13] You and I, or those who follow us, "the saints . . . from [every quarter] of the earth,"[14] "shall be quickened and . . . caught up to meet him,"[15] and those who have died in righteousness, they too will "be caught up to meet him in the midst . . . of heaven."[16]
>
> Then, a seemingly impossible experience: "All flesh," the Lord says, "shall see me together."[17] How will it happen? We do not know. But I testify it will happen—exactly as prophesied. We will kneel in reverence, "and the Lord shall utter his voice, and all the ends of the earth shall hear it."[18]
>
> "It shall be . . . as the voice of many waters, and as the voice of a great thunder."[19] "[Then] the Lord, . . . the Savior, shall stand in the midst of his people."[20]
>
> There will be unforgettable reunions with the angels of heaven and the Saints upon the earth.[21] But most important, as Isaiah declares, "All the ends of the earth shall see the salvation of our God,"[22] and He "shall reign over all flesh."[23]

In this final section of our book on Zion, we will explore the process and the glory of that day when the Zion of our God will come down to earth.

Notes

1. Matthew 6:9–10; see also Luke 11:2.
2. Revelation 22:20.
3. "Come, O Thou King of Kings," *Hymns,* no. 59.
4. Neil L. Andersen, "Thy Kingdom Come," *Ensign* or *Liahona,* May 2015, 119.
5. While general conference overall is translated into 94 languages, not all languages are transmitted simultaneously, nor for all sessions. For the Sunday afternoon session of this general conference [in April 2015], 75 languages were transmitted live.
6. On Tuesday, March 31, 2015, the First Presidency's office sent me [Elder Neil L. Andersen] an email explaining that I would speak on Sunday afternoon, April 5, immediately following the congregational hymn "Come, O Thou King of Kings." The text of this great Restoration hymn, written by Parley P. Pratt, is a humble plea to the Savior to return to the earth. It embodied the message of my conference talk perhaps more powerfully than any other hymn we sing. I was deeply moved by the significance of believing Saints everywhere joining together on Easter Sunday, raising our voices to God and in unison singing, "Come, O thou King of Kings! We've waited long for thee." Realizing that I personally had no input on the music selection for general conference, I wondered if those responsible for the music had read my conference talk entitled "Thy Kingdom Come" and then chosen this hymn about the Second Coming of the Savior. I later learned that the Tabernacle Choir directors had recommended the hymn to the First Presidency in early March, weeks prior to my talk being sent to the First Presidency for translation. The last time that "Come, O Thou King of Kings" was sung as a congregational hymn in general conference was October 2002. We each try to do our part, but He is the grand architect.
7. Doctrine and Covenants 100:16.
8. 1 Nephi 14:14.
9. Neil L. Andersen, "Thy Kingdom Come," 122.
10. Luke 2:12.
11. Doctrine and Covenants 45:44.
12. 1 Thessalonians 4:16.
13. Doctrine and Covenants 133:49.
14. Doctrine and Covenants 45:46.
15. Doctrine and Covenants 88:96.

16. Doctrine and Covenants 88:97.
17. Doctrine and Covenants 101:23.
18. Doctrine and Covenants 45:49.
19. Doctrine and Covenants 133:22.
20. Doctrine and Covenants 133:25.
21. See Moses 7:63.
22. Isaiah 52:10.
23. Doctrine and Covenants 133:25.

CHAPTER 13

The Second Coming of Jesus Christ

(ISA. 6; EZEK. 1; DAN. 7; 10; ZECH. 14; MAL. 3–4; 1 THES. 4; REV. 1; 4; 19; D&C 45; 76; 88; 101; 110; 133; JS—MATTHEW)

The ultimate reward of a Zion people is to have the Lord Jesus Christ dwell among them. This was the case in the Zion of Enoch and the Zion of Melchizedek. It could have been the case with the children of Israel under Moses if they had chosen to become a Zion people. And now, in this final dispensation, it will also be our privilege to welcome Him.

SEVERAL COMINGS OF THE LORD

When we speak of Christ's Second Coming, we must be clear about the precise appearance to which we are referring.

IN HIS GLORY, © DEL PARSON, USED BY PERMISSION

Multiple appearances have been prophesied. From the scriptures we learn that when the Lord returns, He will make some appearances to specific groups and then culminate His return by His appearance in great power, majesty, and glory in such a manner that all the world will see Him (see D&C 133:17–22; 101:22–23).

Several appearances of the Lord in the beginning of this dispensation were private visitations given as part of the Restoration—in the Sacred Grove, in the Kirtland Temple, etc. In addition, the prophets have mentioned four final appearances of the Lord: two of these will be to the Saints, one will be to the Jews, and the fourth will be His final coming in the sight of all the world.

The Appearance at the City of New Jerusalem

Christ will appear at New Jerusalem

- **The Lord "shall suddenly come to his temple"** (D&C 133:2), a temple yet to be built in Jackson County, Missouri (see D&C 84:1–5; 97:10, 15–16).

  President Charles W. Penrose affirmed:

  > Among the [Saints of God] the Lord will make His appearance first; and that appearance will be unknown to the rest of mankind. He will come to the Temple prepared for Him, and His faithful people will behold His face, hear His voice, and gaze upon His glory. From His own lips they will receive further instructions for the development and beautifying of Zion and for the extension and sure stability of His kingdom.[1]

The Appearance at Adam-ondi-Ahman

- **The Lord will appear to the Saints in a grand council at Adam-ondi-Ahman** in Daviess County, Missouri. In attendance will be those who have held priesthood keys during all gospel dispensations and others who are specially invited.

  The Prophet Joseph Smith remarked:

  > Daniel in his seventh chapter speaks of the Ancient of Days; he means the oldest man, our father Adam, Michael; he will call his children together and hold a council with them to prepare them for the coming of the Son of Man [see Daniel 7:9–14]. He (Adam) is the father of the human family, and presides over the spirits of

all men, and all that have had the keys must stand before him in this grand council.[2]

And President Joseph Fielding Smith elaborated:

Christ will appear at Adam-ondi-Ahman

> Not many years hence there shall be gathering of high priests and righteous souls in [the] valley of Adam-ondi-Ahman. At this gathering Adam, the Ancient of Days, will . . . be present. At this time the vision which Daniel saw will be enacted. The Ancient of Days will sit. There will stand before him those who have held the keys of all dispensations, who shall render up their stewardships to the first Patriarch of the race, who holds the keys of salvation. This shall be a day of judgment and preparation. . . .
>
> . . . In this council Christ will take over the reigns of government, officially, on the earth, and "the kingdom and dominion, and the greatness of the kingdom under the whole heaven, shall be given to the people of the saints of the Most High . . ." [Daniel 7:27].
>
> Until this grand council is held, Satan shall hold rule in the nations of the earth; but at that time thrones are to be cast down and man's rule shall come to an end. . . .
>
> Then shall He give the government to the Saints of the Most High. . . . [This council] shall precede the coming of Jesus Christ as a thief in the night, unbeknown to all the world.[3]

The Appearance at the Mount of Olives

- **The Savior's appearance to the Jews** will occur when Jerusalem and its environs are besieged by many nations (the armies of Gog). At the close of a long and costly war, known as the battle of Armageddon, the Jews will flee for safety to the Mount of Olives. There the Savior will make His appearance (see D&C 45:48–53; Zechariah 12:9–14; 13:6; 14:1–9).

Elder Parley P. Pratt recorded:

> Zechariah, [in] chapter 14, . . . said, in plain words, that the Lord shall come at the very time of the overthrow of that army [the Jews' enemies]; yes, in fact, even while they are in the act of taking Jerusalem, and have already succeeded in taking one-half the city, spoiling their houses, and ravishing their women.

The resurrected Christ will descend

The Mount of Olives

> Then, behold, their long-expected Messiah, suddenly appearing, shall stand upon the Mount of Olives, a little east of Jerusalem, to fight against those nations and deliver the Jews. Zechariah says the Mount of Olives shall cleave in twain, from east to west, and one-half of the mountain shall remove to the north while the other half falls off to the south, suddenly forming a very great valley into which the Jews shall flee for protection from their enemies as they fled from the earthquake in the days of Uzziah, king of Judah; while the Lord cometh and all the Saints with Him. . . .
>
> [And] what will be their astonishment when they are about to fall at the feet of their Deliverer and acknowledge Him their Messiah! They [will] discover the wounds which were once made in His

hands, feet, and side; and on inquiry, at once recognize Jesus of Nazareth, the King of the Jews, the man so long rejected.[4]

The Appearance to the Whole World

HALLEY'S COMET, COURTESY OF NASA

As the Lord's Second Coming approaches, signs will precede this epochal event. One of the last of these signs is the sign of the Son of Man (see D&C 88:93; Joseph Smith—Matthew 1:36). The Prophet Joseph Smith predicted: "Then will appear one grand sign of the Son of Man in heaven. But what will the world do? They will say it is a planet, a comet, etc. But the Son of Man will come as the sign of the coming of the Son of Man, which will be as the light of the morning cometh out of the east [see Joseph Smith—Matthew 1:26]."[5]

Following the sign of the Son of Man there will be "silence in heaven for the space of half an hour; and immediately after shall the curtain of heaven be unfolded," and the Lord will make His glorious appearance (D&C 88:95). So great will be the glory and power of His coming that the mountains will flow down, the waters of the seas will boil, all nations will tremble, the sun shall hide his face in shame, the moon shall whithhold its light, the stars shall be hurled from their places, and the elements shall melt with fervent heat (see D&C 133:40–42, 49; 101:25). All that is corruptible shall be consumed and destroyed by the brightness of His glorious presence (see D&C 5:19; 101:24). The Lord will wear red apparel, signifying His great atoning sacrifice and also His judgments upon the wicked (see D&C 133:48–53; Isaiah 63:1–9).

WHAT WILL HE LOOK LIKE?

- **1 John 3:2 "We shall be like him."** In his first epistle, the same John who wrote the book of Revelation made two important statements about what the resurrected Christ will look like at His Second Coming:

  — "We shall see him as he is."

— "We shall be like him."

© DEL PARSON, USED BY PERMISSION IN HIS GLORY,

Other than the brightness of His glory, Christ looks like us, and we look like Him. He is not merely a bright light of some disembodied essence; He is a glorious personage who, like us, has a head, hands, and feet.

- **D&C 130:22 Christ has a tangible body of flesh and bones, as does our Father in Heaven.** The man-made decrees of fourth-century Christian priests notwithstanding, the Lord does have a body, parts, and passions (for example, He loves us). And when He appears at the Second Coming, that fact will be obvious.

APOCALYPTIC VISIONS OF CHRIST

We can learn much about Christ from prophetic visions of Him recorded in the scriptures. Such visions of the Lord are remarkably similar.

Isaiah's Vision of the Lord

- **Isaiah 6:1; 2 Nephi 16:1 Isaiah saw the Lord.** The vision occurred "in the year that king Uzziah died" (ca. 740 B.C.).[6] In this vision Isaiah "saw . . . the Lord sitting upon a throne, high and lifted up." "Both John and Nephi testified that the Lord whom Isaiah saw was the premortal Jesus Christ [Jehovah] (see John 12:41; 2 Nephi 11:2–3)."[7]
- **Isaiah 6:2; 2 Nephi 16:2 Isaiah describes the holy beings that surround God's throne.** The term *seraphim* "probably [means] *fiery beings.* [They are] angelic beings [and] . . . are attendants in Jehovah's court, the ministers of the heavenly sanctuary, joining in adoration before the throne."[8] Moreover, seraphim are likely among the glorious beings that the Prophet Joseph Smith said "dwell in everlasting burnings."[9]

There are a number of metaphors in this scripture that, if taken literally, would seem very strange, but if interpreted symbolically are quite beautiful:

— Seraphim have symbolic wings ("veils" or "covers" in Hebrew).[10] The Prophet Joseph Smith made it clear that "an angel of God never has [actual] wings."[11]

— With these symbolic wings, seraphim can veil or cover their faces ("presence" in Hebrew). They can also hide their feet or legs ("footing" or "location" in Hebrew).[12]

— Seraphim have power to "fly," meaning "to move freely through space."[13] Elder Bruce R. McConkie wrote:

> "*Seraphs* are angels who reside in the presence of God, giving continual glory, honor, and adoration to Him. . . . The fact that these holy beings were shown to him [Isaiah] as having wings was simply to symbolize their 'power, to move, to act, etc.' as was the case also in visions others had received (D&C 77:4)."[14]

- **Isaiah 6:3; 2 Nephi 16:3 The seraphim shout praise unto the Lord.** Isaiah heard one cry unto another, "Holy, holy, holy, is the Lord of hosts: the whole earth is full of his glory." In Hebrew, the way to give superlative emphasis to a statement is to repeat it three times. Thus, "holy, holy, holy" in Hebrew is the equivalent of saying "most holy" in English.[15]

- **Isaiah 6:4; 2 Nephi 16:4 Their praise shakes the temple's foundation.** To say that "the posts of the door moved at the voice of him that cried" was a Hebrew way of saying the "foundations of the thresholds trembled" (Isaiah 6:4, footnote *a*).

- **Isaiah 6:4; 2 Nephi 16:4 The glory of the Lord fills the room.** Isaiah said "the house was filled with smoke," a Hebrew figure of speech meaning that the "presence, power, and glory of the Lord"[16] were there. The Prophet Joseph Smith declared: "God Almighty Himself dwells in eternal fire; flesh and blood cannot go there, for all corruption is devoured by the fire. 'Our God is a consuming fire.' [See Hebrews 12:29; Deuteronomy 4:24.] When our flesh is quickened by the Spirit, there will be no blood in this tabernacle. Some dwell in higher glory than others. . . . Immortality dwells in everlasting burnings."[17]

- **Isaiah 6:5–7; 2 Nephi 16:5–7 Isaiah's sins are forgiven.** Recognizing that he was in the presence of holy beings, Isaiah cried out, "Woe is me! for I am undone"—a figure of speech indicating Isaiah's overwhelming feelings of unworthiness before God. "I am a man of unclean lips, and . . . mine eyes have seen the King, the Lord of hosts" (v. 5).

A hot coal on Isaiah's lips

In response, one of the seraphim flew to him, "having a live coal in his hand, which he had taken with the tongs from off the altar: and he laid it upon my mouth, and said, Lo, this hath touched thy lips; and thine iniquity is taken away, and thy sin purged" (vv. 6–7). The hot coals of the altar of sacrifice symbolized "cleansing" or "purging" to the Hebrews. Thus Isaiah's "unclean lips" (sins) were forgiven.

Ezekiel's Vision of the Lord

- **Ezekiel 1:26–28 A firmament or expanse above or over the creatures.** "And above the firmament that was over their heads was the likeness of a throne, as the appearance of a sapphire stone: and upon the likeness of the throne was the likeness as the appearance of a man above upon it" (v. 26). This "man" (Christ) was surrounded by glory ("the colour of amber, as the appearance of fire") all "round about" him (v. 27). Ezekiel described this brightness as being like "the bow that is in the cloud in the day of rain," and then stated plainly that it was "the glory of the Lord. And when I saw it, I fell upon my face, and I heard a voice of one that spake" (v. 28).

Ezekiel saw the Lord upon His throne

Notice the color amber associated with the Lord's appearance (v. 27). This is likewise featured in other visions of Christ found in the scriptures.

Daniel's Vision of the Lord

- **Daniel 10:1–7 Daniel saw the Lord.** The vision came after three weeks of worrying and fasting, during which Daniel "ate no pleasant bread [desirable foods[18]], neither came flesh nor wine in my mouth, neither did I anoint myself at all, till three whole weeks were fulfilled" (vv. 1–3).

  Then, in the twenty-fourth day of the first month, "as I was by the side of the great river, which is Hiddekel [the Tigris[19]] . . . I lifted up mine eyes, and looked, and behold a certain man clothed in linen, whose loins were girded with fine gold" (vv. 4–5). "His body also was like the beryl, and his face as the appearance of lightning, and his eyes as lamps of fire, and his arms and his feet like in colour to polished brass, and the voice of his words like the voice of a multitude" (v. 6).

  "I Daniel alone saw the vision: for the men that were with me saw not the vision; but a great quaking fell upon them, so that they fled to hide themselves" (v. 7).

Other Apocalyptic Visions of Christ

The following visions are also of Jesus Christ, and their descriptions are very much alike.

- **Exodus 24:9–10 Moses, Aaron, Nadab, Abihu, and seventy of the elders of Israel saw the Lord.**

  9 Then went up Moses, and Aaron, Nadab, and Abihu, and seventy of the elders of Israel:

10 And they saw the God of Israel: and there was under his feet as it were a paved work of a sapphire stone, and as it were the body of heaven in his clearness [or clear as the very heavens[20]].

- **Revelation 1:12–18 While on the Isle of Patmos, John saw the Lord.**

12 And I turned to see the voice that spake with me. . . .

13 And in the midst . . . one like unto the Son of man, clothed with a garment down to the foot, and girt about the paps with a golden girdle.

14 His head and his hairs were white like wool, as white as snow; and his eyes were as a flame of fire;

15 And his feet like unto fine brass, as if they burned in a furnace; and his voice as the sound of many waters.

16 And . . . his countenance was as the sun shineth in his strength.

17 And when I saw him, I fell at his feet as dead. And he laid his right hand upon me, saying unto me, Fear not; I am the first and the last:

18 I am he that liveth, and was dead; and, behold, I am alive for evermore, Amen; and have the keys of hell and of death.

- **Revelation 4:1–3 John later saw the Lord in heaven, seated upon His throne.**

1 After this I looked, and, behold, a door was opened in heaven: and the first voice which I heard was as it were of a trumpet talking with me; which said, Come up hither, and I will shew thee things which must be hereafter.

2 And immediately I was in the spirit: and, behold, a throne was set in heaven, and one sat on the throne.

3 And he that sat was to look upon like a jasper and a sardine stone: and there was a rainbow round about the throne, in sight like unto an emerald.

- **D&C 76:19–24 Joseph Smith and Sidney Rigdon saw the Lord in the heavens.**

19 And while we meditated upon these things, the Lord touched the eyes of our understandings and they were opened, and the glory of the Lord shone round about.

20 And we beheld the glory of the Son, on the right hand of the Father, and received of his fulness;

21 And saw the holy angels, and them who are sanctified before his throne, worshiping God, and the Lamb, who worship him forever and ever.

22 And now, after the many testimonies which have been given of him, this is the testimony, last of all, which we give of him: That he lives!

23 For we saw him, even on the right hand of God; and we heard the voice bearing record that he is the Only Begotten of the Father—

24 That by him, and through him, and of him, the worlds are and were created, and the inhabitants thereof are begotten sons and daughters unto God.

- **D&C 110:1–4 In the Kirtland Temple, Joseph Smith and Oliver Cowdery saw Christ standing on the pulpit.**

1 The veil was taken from our minds, and the eyes of our understanding were opened.

2 We saw the Lord standing upon the breastwork of the pulpit, before us; and under his feet was a paved work of pure gold, in color like amber.

3 His eyes were as a flame of fire; the hair of his head was white like the pure snow; his countenance shone above the brightness of the sun; and his voice was as the sound of the rushing of great waters, even the voice of Jehovah, saying:

4 I am the first and the last; I am he who liveth, I am he who was slain; I am your advocate with the Father.

- **Revelation 19:13; D&C 133:46, 48, 50–51; Isaiah 63:2–3 "A vesture dipped in blood."** It is a common misconception that Christ will be clothed in white at His Second Coming. According to the book of

Revelation, the Doctrine and Covenants, and Isaiah, it is clear that the Savior will be dressed in red apparel at His Second Coming, symbolic of His taking upon Himself the sins of the world and of coming in His judgment.

The foregoing visions of Christ give us some idea of what He will look like at the Second Coming. We can expect a celestial personage with a glorified body that shines like the brightness of the sun. There will be no mistaking who He is when He comes again to rule and reign among His Zion people on earth.

THE RAPTURE

When the Lord descends, He will not be alone. He will be accompanied by the angels of heaven. And all of the righteous on earth will also be caught up to meet Him in the clouds. This is what is called "the Rapture," an event seldom named as such in our Church but frequently mentioned by the rest of the Christian world. Those who are worthy of celestial glory—both the resurrected Saints and the Saints who will be "quickened" or changed from mortality to immortality "in the twinkling of an eye" (see 1 Thes. 4:16–18; 3 Nephi 28:8; D&C 88:96–98; 101:31)—will be part of the heavenly hosts who will welcome the Savior as He descends to the earth in power and glory.

- **D&C 88:93, 95–98 The Rapture.**

93 And immediately there shall appear a great sign in heaven, and all people shall see it together. . . .

95 And there shall be silence in heaven for the space of half an hour; and immediately after shall the curtain of heaven be unfolded, as a scroll is unfolded after it is rolled up, and the face of the Lord shall be unveiled;

96 And the saints that are upon the earth, who are alive, shall be quickened and be caught up to meet him.

97 And they who have slept in their graves shall come forth, for their graves shall be opened; and they also shall be caught up to meet him in the midst of the pillar of heaven—

98 They are Christ's, the first fruits, they who shall descend with him first, and they who are on the earth and in their graves, who are first caught up to meet him; and all this by the voice of the sounding of the trump of the angel of God.

In speaking of the Second Coming and the Rapture, Elder Neil L. Andersen cited several scriptures:

> Those awaiting the Savior's coming will "look for [Him]." And He has promised, "I will come"! The righteous will see Him "in the clouds of heaven [with all the holy angels], clothed with power and great glory" [D&C 45:44]. "An angel shall sound his trump, and the saints . . . from the four quarters of the earth" [D&C 45:45, 46] will "be caught up to meet him" [D&C 88:96]. Those "that have slept," meaning those worthy Saints who have died, "shall [also] come forth to meet [Him]" [D&C 45:45; see also D&C 29:13; 88:96–97].[21]

GEOGRAPHICAL CHANGES

Elder Neal A. Maxwell foretold, "When Christ comes again, it will not be to the meekness of the manger; it will be as the recognized Redeemer and the Lord of the universe!"[22] The scriptures explain the effect of the fulness of His glory upon the earth and its inhabitants when He returns the second time:

- Mountains will flow down at His presence (see D&C 133:40, 44; Micah 1:4).
- The waters upon the earth will boil (see D&C 133:41).
- All nations will tremble at His presence (see D&C 133:42).
- The sun will hide, the moon will withhold its light, and stars will be hurled from their places (see D&C 133:49).
- The wicked will be burned by the brightness or fire of the glory of the Lord (see Malachi 4:1–3; 2 Thes. 2:8).

- **D&C 133:22–24 The continents will reunite.** The noise of these changes will be like "the voice of many waters, and as the voice of a great thunder," as the Lord "shall break down the mountains, and the valleys shall not be found" (v. 22). "He shall command the great deep [the ocean], and it shall be driven back into the north countries, and the islands shall become one land" (v. 23). "And the land of Jerusalem [in the Eastern Hemisphere] and the land of Zion [in the Western Hemisphere] shall be turned back into their own place, and the earth shall be like as it was in the days before it was divided" (v. 24).

President Joseph Fielding Smith observed:

> We read in Genesis that in the beginning all of the land surface was in one place as it was in the days of Peleg [see Genesis 10:25], that the earth was divided. . . . The dividing of the earth was not an act of division by the inhabitants of the earth by tribes and peoples, but a breaking asunder of the continents, thus dividing the land surface and creating the Eastern Hemisphere and Western Hemisphere. By looking at a wall map of the world, you will discover how the land surface along the northern and southern coast of the American Hemisphere and Europe and Africa has the appearance of having been together at one time. Of course, there have been many changes on the earth's surface since the beginning.
>
> We are informed by revelation that the time will come when this condition will be changed and that the land surface of the earth will come back again as it was in the beginning and all be in one place [see D&C 133:18–20].[23]

A DAY OF GREAT DREAD FOR THE WICKED

- **Malachi 3:13–14 Some discouraged Saints consider it "vain" (pointless) to serve God,** because it appears that the wicked prosper despite their wickedness. To such Saints the Lord says, "Your words have been stout [or strong[24]] against me" (v. 13). "Ye have said, It is vain to serve God: and what profit is it that we have kept his ordinance, and that we have walked mournfully before the Lord of hosts?" (v. 14).

  In connection with this scripture, President Spencer W. Kimball shared the following experience:

  > Some time ago a sister said to me, "Why is it, Brother Kimball, that those who do the least in the building of the kingdom seem

to prosper most? We drive a Ford; our neighbors drive a Cadillac. We observe the Sabbath and attend our meetings; they play golf, hunt, fish, and play.

We abstain from the forbidden while they eat, drink, and are merry and are unrestrained. We pay tithing and other church donations; they have their entire large income to lavish upon themselves. We are tied home with our large family of small children, often ill; they are totally free for social life—to dine and dance. We wear cottons and woolens, and I wear a three-season coat, but they wear silks and costly apparel, and she wears a mink coat. Our meager income is always strained and never seems adequate for necessities, while their wealth seems enough to allow them every luxury. And yet the Lord promises blessings to the faithful! It seems to me that it does not pay to live the gospel—that the proud and the covenant breakers are the ones who prosper."

Then I said to her, "Yours is an ancient question. Job and Jeremiah made the same complaint." And I quoted for her the Lord's answer through Malachi: [Malachi 3:13–18; 4:1–2].

Then I said to the disconsolate sister, "But for many rewards you need not wait until the judgment day. You have many blessings *today.* You have your family of lovely, righteous children. What a rich reward for the so-called sacrifices! The blessings that you enjoy cannot be purchased with all your neighbor's wealth."[25]

- **Malachi 3:2 The wicked will not be able to abide the day of Christ's Second Coming.** Malachi asked, "Who may abide the day of his coming? and who shall stand when he appeareth?" Then he answered that anyone can be prepared to meet the Savior through sincere repentance, "for he is like a refiner's fire, and like fullers' soap."

A fuller's soap was the most thorough cleansing agent available in ancient times, turning filthy clothes into the whitest white.

ILLUSTRATION FROM THE CHILDREN'S BIBLE

The refiner's fire

A refiner's fire separates out the dross from the gold, purifying the metal through intense heat.

- **Malachi 3:5 The Lord will send judgment and destruction upon the wicked.** He will be "a swift witness" against those He detests: "against the sorcerers, and against the adulterers, and against false swearers, and against those that oppress the hireling in his wages, the widow, and the fatherless, and that turn aside the stranger from his right, and fear not me, saith the Lord of hosts." All of these will have reason to fear on the day of the Lord's coming.
- **Malachi 4:1 The proud and the wicked will become as "stubble."** "For, behold, the day cometh, that shall burn as an oven; and all the proud, yea, and all that do wickedly, shall be stubble: and the day that cometh shall burn them up, saith the Lord of hosts, that it shall leave them neither root nor branch."

President Joseph Fielding Smith stated:

> The great and dreadful day of the Lord is the day when judgments are poured out upon the wicked and the earth is cleansed of its iniquity. It is not to be a dreadful day to the righteous, but it certainly will be to all that do wickedly, for they will be as stubble and will be burned when the Lord comes in His glory, and they shall be left with "neither root nor branch" (Malachi 4:1).[26]

In Malachi 4:1, the phrases "day . . . that shall burn as an oven" and "the proud . . . and all that do wickedly, shall be stubble" are meaningful as figures of speech, but they may also be taken literally with regard to the burning that will happen at the Lord's Second Coming.

President Joseph Fielding Smith added:

> All through the scriptures we have the word of the Lord that at His coming the wicked and the rebellious will be as stubble and will be consumed. Isaiah has so prophesied. Malachi is very definite when he says: [Malachi 4:1]. Surely the words of the Lord are not to be received lightly or considered meaningless. We are all commanded to labor "while it is called today." None shall be spared from this burning who "remain in Babylon." Babylon is the world; those who remain in Babylon are those who follow the

> practices of the world, and who do not accept in their hearts the word of the Lord.[27]
>
> When Christ comes the second time it will be in the clouds of heaven, and it shall be *the day of vengeance against the ungodly,* when those who have loved wickedness and have been guilty of transgression and rebellion against the laws of God will be destroyed. All during the ministry of Christ wickedness ruled and seemed to prevail, but when He comes in the clouds of glory as it is declared in this message of Malachi to the world, and which was said by Moroni to be near at hand, then Christ will appear as the *refiner* and *purifier* of both man and beast and all that pertains to this earth, for the earth itself shall undergo a change and receive its former *paradisiacal glory.*[28]

And Elder Theodore M. Burton commented:

> When Malachi prophesied of the Second Coming of Christ, he spoke of "the proud, yea, and all that do wickedly." Of whom was he speaking? First, of those who rejected Christ because of the pride of their hearts, and second, of those who, having accepted Jesus, were not valiant in keeping His commandments.
>
> Malachi went on to say they "shall burn as stubble." This means that they shall be destroyed. By whom? Malachi explains, "They that come shall burn them, saith the Lord of Hosts." . . .
>
> But what is meant by the expression "that it shall leave them neither root nor branch"? This expression simply means that wicked and indifferent persons who reject the gospel of Jesus Christ will have no family inheritance or patriarchal lineage—neither root (ancestors or progenitors) nor branch (children or posterity). Such persons cannot be received into the celestial kingdom of glory of resurrected beings, but must be content with a lesser blessing.[29]

- **Malachi 4:1 is referred to numerous times in the Doctrine and Covenants** and in other scriptures, which gives some indication of the importance of this passage.

  — **D&C 5:19** The wicked will be consumed away and utterly destroyed.

—	**D&C 29:9**	The proud and the wicked will be burned up like stubble.
—	**D&C 64:23**	He that is tithed shall not be burned at Christ's Second Coming.
—	**D&C 64:24**	The Lord will burn up the proud and the wicked.
—	**D&C 101:24**	Every corruptible thing will be consumed by fire—men, beasts, fowls, and fish.
—	**D&C 112:24**	It will be a day of wrath, burning, desolation, and weeping.
—	**D&C 133:64**	Those who are burned will be left with neither root nor branch.
—	**2 Thes. 2:8–10**	All the wicked will be destroyed by the brightness of His coming.
—	**2 Peter 3:10**	It will come unexpectedly—"as a thief in the night" to the wicked.

A DAY OF GREAT JOY FOR THE RIGHTEOUS

The Second Coming will be a fearful, mournful time for the wicked, but it will be a day of peace for the righteous.

- **D&C 45:57–59 Blessings for the righteous.**

57 For they that are wise and have received the truth, and have taken the Holy Spirit for their guide, and have not been deceived—verily I say unto you, they shall not be hewn down and cast into the fire, but shall abide the day.

58 And the earth shall be given unto them for an inheritance; and they shall multiply and wax strong, and their children shall grow up without sin unto salvation.

59 For the Lord shall be in their midst, and his glory shall be upon them, and he will be their king and their lawgiver.

- **Malachi 4:2–3 The Second Coming will be a day of healing and of power over the wicked.** While the wicked fear and suffer, the righteous will rejoice: "But unto you that fear my name shall the Sun of righteousness arise with healing in his wings; and ye shall go forth, and grow up as calves of the stall" (v. 2). The wicked will be "tread down" by the righteous, becoming "ashes under the soles of your feet in [that] day" (v. 3).

A number of glorious events will accompany the return of the Lord Jesus Christ:

— **D&C 45:39**	The righteous will look forward to that great day.
— **Moses 7:62**	Righteousness and truth will sweep the earth; a Holy City (the New Jerusalem) will be built.
— **1 Thes. 4:16–18**	The dead and living who are worthy of celestial glory will rise and ascend to meet Christ in the air.
— **1 Thes. 5:1–9**	Destruction will not overtake the righteous, but it will overtake the wicked.
— **A of F 1:10**	Christ will reign personally on the paradisiacal earth.

President Ezra Taft Benson assured:

> As we live the commandments of God, we can look forward with joyful anticipation to the Second Coming of the Lord Jesus Christ and know that through our efforts we are worthy, with our loved ones, to dwell in His presence for all eternity. Surely nothing is too hard to gain this great goal. We cannot let down for a moment. We must prove, every day of our lives, that we are willing to do the will of the Lord—to spread the restored gospel, to bear testimony to the world, to share the gospel with others.[30]

- **Malachi 3:16–18 The names of the righteous are written in a "book of remembrance."** A book of remembrance is written before the Lord "for them that feared the Lord, and that thought upon his name" (v. 16). "And they shall be mine, saith the Lord of hosts, in that day when I make up my jewels [or royal treasure[31]]; and I will spare them, as a man spareth his own son that serveth him" (v. 17). When the Lord returns,

He will "discern between the righteous and the wicked, between him that serveth God and him that serveth him not" (v. 18).

There are many scriptural references to a book of remembrance that contains a record of our lives:

— **Rev. 20:12**	We will all be judged from the "book of life."
— **D&C 128:6–7**	The book is kept in heaven and contains our works.
— **D&C 88:2**	It also contains the names of the sanctified.
— **D&C 88:2**	Our prayers are likewise recorded therein.
— **Psalm 69:28**	It is possible to be "blotted out" from the book.
— **Rev. 13:8** **Rev. 17:8** **Rev. 22:19**	Those who follow Satan and alter the Lord's words shall have their names blotted out from the book.
— **Rev. 13:8**	Those whose names are not written in the book worship Satan.
— **Rev. 17:8**	The wicked will be surprised when Satan is revealed.
— **Rev. 3:5**	Those who overcome the world are not blotted out from the book.
— **Rev. 21:27**	Only the righteous may enter the Holy City (the New Jerusalem) and enjoy Christ's presence there.
— **D&C 88:2**	Those whose names are written in the book of life shall inherit eternal life in the celestial world.

The Bridegroom

- **D&C 88:92 "The Bridegroom cometh."** "Angels shall fly through the midst of heaven, crying with a loud voice, sounding the trump of God, saying: Prepare ye, prepare ye, O inhabitants of the earth; for the judgment of our God is come. Behold, and lo, the Bridegroom cometh; go ye out to meet him." This will fulfill the parable of the ten virgins (see D&C 45:56–57). Some of the Saints will be prepared for the Lord's coming and some will not.

The Metaphor of Marriage

JEWISH ENCYCLOPEDIA, 1901–6

Traditional Jewish wedding ceremony in the 19th century

Jesus considers His relationship with us to be sacred, like a marriage. He uses the metaphor of marriage when discussing covenants and blessings. Those who seek after other gods are idolatrous and unfaithful. Christ always keeps His covenants with us, and He expects us to keep our covenants with Him. If we are faithful we become joint-heirs with Him in all things.

Isaiah 54 centers around the metaphor of marriage. The Savior read and explained this chapter to the Nephites when He visited them (see 3 Nephi 22), making it all the more powerful as an explanation of the sacredness of our covenants with Him. He considers it a very personal bond between Himself and us.

Elder Jeffrey R. Holland taught:

> The imagery of Jehovah as bridegroom and Israel as bride is among the most commonly used metaphors in scripture, being used by the Lord and His prophets to describe the relationship between Deity and the children of the covenant. . . . Christ has, on occasion, been rightfully angry with backsliding Israel, but that has always been brief and temporary—"a small moment." Compassion and mercy always return and prevail in a most reassuring way. . . . The Lord's kindness and peace will never be taken from His covenant people.[32]

A Marriage and a Feast

The parable of the ten virgins (see Matthew 25:1–13) speaks of a marriage which the righteous are welcome to attend, but not the wicked and the unprepared. The marriage features the blessings of exaltation that are in store for the faithful.

- **Isaiah 25:6 A feast for the faithful.** "And in this mountain shall the Lord of hosts make unto all people [or nations[33]] a feast of fat things, a feast of wines on the lees, of fat things full of marrow, of wines on the lees well refined."

  This feast is sometimes referred to as the "bridal feast" or the "messianic banquet." It is related to the sacred, communal meal that occurred in connection with temple sacrifices and rituals, usually at the conclusion of a covenant ceremony (see Exodus 24:7–11; 1 Kings 8:62–66). Having sought forgiveness through blood sacrifice of an animal, the participants then took a portion of the meat home and ate it in celebration of the occasion and as part of the symbolism of partaking of the source of their redemption.

  — **Revelation 19:9** There is to be yet another messianic sacramental meal ("the marriage supper of the Lamb") when the Lord comes again at the end of the world.

  — **Revelation 7:15, 17** Those before the throne of God serve Him day and night in His temple. The Lord dwells among them, feeds them, leads them unto living fountains of waters, and wipes away all tears from their eyes.

  — **D&C 58:6–12** The same concept of the "supper of the Lord" is found in the Doctrine and Covenants.

  — **D&C 27:5–14** The list of invited guests includes Moroni, Elias, John the Baptist, Elijah, Joseph, Jacob, Isaac, Abraham, Adam, Peter, James, John the Beloved, and anyone else who is willing to qualify— "all those whom my Father hath given me out of the world."

  — **Luke 14:15–24** In this scripture the Lord gave the parable of the great supper. Those whom the Father hath given Christ out of the world are the faithful Saints of all ages.

A GREAT OR A DREADFUL DAY?

When the long-awaited day of the Second Coming arrives, the Lord's people will be richly blessed for their faithfulness and endurance (see D&C 54:10; 133:52–53). They will be caught up to meet the Lord in the clouds and rewarded according to their deeds while the wicked are destroyed and cast into outer darkness (see D&C 88:96–97; 101:90–91). This will be the "great and dreadful day of the Lord."[34]

The entire point of this book is to remind those who are seeking to be righteous of the great blessings that will be theirs at the Second Coming and in the Zion society of which they will be a part. We need not focus on the great destruction that will come to the wicked. For us, it should be a day of great joy—a day when our dead loved ones will be resurrected, and we will delight in a thousand years of peace and joy and safety. We shall be with and worship the Lord, our King. And He shall reign forever, both on earth and in heaven.

Notes

1. Charles W. Penrose, "The Second Advent," *Millennial Star,* Sept. 10, 1859, 582–83.
2. *Teachings of Presidents of the Church: Joseph Smith* (2007), 104. See also Doctrine and Covenants 116.
3. Joseph Fielding Smith, *The Way to Perfection,* 16th ed. (1975), 289, 290, 291.
4. Parley P. Pratt, *Key to the Science of Theology; A Voice of Warning* (1978), 32, 33.
5. *Teachings of Presidents of the Church: Joseph Smith,* 252–53.
6. See "The Establishment of Zion (Isaiah 1–12)," *Old Testament Student Manual: 1 Kings–Malachi,* 3rd ed. (Church Educational System manual, 2003), 143.
7. "The Establishment of Zion (Isaiah 1–12)," 143.

8. Bible Dictionary in the Latter-day Saint edition of the King James Version of the Bible, "Seraphim."

9. *Teachings of Presidents of the Church: Joseph Smith,* 221.

10. See Avraham Gileadi, "Isaiah: Four Latter-day Keys to an Ancient Book," in Monte S. Nyman, ed., *Isaiah and the Prophets: Inspired Voices from the Old Testament* (1984), 129.

11. Joseph Smith, in *History of the Church,* 3:392.

12. See Avraham Gileadi, "Isaiah: Four Latter-day Keys to an Ancient Book," 129.

13. See Avraham Gileadi, "Isaiah: Four Latter-day Keys to an Ancient Book," 129.

14. Bruce R. McConkie, *Mormon Doctrine,* 2nd ed. (1966), 702, 703.

15. See Avraham Gileadi, "Isaiah: Four Latter-day Keys to an Ancient Book," 129.

16. "Lesson 31: 2 Nephi 11 and 16," *Book of Mormon Seminary Teacher Manual* (Church Educational System manual, 2012), 106.

17. Joseph Smith, in *History of the Church,* 6:366.

18. See Daniel 10:3, footnote *a.*

19. See Daniel 10:4, footnote *a.*

20. See Exodus 24:10, footnote *c.*

21. Neil L. Andersen, "Preparing the World for the Second Coming," *Ensign* or *Liahona,* May 2011, 52.

22. Neal A. Maxwell, in "Special Witnesses of Christ," *Ensign,* Apr. 2001, 6.

23. Joseph Fielding Smith, *Answers to Gospel Questions,* comp. Joseph Fielding Smith Jr., 5 vols. (1957–66), 5:73–74.

24. See Malachi 3:13, footnote *a.*

25. Spencer W. Kimball, *Faith Precedes the Miracle* (1972), 221–22.

26. Joseph Fielding Smith, *Church History and Modern Revelation,* 2 vols. (1953), 2:51.

27. Joseph Fielding Smith, *Church History and Modern Revelation,* 1:238.

28. Joseph Fielding Smith, *Doctrines of Salvation,* comp. Bruce R. McConkie, 3 vols. (1954–56), 3:11.

29. Theodore M. Burton, in Conference Report, Oct. 1967, 81.

30. *The Teachings of Ezra Taft Benson* (1988), 341.

31. See Malachi 3:17, footnote *b.*

32. Jeffrey R. Holland, *Christ and the New Covenant: The Messianic Message of the Book of Mormon* (1997), 290.

33. See Isaiah 25:6, footnote *a.*

34. See Malachi 4:5; 3 Nephi 25:5; Doctrine and Covenants 2:1; 110:14, 16; 128:17; 138:46; Joseph Smith—History 1:38.

CHAPTER 14

The Celestial Cities of Our God

(ISAIAH 54; REVELATION 21; 3 NEPHI 20–22; ETHER 13; D&C 45; 97; 133; MOSES 7; ARTICLES OF FAITH 1:10)

We look forward to the coming of Christ to dwell among His Zion people. Where will He go after He arrives? And how will He rule and reign on the earth?

CHOSEN CITIES ON CHOSEN LANDS

The answer to these questions is the two Jerusalems—the old Jerusalem in the land of Israel and the New Jerusalem on the American continent. Zion will be spread all over the world, wherever there is a stake of Zion organized. But our Lord will reign from these two celestial cities.

The New Jerusalem

- **Ether 13:2 The American continent is a chosen land.** The prophet Ether told the Jaredites "of all things, from the beginning of man; and that after the waters [of the Flood in Noah's day] had receded from off the face of this land it became a choice land above all other lands, a chosen land of the Lord; wherefore the Lord would have that all men should serve him who dwell upon the face thereof."

- **Ether 13:3–4, 6–7 The New Jerusalem will be built as a holy city upon this land (the Americas) by and for the house of Joseph** before the Second Coming. The Zion society that exists in heaven (inhabited by the people of Enoch and the people of Melchizedek) will "come down out of heaven [along with] the holy sanctuary of the Lord" (v. 3). Ether prophesied concerning the New Jerusalem, which will "be built up upon this land, unto the remnant of the seed of Joseph" (vv. 4, 6).

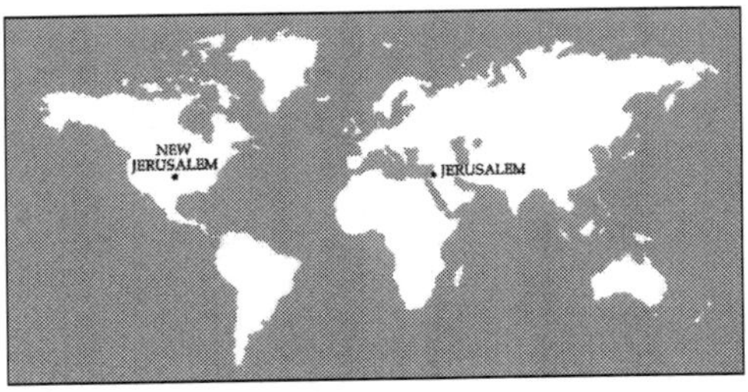

  Ether also taught that when Joseph brought his father Jacob (Israel) down into Egypt to preserve his life from famine, it was "a type" (symbol) of when the Lord later "brought a remnant of the seed of Joseph [Lehi's family] out of the land of Jerusalem, that he might be merciful unto the seed of Joseph that they should perish not" (vv. 6–7).

- **Ether 13:8–9 The New Jerusalem will stand until the earth is celestialized.** "The remnant of the house of Joseph shall be built upon this land; and it shall be a land of their inheritance; and they shall build up a holy city unto the Lord, like unto the Jerusalem of old; and they shall no more be confounded, until the end come [at the end of the Millennium] when the earth shall pass away[,] . . . and all things have become new."

- **Ether 13:10 Those who inhabit the New Jerusalem will be pure and righteous.** They will be those "whose garments are white through the blood of the Lamb; and . . . who are numbered among the remnant of the seed of Joseph . . . of the house of Israel."

- **3 Nephi 21:22–25 The Gentiles will help build the New Jerusalem.** Speaking of the Gentiles upon the American continent, the Lord said, "If they will repent and hearken unto my words, and harden not their hearts, I will establish my church among them, and they shall come in unto the covenant and be numbered among this the remnant of Jacob, unto whom I have given this land for their inheritance" (v. 22).

These converted Gentiles "shall assist my people, the remnant of Jacob, and also as many of the house of Israel as shall come, that they may build a city, which shall be called the New Jerusalem" (v. 23). This will involve all who are "gathered in, who are scattered upon all the face of the land, in unto the New Jerusalem" (v. 24). "And then shall the power of heaven come down among them; and I also will be in the midst" (v 25).

- **The tenth article of faith says:**

> We believe in the literal gathering of Israel and in the restoration of the Ten Tribes; that Zion (the New Jerusalem) will be built upon the American continent; that Christ will reign personally upon the earth; and, that the earth will be renewed and receive its paradisiacal glory.

This statement, which sometimes draws derision from those who oppose our teachings, sparks much interest and discussion among faithful Church members. Some of it is useful, but some of it is pure speculation—sometimes even the piecing together of divergent prophecies into one conglomerate prediction that uses a piece of truth here and a piece of truth there to construct an idea.

It has been said that a camel is a horse designed by a committee. And many views of latter-day prophecy are "camels" concocted from divergent and unrelated statements of the prophets. We should be careful not to teach such "philosophies of men" in our homes and Church classes.

President Harold B. Lee instructed:

> The Lord has clearly placed the responsibility for directing the work of gathering in the hands of the leaders of the Church, to whom He will reveal His will where and when such gatherings would take place in the future. It would be well, before the frightening events concerning the fulfillment of all God's promises and predictions are upon us, that the Saints in every land prepare themselves and look forward to the instruction that shall come to them from the First Presidency of this Church as to where they shall be gathered. They should not be disturbed in their feelings

until such instruction is given to them as it is revealed by the Lord to the proper authority.[1]

- **Reliable predictions.** Here are some reliable predictions, which come from latter-day prophets and apostles, and which avoid the kind of wild speculation we sometimes hear.

  Elder Bruce R. McConkie summarized how the cities of our God relate to one another. He said we must know these five facts:

  1. Ancient Jerusalem, the city of much of our Lord's personal ministry among men, shall be rebuilt in the last days and become one of the two great world capitals, a millennial city from which the word of the Lord shall go forth.
  2. A New Jerusalem, a new Zion, a city of God shall be built on the American continent.
  3. Enoch's city, the original Zion, "the City of Holiness, . . . was taken up into heaven" [see Moses 7:13–21].
  4. Enoch's city, with its translated inhabitants now in their resurrected state, shall return, as a New Jerusalem, to join with the city of the same name which has been built upon the American continent.
  5. When this earth becomes a celestial sphere "that great city, the holy Jerusalem," shall again descend "out of heaven from God," as this earth becomes the abode of celestial beings forever [see Revelation 21:10–27].[2]

Where Will the New Jerusalem Be Built?

The Prophet Joseph Smith revealed:

> The tribe of Judah will return to Old Jerusalem. The city of Zion spoken of by David, in the [102nd] Psalm, will be built upon the land of America. "And the ransomed of the Lord

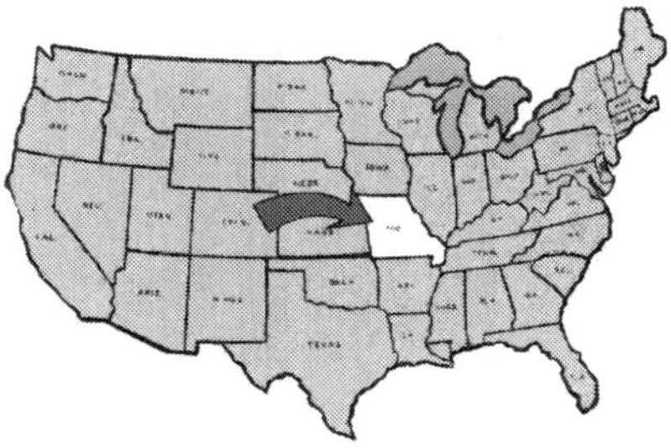

The New Jerusalem will be built in western Missouri

shall return, and come to Zion with songs and everlasting joy upon their heads" [Isaiah 35:10]; and then they will be delivered from the overflowing scourge that shall pass through the land. But Judah shall obtain deliverance at Jerusalem."[3]

And President Alvin R. Dyer stated, "The Zion of God, or the place where the city of the New Jerusalem shall be built, which shall be the first of the cities of Zion, shall . . . be established in Jackson County, Missouri."[4]

Why is this the location for the New Jerusalem? For the answer to this question we must go back to the beginning—to the Garden of Eden.

The Location of the Garden of Eden

- **Moses 3:8 "Eastward in Eden."** President Brigham Young taught:

> In the beginning, after this earth was prepared for man, the Lord commenced His work upon what is now called the American continent, where the Garden of Eden was made.[5]

"Eastward" has symbolic meaning. The scriptures inform us that God planted a garden "eastward in Eden" (Genesis 2:8; Moses 3:8; Abraham 5:8). When Adam and Eve partook of the forbidden fruit, it was to the east of the Garden of Eden that they were driven.

Dr. Alonzo L. Gaskill wrote:

> If something moves eastward, it is symbolically moving "toward God." Thus the Fall was not a tragedy wherein all was lost and thrown into chaos as a result of Adam and Eve's transgression. On the contrary, their expulsion from Eden began their mortal journey along the only path that would prepare them for eternal glory; it was a movement toward God in the truest sense.[6]

President Heber C. Kimball affirmed: "The spot chosen for the Garden of Eden was Jackson County, in the State of Missouri, where [the city of] Independence now stands; it was occupied in the morn of creation by Adam."[7]

And President Joseph Fielding Smith declared:

> In accord with the revelations given to the Prophet Joseph Smith, we teach that *the Garden of Eden was on the American continent located where the City Zion, or the New Jerusalem, will be built* [see D&C 57:1–3; 84:1–3]. When Adam and Eve were driven out of the Garden, they eventually dwelt at a place called *Adam-ondi-Ahman,* situated in what is now Daviess County, Missouri.[8] Three years before the death of Adam he called the righteous of his posterity at this place and blessed them [see D&C 107:53–57], and it is at this place where Adam, or Michael, will sit as we read in the 7th chapter of Daniel [see Daniel 7:9–14, 21–22, 26–27].[9]

Who Will Assist in Building the New Jerusalem?

- **The Latter-day Saints.** In 1857, President Heber C. Kimball predicted: "We never shall leave these valleys [in the Rocky Mountains]—till we get ready; no, never; no, never[!] We will live here till we go back to Jackson County, Missouri. I prophesy that, in the name of Israel's God."[10]
- **The Lamanites and other descendants of Joseph.** The New Jerusalem cannot be built until the Lamanites and other descendants of Joseph, as a people, are converted and ready to build it. Elder Orson Pratt observed:

> The Latter-day Saints in these [Rocky] Mountains never can have the privilege of going back to Jackson County and building that city which is to be called the New Jerusalem, . . . until quite a large portion of the remnants of Joseph [Lamanites and others] go back with us. Now then, here is a work for us, and we have no need to pray [to] the Father to return us to Jackson County until that work is done.[11]

- **The lost ten tribes** will also gather to the New Jerusalem (see D&C 133:30–33). These tribes shall bring with them "rich treasures" to give "unto the children of Ephraim, my servants" (the priesthood leaders of the Church) (v. 30). "And the boundaries [mountains] of the everlasting hills shall tremble at their presence" (v. 31). "And there shall they fall down and be crowned with glory, even in Zion, by the hands of the servants of the Lord, even the children of Ephraim" (v. 32). This means that they will receive their temple blessings from the priesthood leaders of "Ephraim" (this Church). "And they shall be filled with songs of everlasting joy" (v. 33).

The Ten Tribes Will Return

We discussed the return of the lost ten tribes in chapter 11 of this book. This great event will be part of the redemption of Zion. We will repeat two scriptures here in order to understand how the return of the tribes of Israel relates to the two holy cities of Jerusalem.

- **Deuteronomy 30:1–5 Eventually, all of the tribes of Israel will return to the Old Jerusalem,** to receive with Judah the lands of their first inheritance. But first, "they who are in the north countries" (D&C 133:26) will come to "the boundaries of the everlasting hills" (D&C 133:31) to receive their priesthood and temple blessings.

- **D&C 133:26–33 The lost ten tribes will first gather to the New Jerusalem.**

  "And they who are in the north countries shall come in remembrance before the Lord; and their prophets shall hear his voice, and shall no longer stay themselves; and they shall smite the rocks, and the ice shall flow down at their presence. And an highway shall be cast up in the midst of the great deep" (vv. 26–27).

  "Their enemies shall become a prey unto them" (v. 28). "And in the barren deserts there shall come forth pools of living water; and the parched ground shall no longer be a thirsty land" (v. 29).

These tribes shall bring with them "rich treasures" to give "unto the children of Ephraim, my servants" (the priesthood leaders of the Church) (v. 30). "And the boundaries [mountains] of the everlasting hills shall tremble at their presence" (v. 31). "And there shall they fall down and be crowned with glory, even in Zion, by the hands of the servants of the Lord, even the children of Ephraim" (v. 32). This means that they will receive their temple blessings from the priesthood leaders of "Ephraim" (this Church). "And they shall be filled with songs of everlasting joy" (v. 33).

Elder Orson Pratt asked:

> How long will they who come from the north countries tarry in the heights of Zion? ... They will dwell in Zion a good while, and during that time, there will be twelve thousand chosen out of each of these ten tribes, besides twelve thousand that will be chosen from Judah, Joseph, and the remaining tribes, one hundred and forty-four thousand in all.... For what purpose? ... These parties ... will go forth among all people, nations, and tongues, and gather up and hunt out the house of Israel, wherever they are scattered, and bring as many as they possibly can into the Church ..., preparatory to the great day of the coming of the Lord. One hundred and forty-four thousand missionaries! Quite a host. All this has got to take place.[12]

The Old Jerusalem

- **Ether 13:5, 11 The Old Jerusalem will be a holy city for the Jews and the other tribes of Israel** (v.5). The inhabitants of the city will include the Jews and those of the lost ten tribes "who were scattered and gathered in from the four quarters of the earth, and from the north countries," who are also "partakers of the fulfilling of the covenant which God made with their father, Abraham [meaning members of the Church]" (v. 11).

PUBLIC DOMAIN

A temple will stand in Old Jerusalem

- **D&C 133:35 The sons of Judah will be "sanctified in holiness before the Lord,** to dwell in his presence day and night, forever and ever." The Lord will sit upon His throne in the House of the Lord that will stand in the city of Old Jerusalem.

- **3 Nephi 20:29–34 The Old Jerusalem will be restored as a land of inheritance for the Jews and the gospel will be preached to them.** Speaking of His people of the tribe of Judah (the Jews), whose ancestral home is in the land of Israel, the Lord promised that He will "remember the covenant which I have made with my people; and I have covenanted with them that I would gather them together in mine own due time, that I would give unto them again the land of their fathers for their inheritance, which is the land of Jerusalem, which is the promised land unto them forever, saith the Father. . . . Then will the Father gather them together again, and give unto them Jerusalem for the land of their inheritance" (vv. 29, 33).

  Equally important, "the time cometh, when the fulness of my gospel shall be preached unto them; and they shall believe in me, that I am Jesus Christ, the Son of God, and shall pray unto the Father in my name" (vv. 30–31). Then, quoting Isaiah, the Lord promised that their "watchmen" (priesthood leaders) will again "lift up their voice, and with the voice together shall they sing; for they shall see eye to eye. . . . Then shall they break forth into joy—Sing together, ye waste places of Jerusalem; for the Father hath comforted his people, he hath redeemed Jerusalem" (vv. 32, 34; compare Isaiah 52:8–9).

- **3 Nephi 21:1 Zion will be established again among the Savior's people after they have been gathered.** Jesus said, "I give unto you a sign, that ye may know the time when these things shall be about to take place—that I shall gather in, from their long dispersion, my people, O house of Israel, and shall establish again among them my Zion." The coming forth of the Book of Mormon was an important milestone in the gathering of Israel.[13]

  To understand the sign Jesus gave in 3 Nephi 21, we must have a correct understanding of what *Zion* means. It often refers to specific places, but it is also a condition of the heart and mind (see D&C 97:21; Moses 7:18). In this case, it seems likely that the Lord is referring to both a place (the Old Jerusalem) and also the establishment of a Zion people in that land—something that the Lord has tried to establish among them since the days of Moses, but without success because of their wickedness and unbelief (see D&C 84:23– 25). In the latter days, Zion will finally be established among them, in preparation for the arrival of their long-awaited Messiah and King.

- **Isaiah 54:4–13; 3 Nephi 22:4–13 As the waters of Noah."** In the Middle East in ancient times, the inability to bear children was considered an awful curse. But Isaiah prophesied that in the latter days Israel will forget the shame of her "childless" years, and, as her children are gathered, she will rejoice in her new and prosperous condition.

  "Fear not," said the Lord through Isaiah, "for thou shalt not be ashamed: neither be thou confounded; for thou shalt not be put to shame: for thou shalt forget the shame of thy youth, and shalt not remember the reproach of thy widowhood any more. For thy Maker is thine husband; the Lord of hosts is his name; and thy Redeemer the Holy One of Israel; The God of the whole earth shall he be called," and He "hath called thee as a woman forsaken and grieved in spirit, and a wife of youth, when thou wast refused [because thou wast despised[14]], saith thy God" (vv. 4–6). "For a small moment have I forsaken thee; but with great mercies will I gather thee. In a little wrath I hid my face from thee for a moment; but with everlasting kindness will I have mercy on thee, saith the Lord thy Redeemer" (vv. 7–8).

  This promise was as certain as the one made to Noah concerning the waters of the Flood: "For this [the promise of gathering in the last days] is as the waters of Noah unto me," the Lord said, "for as I have sworn that the waters of Noah should no more go over the earth; so have I sworn that I would not be wroth with thee, nor rebuke thee [forever]" (v. 9). Though the mountains might depart, and the hills be removed, the Lord's promised "kindness shall not depart from thee, neither shall the covenant of my peace be removed, saith the Lord that hath mercy on thee" (v. 10). Instead of being "afflicted, tossed with tempest, and not comforted," the Lord said He would "lay thy stones with fair colours, and lay thy foundations with sapphires. And I will make thy windows of agates, and thy gates of carbuncles, and all thy borders of pleasant stones" (vv. 11–12). These are promises of material wealth and peaceful security. Even more important, the Lord promised that "all thy children shall be taught of the Lord; and great shall be the peace of thy children" (v. 13).

— **Revelation 21:19–21** The Apostle John on the Isle of Patmos gave a similar description of the city of Zion: "And the foundations of the wall of the city were garnished with all manner of precious stones. The first foundation was jasper; the second, sapphire; the third, a chalcedony; the fourth, an emerald; the fifth, sardonyx; the sixth, sardius; the seventh, chrysolite; the eighth, beryl; the ninth, a topaz; the tenth, a chrysoprasus; the eleventh, a jacinth; the twelfth, an amethyst. And the twelve gates were twelve pearls; every several gate was of one pearl: and the street of the city was pure gold, as it were transparent glass."

The beautiful and celestial City of Zion

The City of Enoch

- **Moses 7:17–18 Enoch's people became a "Zion" people.** Their righteousness reached a point where the "glory of the Lord . . . was upon his people. And the Lord blessed the land, and they were blessed upon the mountains, and upon the high places, and did flourish" (v. 17). The Lord gave Enoch's righteous people a new name: "ZION, because they were of one heart and one mind, and dwelt in righteousness; and there was no poor among them" (v. 18).

  — Other groups of righteous people (such as Melchizedek's people,[15] and the Nephites for 200 years following the resurrected Christ's visit to them[16]) also achieved this "Zion" state. In contrast, the children of Israel in Moses's day,[17] and also the Latter-day Saints in the 1830s,[18] failed to become a Zion people.

- **Moses 7:19–21 Enoch established the city of Zion, which was translated.** Enoch built a city which was called "the City of Holiness, even ZION" (v. 19). Thus, both the *people* and the *place* where they dwelt were designated as Zion. The Lord blessed them with safety and peace, "but the residue of the people [He] cursed" (v. 20). And eventually, "in process of time," the city and people of Zion were "taken up into heaven" (translated) (v. 21).

Enoch's city of Zion was taken up

— The name "City of Holiness" is more meaningful if we remember that our Heavenly Father's name is "Man of Holiness" (Moses 6:57).

- **Moses 7:67–69 "Zion is fled."** We are told that "the Lord showed Enoch all things, even unto the end of the world" (v. 67). We are also told that "Enoch and all his people walked with God, and he dwelt in the midst of Zion" while the city was on the earth (v. 69). And then, after 365 years of its existence, the city of "Zion was not, for God received it up into his own bosom; and from thence went forth the saying, ZION IS FLED" (vv. 68–69).

— **JST, Genesis 9:21–25; D&C 45:12 The city of Enoch is the same city that will return again at the Lord's Second Coming.** The rainbow is usually associated with God's covenant to Noah after the Flood. But actually, the rainbow was set in heaven as a reminder of God's covenant to Enoch and to Noah:

21 And the bow shall be in the cloud; and I will look upon it, that I may remember the everlasting covenant, which I made unto thy father Enoch; that, when men should keep all my commandments, Zion [the Zion of the Lord in Enoch's time; see Moses 7] should again come on the earth, the city of Enoch which I have caught up unto myself.

22 And this is mine everlasting covenant, that when thy posterity shall embrace the truth, and look upward, then shall Zion look downward, and all the heavens shall shake with gladness, and the earth shall tremble with joy;

23 And the general assembly of the church of the firstborn shall come down out of heaven, and possess the earth, and shall have place

until the end come. And this is mine everlasting covenant, which I made with thy father Enoch.

24 And the bow shall be in the cloud, and I will establish my covenant unto thee, which I have made between me and thee, for every living creature of all flesh that shall be upon the earth.

25 And God said unto Noah, This is the token of the covenant which I have established between me and thee; for all flesh that shall be upon the earth.

THE NEW JERUSALEM, GUSTAVE DORÉ, 1865

Enoch's Zion will return

President Brigham Young noted:

> Enoch had to talk with and teach his people during a period of three hundred and sixty years, before he could get them prepared to enter into their rest, and then he obtained power to translate himself and his people.[19]

Living in the Celestial Cities

- **D&C 45:67 "The glory of the Lord shall be there."** "And the glory of the Lord shall be there, and the terror of the Lord also shall be there, insomuch that the wicked will not come unto it, and it shall be called Zion."

- **Joel 2:28–29 The Spirit will be poured out upon "all flesh."** The Lord will "pour out [His] spirit upon all flesh; and your sons and your daughters shall prophesy, your old men shall dream dreams, your young men shall see visions: and also upon the servants and upon the handmaids in those days will I pour out my spirit."

Concerning this passage, President Joseph Fielding Smith explained:

> *The Lord has already commenced to pour out His Spirit upon all flesh,* and we do find even now that the sons and daughters prophesy; the old men dream dreams, and the young men see visions.

Now, my brethren and sisters, *I am not going to confine this prophecy to the members of the Church.* The Lord said He would pour out His Spirit upon *all* flesh. *That does not mean that upon all flesh the Holy Ghost should be sent,* and that they should be participants in the blessings which those are privileged to receive who have been baptized and endowed and become members of the Church [see John 14:17]; but *the Lord would pour out His blessings and His Spirit upon all people and use them to accomplish His purposes* [see D&C 88:6–13].[20]

- God's celestial cities will be places of unimaginable joy, of peace, of safety, and of living under the rule of our Eternal King, the Lord Jesus Christ.

Our resurrected loved ones will be there. The lamb and the lion will be at peace, and young children will play with them both.[21] They will grow up in perfect felicity in the celestial cities of our God.

Notes

1. Harold B. Lee, *Ye Are the Light of the World* (1974), 167.
2. Bruce R. McConkie, *Doctrinal New Testament Commentary,* 3 vols. (1965–73), 3:580–81.
3. Joseph Smith, in *History of the Church,* 1:315. See also Joel 2:32; Isaiah 26:20–21; Jeremiah 31:12; Psalm 1:5; Ezekiel 34:11–13.
4. Alvin R. Dyer, *The Center Place of Zion,* Brigham Young University Speeches of the Year (Feb. 7, 1967), 7.
5. *Teachings of Presidents of the Church: Brigham Young* (1997), 94.
6. Alonzo L. Gaskill, *The Lost Language of Symbolism* (2003), 152.
7. Heber C. Kimball, "Discourse," *Deseret News,* Aug. 5, 1863, 33.

8. See Doctrine and Covenants 116. See also Joseph Smith, in *History of the Church,* 3:34–36, 387–89. See also Alvin R. Dyer, *The Refiner's Fire,* 3rd ed. (1972), 16–18, 115, 158–59, 171–72.
9. Joseph Fielding Smith, *Doctrines of Salvation,* comp. Bruce R. McConkie, 3 vols. (1954–56), 3:74.
10. Heber C. Kimball, "Discourse," *Deseret News,* Sept. 9, 1857, 211. See also Heber C. Kimball, in Orson F. Whitney, *Life of Heber C. Kimball* (1945), 398.
11. Orson Pratt, "Discourse," *Deseret News,* Mar. 3, 1875, 69.
12. Orson Pratt, "Discourse," *Deseret News,* June 30, 1875, 341.
13. See 3 Nephi 21, chapter summary.
14. See Isaiah 54:6, footnote *d.*
15. See Joseph Smith Translation, Genesis 14:25–40 (in the Bible appendix). See also Alma 13:14–19.
16. See 4 Nephi 1:2–3, 15–16, 22–26.
17. See Doctrine and Covenants 84:23–25.
18. See Doctrine and Covenants 101; 103; 105.
19. *Teachings of Presidents of the Church: Brigham Young,* 94.
20. Joseph Fielding Smith, *Doctrines of Salvation,* 1:176.
21. See Isaiah 11:6–9; 65:25; 2 Nephi 21:6–9; 30:12–15.

Conclusion

The Lord Is Waiting for Us to Establish Zion

As we contemplate the glorious blessings of Zion, we must confess that we are not yet ready for them. If we were, Zion would already be established and our Lord would have come to dwell among us. We still have much work to do.

The Lord will only reign over a Zion people. Until we are ready to receive Him, He cannot come. In that sense, we can truly say: We are not waiting for the Savior; He is waiting for us.

President Spencer W. Kimball affirmed:

> This day will come; it is our destiny to help bring it about! Doesn't it motivate you to lengthen your stride and quicken your pace as you do your part in the great sanctifying work of the kingdom? It does me. It causes me to rejoice over the many opportunities for service and sacrifice afforded me and my family as we seek to do our part in establishing Zion.[1]

The Lord Will Come Only to a Zion People

The last and most important definition of a Zion people is "those who will welcome the Lord at His Second Coming." Hopefully, some of those will be ourselves and our descendants.

One thing is certain—Jesus will not come to inherit a non- Zion people or kingdom. So, while we may believe we are waiting for Him, it may be more accurate to say He is waiting for us.

Only when we have become a Zion people will we be worthy and ready to receive Him. Thus, the Saints can have an effect on bringing about the Lord's purposes and hastening His work for the redemption of Zion.

In June 1834 the Lord indicated that Zion might already have been established were it not for the transgressions of His people (see D&C 105:1–10).

It is not the Lord who causes delays in bringing forth the establishment of Zion and the fulness of blessings upon the Saints. The rate at which His promises to His people are fulfilled and His blessings come to them is determined by their willingness to respond to His counsel and do what they have been asked to do through His prophets.

President Spencer W. Kimball asked:

> What does this mean to us? It means that if the members of the Church do real proselyting in their home wards that the number of converts could grow to astronomical figures and even hasten the time when the Lord will be returning to the earth in His second advent.[2]

How Long Will it Take to Establish Zion?

This depends entirely upon us. Ever since the days of the Prophet Joseph Smith, the Saints have been making solemn, holy covenants in temples to make whatever sacrifices are necessary and to consecrate all that we possess to the building up of the kingdom of God and the establishment of Zion.

In 1978, President Spencer W. Kimball had much to say about our becoming a Zion people when he invited us to "lengthen our stride" to bring all these things to pass. Among other things, he said:

> The length of time required "to accomplish all things pertaining to Zion" [D&C 105:37] is strictly up to us and how we live, for creating Zion "commences in the heart of each person."[3] That

it would take some time to learn our lessons was seen by the prophets. . . .

Unfortunately we live in a world that largely rejects the values of Zion. Babylon has not and never will comprehend Zion. . . . Zion can be built up only among those who are pure in heart, not a people torn by covetousness or greed, but a pure and selfless people. Not a people who are pure in appearance, rather a people who are pure in heart. Zion is to be in the world and not of the world, not dulled by a sense of carnal security, nor paralyzed by materialism. No, Zion is not things of the lower, but of the higher order, things that exalt the mind and sanctify the heart.[4]

Satan is not sitting idly by as we seek to establish Zion. He would divert us toward other priorities and seek to hedge up our way in every way possible.

President Kimball warned the Saints in 1976:

The Lord has blessed us as a people with a prosperity unequaled in times past. The resources that have been placed in our power are good, and necessary to our work here on the earth. But I am afraid that many of us have been surfeited with flocks and herds and acres and barns and wealth and have begun to worship them as false gods, and they have power over us. Do we have more of these good things than our faith can stand?

Many people spend most of their time working in the service of a self-image that includes sufficient money, stocks, bonds, investment portfolios, property, credit cards, furnishings, automobiles, and the like to *guarantee* carnal security throughout, it is hoped, a long and happy life. Forgotten is the fact that our assignment is to use these many resources in our families and quorums to build up the kingdom of God—to further the missionary effort and the genealogical and temple work; to raise our children up as fruitful servants unto the Lord; to bless others in every way, that they may also be fruitful.[5]

President Brigham Young observed in 1864:

> If the people neglect their duty, turn away from the holy commandments which God has given us, seek their own individual wealth, and neglect the interests of the kingdom of God, we may expect to be here quite a time—perhaps a period that will be far longer than we anticipate.[6]

President Spencer W. Kimball further instructed:

> Zion is "every man seeking the interest of his neighbor, and doing all things with an eye single to the glory of God" (D&C 82:19). As I understand these matters, Zion can be established only by those who are pure in heart, and who labor for Zion, for "the laborer in Zion shall labor for Zion; for if they labor for money they shall perish" (2 Nephi 26:31).
>
> As important as it is to have this vision in mind, defining and describing Zion will not bring it about. That can only be done through consistent and concerted daily effort by every single member of the Church. No matter what the cost in toil or sacrifice, we must "do it." That is one of my favorite phrases: "Do It."[7]

We Have a Great Responsibility

Elder Bruce R. McConkie wrote:

> *Zion* is the name given by the Lord to His Saints; it is the name by which the Lord's people are always identified. Of the Saints in Enoch's day the record says: *"And the Lord called his people ZION, because they were of one heart and one mind, and dwelt in righteousness; and there was no poor among them"* (Moses 7:18).[8]

Have we reached this blessed state? No. Not yet. But there is no doubt that the Lord expects us to do so. Even before the Church was organized, the Lord commanded the Saints to "seek to bring forth and establish the cause of Zion" (see D&C 6:6; 11:6; 12:6; 14:6). On the day of the Church's organization, the Lord commended the Prophet Joseph Smith for his diligence in seeking to bring forth Zion (see D&C 21:7–8). And after the

Church was organized, various brethren were commanded to labor in Zion with all their power and strength (see D&C 24:7; 30:11; 93:53).[9]

When we consider our blessed state as Latter-day Saints, it ought to remind us that we have much to do. In my own patriarchal blessing I am reminded: "Thou are obligated to act upon the favorable circumstances of thy birth." I am sure that I am not alone in this expectation.

As the rightful heirs of the covenants and blessings of Abraham, we are responsible to bless "all the families of the earth" by our efforts (Abraham 2:11). This includes our Father's children on both sides of the veil. Of course, if we are not making an effort, then this promise cannot be fulfilled. We must, as President Kimball said, "Do it."

Elder Bruce R. McConkie declared:

> The Lord has laid upon us the responsibility to lay the foundation for that which is to be. We have been commissioned to prepare a people for the Second Coming of the Son of Man. We have been called to preach the gospel to every nation and kindred and tongue and people. We have been commanded to lay the foundations of Zion and to get all things ready for the return of Him who shall again crown the Holy City with His presence and glory.[10]

Zion Commences in Our Hearts

The Prophet Joseph Smith stated that "we ought to have the building up of Zion as our greatest object."[11] If this our goal, we must begin in our homes. That can be done without any general announcement from the heads of the Church. Each must choose for himself to live this celestial law.

President Brigham Young remarked:

> When we conclude to make a Zion we will make it, and this work commences in the heart of each person. When

the father of a family wishes to make a Zion in his own house, he must take the lead in this good work, which it is impossible for him to do unless he himself possesses the spirit of Zion. Before he can produce the work of sanctification in his family, he must sanctify himself, and by this means God can help him to sanctify his family. . . .

There is not one thing wanting in all the works of God's hands to make a Zion upon the earth when the people conclude to make it. We can make a Zion of God on earth at our pleasure, upon the same principle that we can raise a field of wheat, or build and inhabit. There has been no time when the material has not beet here from which to produce corn, wheat, etc., and by the judicious management and arrangement of this ever-existing material a Zion of God can always be built on the earth.[12]

It is a matter of choosing to establish Zion. Our leaders will not command it. We must voluntarily begin the process.

Establishing Zion in Jackson County

Ultimately, the latter-day Zion will be built in Jackson County, Missouri. It is true that every stake of Zion is also part of Zion. But the City of our God will be built where the Lord has decreed it shall be built.

Elder Orson F. Whitney asked:

Will our mission end here [in Utah]? Is the State of Utah the proper monument of the "Mormon" people? No. . . . The monument to "Mormonism" will stand in Jackson County, Missouri. There the great City will be built: there Zion will arise and shine, "the joy of the whole earth," and there the Lord will come to His Temple in His own time, when His people shall have made the required preparation.[13]

This will not be just a matter of "going there" when called to do so. If we have learned anything at all from the Latter- day Saints' first experience in Jackson County, it is that the Lord will not tolerate wickedness and sloth on that sacred land. It is a fantasy to think that we can go there without first becoming a Zion people who live the celestial law of consecration and in every other way behave like Saints.

Elder Orson Pratt taught:

> When we go back to Jackson County, we are to go back with power. Do you suppose that God will reveal His power among an unsanctified people, who have no regard nor respect for His laws and institutions, but who are filled with covetousness? No. When God shows forth His power among the Latter-day Saints, it will be because there is a union of feeling in regard to doctrine, and in regard to everything that God has placed in their hands; and not only a union but a sanctification on their part, that there shall not be a spot or wrinkle as it were, but everything shall be as fair as the sun that shines in the heavens.[14]

How May We Prepare to Establish Zion?

President Spencer W. Kimball summarized how we can prepare for the days ahead:

> May I suggest three fundamental things we must do if we are to "bring again Zion,"[15] three things for which we who labor for Zion must commit ourselves.
>
> First, we must eliminate the individual tendency to selfishness that snares the soul, shrinks the heart, and darkens the mind. . . .
>
> Second, we must cooperate completely and work in harmony one with the other. There must be unanimity in our decisions and unity in our actions. After pleading with the saints to "let every man esteem his brother as himself" (D&C 38:24), the Lord concludes His instructions on cooperation to a conference of the membership in these powerful words:

"Behold, this I have given unto you as a parable, and it is even as I am. I say unto you, be one; and if ye are not one ye are not mine" (D&C 38:27).

If the Spirit of the Lord is to magnify our labors, then this spirit of oneness and cooperation must be the prevailing spirit in all that we do. . . .

Third, we must lay on the altar and sacrifice whatever is required by the Lord. We begin by offering a "broken heart and a contrite spirit." We follow this by giving our best effort in our assigned fields of labor and callings. We learn our duty and execute it fully. Finally we consecrate our time, talents, and means as called upon by our file leaders and as prompted by the whisperings of the Spirit. In the Church, as in the welfare system also, we can give expression to every ability, every righteous desire, every thoughtful impulse. Whether a volunteer, father, home teacher, bishop, or neighbor, whether a visiting teacher, mother, homemaker, or friend—there is ample opportunity to give our all. And as we give, we find that "sacrifice brings forth the blessings of heaven!"[16] And in the end, we learn it was no sacrifice at all.[17]

Come then, my brothers and sisters, and let us build Zion.

Notes

1. Spencer W. Kimball, "Becoming the Pure in Heart," *Ensign,* May 1978, 80.
2. Spencer W. Kimball, "A Report and a Challenge," *Ensign,* Nov. 1976, 4.
3. *Teachings of Presidents of the Church: Brigham Young* (1997), 113.
4. Spencer W. Kimball, "Becoming the Pure in Heart," 80–81.
5. Spencer W. Kimball, "The False Gods We Worship," *Ensign,* June 1976, 4.
6. Brigham Young, "Remarks," *Deseret News,* June 15, 1864, 294.
7. Spencer W. Kimball, "Becoming the Pure in Heart," 81.
8. Bruce R. McConkie, *Mormon Doctrine,* 2nd ed. (1966), 854.
9. See Bruce R. McConkie, *Mormon Doctrine,* 854.

10. Bruce R. McConkie, "Come: Let Israel Build Zion," *Ensign,* May 1977, 116.
11. *Teachings of Presidents of the Church: Joseph Smith* (2007), 186.
12. *Teachings of Presidents of the Church: Brigham Young,* 113.
13. Orson F. Whitney, in Conference Report, Apr. 1916, 68.
14. Orson Pratt, "Discourse," *Deseret News,* Mar. 19, 1873, 101.
15. See Isaiah 52:8; Mosiah 15:22, 29; 3 Nephi 16:18; D&C 113:8.
16. "Praise to the Man," *Hymns,* no. 27.
17. Spencer W. Kimball, "Becoming the Pure in Heart," 81.

About the Author

Randal S. Chase spent his childhood years in Nephi, Utah, where his father was a dry land wheat farmer and businessman. In 1959 the family moved to Salt Lake City and settled in the Holladay area. Randal served a full-time mission in the Central British (England Central) Mission from 1968 to 1970. He returned home and married Deborah Johnsen in 1971. They are the parents of six children—two daughters and four sons—and an ever-expanding number of grandchildren.

Randal was called to serve as a bishop at the age of 27 in the Sandy Crescent South Stake (in the Salt Lake Valley). He served six years in that capacity and has since served as a high councilor, a stake executive secretary and clerk, and in many other stake and ward callings. Regardless of whatever other callings he has received over the years, one was nearly constant: he has taught Gospel Doctrine classes in every ward he has ever lived in as an adult—a total of 45 years.

Dr. Chase was a well-known media personality on Salt Lake City radio stations in the 1970s. He left on-air broadcasting in 1978 to develop and market a computer-based management, sales, and music programming system to radio and television stations in the United States, Canada, South America, and Australia. After the business was sold in 1984, he supported his family as a media and business consultant in the Salt Lake City area.

Having a great desire to teach young people of college age, he determined in the late 1980s to pursue his doctorate, and received his PhD in Communication from the University of Utah in 1997. He has taught communication courses at that institution as well as at Salt Lake Community College and Dixie State University for 29 years. He served as

Communication Department chair and is currently a full-time professor at Dixie State University in St. George, Utah.

Concurrently with his academic career, Brother Chase has served as a volunteer LDS Institute and Adult Education instructor in the Church Educational System (CES) since 1994, both in Salt Lake City and St. George, where he currently teaches a weekly Adult Education class for three stakes in the Washington area. He has also conducted multiple Church history tours and seminars. During these years of gospel teaching, he has developed an extensive library of lesson plans and handouts which are the predecessors to this book.

Dr. Chase has published a 13-volume series of study guides on the Book of Mormon; Doctrine and Covenants and Church history; Old Testament; New Testament; and Pearl of Great Price, titled *Making Precious Things Plain.* The series is designed to assist teachers and students of the gospel as well as those who simply want to study on their own. This book, titled *Establishing Zion,* is an outgrowth of those volumes.

73376232R00162

Made in the USA
San Bernardino, CA
04 April 2018